The EEC and Eastern Europe

EDITORS:
AVI SHLAIM AND G. N. YANNOPOULOS

The EEC and Eastern Europe

CAMBRIDGE UNIVERSITY PRESS
CAMBRIDGE
LONDON · NEW YORK · MELBOURNE

Published by the Syndics of the Cambridge University Press
The Pitt Building, Trumpington Street, Cambridge CB2 1RP
Bentley House, 200 Euston Road, London NW1 2DB
32 East 57th Street, New York, NY 10022, USA
296 Beaconsfield Parade, Middle Park, Melbourne 3206, Australia

First published 1978

Printed in Great Britain at the
University Press, Cambridge

Library of Congress Cataloguing in Publication Data
Main entry under title:
The EEC and Eastern Europe.
'Most of the papers which comprise this volume were
delivered originally at a conference organized by the
Graduate School of Contemporary European Studies at the
University of Reading in December 1975.'
  1. European Economic Community – Europe, Eastern –
Addresses, essays, lectures. I. Shlaim, Avi.
II. Yannopoulos, George, 1936– III. Reading, Eng.
University. Graduate School of Contemporary European
Studies.
HC241.25.E83E13 382'.9142'0947 78-1954
ISBN 0 521 22072 6

Contents

Contributors

Avi Shlaim, Lecturer in Politics, University of Reading.

G. N. Yannopoulos, Lecturer in Economics, University of Reading.

Peter Marsh, Lecturer in Politics, Manchester Polytechnic.

Peter Wiles, Professor of Russian Economic and Social History, School of Slavonic and East European Studies, University of London.

Alan Smith, Lecturer in Economics and Social Studies of Eastern Europe, School of Slavonic and East European Studies, University of London.

John Pinder, Director of Political and Economic Planning, London.

Philip Hanson, Senior Lecturer, Centre for Russian and East European Studies, University of Birmingham.

Richard Portes, Professor of Economics, Birkbeck College, University of London.

J. Wilczynski, Associate Professor of Economics, Royal Military College, University of New South Wales.

Friedemann Müller, Forschungsinstitut für Internationale Politik und Sicherheit, Munich.

Max Baumer, Forschungsinstitut für Internationale Politik und Sicherheit, Munich.

Hanns-Dieter Jacobsen, Forschungsinstitut für Internationale Politik und Sicherheit, Munich.

Acknowledgements

Most of the papers which comprise this volume were delivered originally at a conference organized by the Graduate School of Contemporary European Studies at the University of Reading in December 1975. The European Educational Research Trust and the Commission of the European Communities generously provided financial support. Many colleagues in the School and in the Departments of Economics and Politics provided invaluable support. Mrs Patricia Sales and Mrs Ann Bedford of the School office responded to the never-ending requests for organizational and secretarial assistance with unflagging enthusiasm, efficiency and skill.

Special thanks are also due to the conference participants for the helpful comments they made on the original papers presented by the contributors and to the editorial staff of the Cambridge University Press for the outstandingly imaginative and constructive part they played in preparing these papers for publication. We would like to express our deep gratitude to all these institutions and individuals. Without their cooperation neither the conference nor this volume would have been possible.

A.S.
G.Y.
Reading, 1977

1

Economic Relations between the EEC and Eastern Europe: an Introduction

G. N. YANNOPOULOS AND AVI SHLAIM

The aim of this introductory chapter is firstly to present in a summary form the main developments in the field of trade (both visible and invisible) and financial transactions between the European Economic Communities (EEC) since its inception and the socialist countries of the Council of Mutual Economic Assistance (CMEA or Comecon); secondly to examine the main issues which are likely to influence, either positively or negatively, the future course of EEC–CMEA relations; and thirdly to link the various contributions together and thus help the reader to see how they are related to each other.

I

It is one of the paradoxes of international politics in the era of détente that relations with allies frequently fail to keep pace with relations with adversaries. Thus the decline of unity within the Atlantic Alliance has been accompanied in recent years by an improvement in the relations between the countries of Western Europe and their traditional adversaries in the East. This improvement has been the product of a subtle process of interaction between the economic dimensions of East–West relations on the one hand and the political and military dimensions on the other.

The EEC offers the countries of Eastern Europe considerable opportunities for trade and economic cooperation, which are vital to their development but of only limited importance to the EEC itself. This economic dependence of the East can be used by the EEC for promoting greater freedom, political stability and military security in Europe – an area in which, having little to offer, it poses essentially as a *demandeur*.[1] This is the broad context in which the specific relations between the EEC and the CMEA take place.

For the student of international economics, the study of EEC–CMEA relations also provides interesting insights into such questions as the impact of the formation of trade blocs on the development of world trade and the difficulties of coordinating external commercial policy among states with separate monetary authorities, treasuries and foreign ministries.

On the first question, i.e. the impact of trade blocs on the evolution of international trade, it is difficult to give a definitive answer. Neither the formation of a customs union among the six Western European countries in the late 1950s nor the creation of formal instruments for economic integration by the CMEA countries during the period 1962–71, had any adverse effect on the development of trade between the EEC countries and the countries of Eastern Europe. On the contrary, the movement towards a customs union in the EEC coincided with a period of rapid expansion in trade with Eastern Europe.

Between 1958 and 1970 EEC exports to the CMEA countries increased by 385 per cent – an increase almost twice as large as the growth of Community exports to third countries. Over the same period, imports of the Community from the CMEA area increased by 300 per cent compared to an increase of total Community imports of 180 per cent. As shown in chapter 8 below (table 1) this pattern continued in the 1970s. Thus, whilst the Community's total trade with the world expanded by 192 per cent between 1970 and 1976, the volume of trade with CMEA countries increased by 249 per cent. Indeed, the trade links between the two 'integration blocs' were further strengthened in the post-1970 period – EEC exports to the CMEA countries, which were 3.35 per cent of all EEC exports in 1970, constituted 4.27 per cent of the total in 1974. During this five-year period, the share of EEC exports to CMEA countries other than the USSR increased progressively. In 1970, about 36.5 per cent of the EEC exports to the CMEA area were absorbed by the Soviet

1 Roger Morgan, 'West–East relations in Europe', *International Affairs*, vol. 49, no. 2 (April 1973).

Union; in 1974 the share was reduced to about 34 per cent. The share of the exports of the centrally planned economies of Europe and the USSR absorbed by the EEC increased from 12.3 per cent in 1970 to 16.3 per cent in 1974. The increase is even larger if we look at the trade of the Soviet Union only. In 1970 10.6 per cent of the Soviet exports were directed to the EEC countries. This share increased to 16.2 per cent in 1974.

It must be noted, however, that the CMEA exports to Western Europe other than the EEC countries were rising since 1970 at an equally fast pace. Thus the developed market economies of Europe absorbed 20.4 per cent of all CMEA exports in 1970 and 27.0 per cent in 1974. The EEC countries receive about 60 per cent of all CMEA exports to Western Europe.

On the basis of such evidence, can one really claim that the process of economic integration in Western Europe has been the pivotal factor in this rapid expansion of trade and economic relations with Eastern Europe? Measurements of the static effects from the formation of a customs union in the EEC indicate that if anything else there were trade diversion effects against Eastern European countries.[2] However, the formation of a customs union brings about dynamic effects which show up in an acceleration in the rate of economic growth of the integrated area. This acceleration in growth rates leads, *inter alia*, to an increase in the demand for imports and so produces positive spillover effects for third countries. Thus, economic integration in Western Europe acts as a stimulant to international trade in general and to East–West trade in particular.

At the same time, economic reform in Eastern Europe, the passing from what Wilczynski[3] called the stage of 'extensive' growth into the stage of 'intensive' growth that demands more rationalization and specialization in production, and the increasing cooperation among CMEA countries in the field of economic planning (e.g. the establishment of the two CMEA banks, the creation of a number of international economic

2 Bella Balassa, 'Trade creation and trade diversion in the European Common Market', *Economic Journal*, vol. 77 (1967), pp. 1–21.

3 Josef Wilczynski, *The Economics of Socialism* (London: Allen and Unwin, 1970).

organizations within the CMEA area and the launching of joint project initiatives),[4] led the policy makers in Eastern Europe to pay increasing attention to international trade as a means of improving the efficiency of their own economies and raising the standards of living of their people. In many cases, economic reforms meant some freedom for socialist enterprises to have direct access to foreign markets.

Indeed, it has been argued persuasively (chapter 3 below) that the Soviet initiatives for détente and the movement for a European Security Conference are part of a strategy to tackle the problem of growth retardation that appeared in the Soviet and Eastern European economies in the 1960s. To take the economy out of the low growth trap into which it was moving, the Soviet authorities and economic planners in Eastern Europe had to accept that international trade can become an engine for growth. Improved economic relations with developed market economies were also necessary in order to speed up technological progress through the use of foreign research and development. Improved trade relations and the use of foreign R and D had to be supported by adequate finance. Given the shortage of hard currencies in the centrally planned economies of Eastern Europe, resort to foreign borrowing was inevitable. Foreign borrowing from Western banks was recognized to be politically less harmful than borrowing from governments. The development of a climate of détente was absolutely essential in order to be able to tap the Eurocurrency markets and have access to Western technology. The road to Helsinki was followed as the only realistic option open to the CMEA countries for improving their economic performance. It is not therefore peculiar that the Eastern Europeans attach so much importance to Basket Two of the Helsinki final act, which calls on signatories to take steps to improve commercial and scientific relations.

Eastern European emphasis on international trade and industrial cooperation with Western Europe is not altogether unrelated to the dynamics of European economic integration. As Pinder shows (chapter 4 below), Soviet economists are more

4 P. H. Gledenning, 'Comecon: progress and prospects', *NATO Review*, no. 3 (June 1977), pp. 15–19.

concerned than are their Western counterparts with the effects of integration on economic development. Because they view integration as 'a higher level of internationalization of production' they become more aware of its impact on relative economic performance. They have not failed to notice that the rate of growth of labour productivity in Eastern Europe was in the 1960s falling behind that of the EEC countries. The faster growth in Western Europe provided a further challenge to the Eastern European countries, since they are interested not simply in maintaining a high growth rate but also in sustaining a growth lead over Western Europe.

Thus a combination of economic developments within the CMEA area and external economic developments, including economic integration in Western Europe, led to more intensive economic relations between the EEC and the Eastern European countries. The climate of détente provided the appropriate environment for the smooth expansion of these relations and for their extension far beyond the traditional trade in goods and services. They now include a set of complex relations known as industrial cooperation, such as co-production, subcontracting, joint ventures, and the supply of complete plants or the licensing of Western technology with payment in finished goods, known as 'compensation' or 'buyback' deals.[5]

Trade relations between Eastern and Western Europe have not yet reached the level they were at before the Second World War. In 1938, about 70 per cent of Eastern European trade was with Western European countries. Thirty years later (1968) it was reduced to about 20 per cent, climbing in 1974 to 27 per cent. Similarly, the share of Western European trade with Eastern Europe, which before the war was between 9 and 10 per cent of their total foreign trade, has now reached about half of that percentage.[6] Despite the re-orientation that has taken place since the war in the foreign trade of Eastern Europe, the share of Western Europe and of the European Community in particular in the external trade of the CMEA countries has been

5 UN ECE, *Analytical Report on Industrial Cooperation among ECE Countries* (Geneva: United Nations, 1973).

6 Albert Masnata, *East–West Economic Cooperation – Problems and Solutions*, English translation (London, 1974).

TABLE 1 EEC share in Western European exports to the CMEA (%)

	1960	1966	1970
EEC (6)	47.2	44.7	51.0
(West Germany)	(20.9)	(18.6)	(21.9)
UK	10.2	11.0	10.5
Denmark	2.8	2.6	1.9

Source: OECD, *Trade Statistics.*

TABLE 2 EEC share in Western European imports from the CMEA (%)

	1960	1966	1970
EEC (6)	41.1	41.9	46.0
(West Germany)	(16.0)	(15.1)	(18.3)
UK	16.4	15.7	14.5
Denmark	3.3	2.9	2.5

Source: OECD, *Trade Statistics.*

rising steadily in the last twenty years. Intra-CMEA trade accounted in 1955 for about 70 per cent of the total Eastern European (including USSR) foreign trade. In 1970 it accounted for 65 per cent of the total and in 1976 for only 52 per cent. More than half of the remaining 48 per cent was accounted for by Western Europe. The EEC part in the Western European exports to the CMEA and the Western European imports from the CMEA showed a clear rising trend, as is indicated in tables 1 and 2. The data in these tables cover the period 1960–70, developments in the most recent period (1971–6) are examined in chapter 8 and chapter 3 below.

In general, trade relationships between the EEC and the CMEA are not symmetrical, in the sense that whereas trade with the EEC countries accounts for a sizeable share of the total external trade of the CMEA, trade with Eastern Europe

TABLE 3 Relative importance of Eastern Europe in the
exports* of the EEC (%)

	1960	1965	1970
Benelux	2.5	1.5	1.5
France	3.2	3.0	3.6
Germany	3.8	3.3	3.8
Italy	4.7	4.6	5.3
Holland	1.6	1.6	1.8
UK	2.1	2.3	3.2
Denmark	3.8	4.2	3.5

* Exports valued at f.o.b. prices
Source: UN ECE, *Economic Bulletin for Europe.*

accounts for a small part of the total foreign trade of the EEC.
If we take exports first, we find that the relative importance of
Eastern Europe in the exports of Italy is the largest among the
EEC countries (table 3). Italian exports to the CMEA (valued at
f.o.b.) fluctuated in the period 1960–70 around 5 per cent of the
country's total exports. Of the other EEC countries, France,
Germany, and Denmark directed annually over the last decade
between 3 and 4 per cent of their total exports to the CMEA
countries. The corresponding shares for the other EEC
countries varied between 2.0 and 3.5 per cent for the UK and
between 1.5 and 2.5 per cent for Benelux and the Netherlands. In the case of Italy, the UK and France, the relative importance of Eastern Europe in their export trade was rising
slightly during the 1960s, whereas for the remaining EEC
countries it either stayed unchanged or showed a slight decline.

In view of the proposed enlargement of the Community it is
worthwhile to look at the relative importance of the CMEA in
the export trade of the three candidate countries. The case
of Spain is very similar to that of the other EEC countries.
Portuguese dependence on Eastern European markets for their
exports was much below that of any of the nine EEC countries.
Greece is entirely different; it depends on the Eastern European
markets to a much larger extent. In the early 1960s about 22 per
cent of Greece's exports were directed to the CMEA countries.

TABLE 4   Relative importance of Eastern Europe in the imports* of the EEC (%)

	1960	1965	1970
Benelux	1.9	1.9	1.6
France	2.5	2.6	2.4
Germany	3.7	3.4	3.7
Italy	5.6	6.0	6.5
Holland	2.2	2.0	1.6
UK	3.0	3.8	4.0
Denmark	4.3	4.1	3.4

* Imports valued at c.i.f. prices.
Source: UN ECE, *Economic Bulletin for Europe*.

The share has been falling steadily since the middle 1960s and in 1976 it stood at half of the 1960 figure.

The big customers of the EEC are the USSR, East Germany, Poland and Czechoslovakia. However, in recent years, the shares of Romania and Bulgaria have been growing fast. These last two CMEA countries are becoming increasingly important buyers of Common Market products.

As far as imports from Eastern Europe are concerned (table 4), we find again that Italy tends to be the largest purchaser, in comparison with other EEC countries, of imported goods from the CMEA area (around 6 to 6.5 per cent of her total imports valued at c.i.f.). The share of Eastern European products in the imports of the UK rose from about 3 per cent at the beginning of the 1960s to about 4 per cent towards the end of the last decade. On the contrary, the corresponding shares in the French, German, Dutch and Benelux imports varied only slightly around a stable trend value. Only in the case of Denmark is there a slight decline over the decade in the share of CMEA products in the total Danish imports (from slightly over 4 per cent in 1960 to slightly less than 3.5 per cent in 1970). If we look now at the three candidate countries, we notice again the higher dependence of Greek imports on the CMEA. But as with exports, the share in imports has been declining throughout the

TABLE 5 Trade balance between the EEC and the CMEA:
1960–70 ($m at current exchange rates)

	EEC (6)	UK	Denmark
1960	132.7	−53.4	−20.0
1961	149.6	−52.4	−25.0
1962	162.0	−63.2	1.8
1963	−88.8	−68.4	4.2
1964	44.3	−191.4	−10.3
1965	79.7	−236.1	−9.1
1966	132.9	−187.3	−23.3
1967	370.1	−146.0	−9.0
1968	569.8	−105.3	−23.6
1969	526.0	−157.2	−17.1
1970	549.4	−167.0	−16.3

Note: c.i.f. prices were adjusted to f.o.b. by reducing the former by 10%.
Source: IMF, *Balance of Payments Yearbook*.

last decade. Indeed, in 1970 the relative importance of Eastern
Europe in the imports of Greece was lower than that of Italy.
  The overall trade balance between the EEC (six countries) and
the CMEA countries during the period 1960–70 showed in all
years (with the exception of 1963) a surplus in favour of the EEC
which has been accelerating since 1967. This overall surplus
results mainly from the individual surpluses of Germany and
France. As a matter of fact, of the total EEC trade balance
surplus in 1970, 49.7 per cent was accounted for by Germany
and 47.3 per cent by France. In contrast to this, Italy remained
a deficit country for most of the period 1960–70. Benelux and
Holland showed deficits in their trade balance with the CMEA
up to 1966 but subsequently (since 1967) became surplus countries. Compared to this trade performance of the original six
EEC member states, the three new members that joined the
Community in the 1970s present an exactly opposite picture
(table 5). The UK showed a persistent deficit in its trade with
Eastern Europe – a deficit which was almost steadily growing.
Denmark too had a trade deficit with the CMEA – with the

exception of 1962–3. The Danish trade deficit was, however, fluctuating rather than getting steadily bigger.

The most dramatic increases in the trade balance deficits of the CMEA countries occurred between 1973 and 1975. During this period Italy's trade balance with the CMEA turned from deficit into surplus, the British deficit was drastically reduced, and the West German and French surpluses increased by 125 per cent and 212 per cent respectively. The growth of the EEC's trade surpluses with the CMEA area during 1974 and 1975 were exceptional and were the result of special circumstances. Eastern European emphasis on increasing the availability of consumption goods meant a reassessment of foreign trade on the part of the CMEA. The recession in Europe led the Western European companies to step up their selling effort in the CMEA, which continued to remain an area of steady demand growth. At the same time recession made it difficult for the Eastern European trading companies to expand their sales in the EEC. That the circumstances of 1974 and 1975 were exceptional is shown by the developments that took place in 1976. In that year the exports of the EEC fell by 6 per cent and those of the whole of the OECD by 2 per cent. At the same time the CMEA countries managed to raise the value of their exports to the EEC by almost 20 per cent and to the West as a whole by 12.5 per cent.

Contrary to these developments in the balance of visible trade, the CMEA has succeeded, steadily since 1960, to improve its position with the EEC in invisible trade. For example, between 1960 and 1970 West Germany's payments on invisible trade with the CMEA increased by a factor of 5.6, compared with an increase of its receipts by a factor of only 3.4. Trends in the other EEC countries are similar,[7] although the difference between the rate of increase in the payments for imports of services from the CMEA and in the receipts from exports is not as large as in the case of West Germany. The improved position of the CMEA in its invisible trade with the EEC is due to reasons which

7 Oleg Betcher, *La balance des paiements de l'Europe occidentale avec l'Europe orientale* (Geneva: Institut universitaire des hautes études internationales, 1976).

TABLE 6   Composition of CMEA exports to the EEC, 1970–4 (%)

	1970	1971	1972	1973	1974
Crude materials, excluding fuels, oils and fats	19.5	18.8	16.7	16.9	16.7
Mineral fuels and related materials	12.8	15.7	15.1	19.3	27.0
Food, beverages and tobacco	21.3	20.2	20.8	18.4	13.1

Source: UN, *Statistical Yearbook* (1976).

are likely to continue in the future. Improvements in invisible trade came from such items as transport, merchandise insurance and tourism. Freight rates charged by the Soviet and Eastern European merchant fleets have been very competitive. Western shipowners are complaining about dumping but such allegations are hard to unravel. The number of tourists from the EEC (six countries) to Eastern Europe increased from 185 305 in 1961 to 1 472 967 in 1970. During the same decade the number of British tourists visiting Eastern Europe increased from 46 669 to 185 934. Despite these developments, trade in services continues to remain of limited importance compared to trade in goods and can thus exert only limited influence on the overall evolution of the balance of payments between the EEC and Eastern Europe.

The composition of the trade of the CMEA with the EEC as well as with the other developed market economies, is similar to that of a developing nation at an intermediate level of development. Approximately 35–40 per cent of CMEA exports to the EEC are raw materials (including mineral fuels); another 15–20 per cent consists of food, beverages and tobacco (table 6).

The sharp rise in the proportion of exports of mineral fuels directed to the EEC is part of a recent policy of the Soviet Union to divert more of its oil exports to hard-currency areas and away from the CMEA in an effort to cover part of its growing deficit with the West. More recent information contained in the 1977

TABLE 7 Western trade with the CMEA by factor intensity
(%): sample of ten industrialized Western countries

	Labour intensive		Resource intensive		Technology intensive	
	Exports	Imports	Exports	Imports	Exports	Imports
1965–8	27	27	22	60	51	13
1971–4	30	26	24	59	46	15

Source: R. Ensor, 'Why future credits depend on East bloc exports', *Euromoney*
(January 1977), p. 42.

Soviet Foreign Trade Statistical Yearbook shows that oil exports to
the EEC during 1976 totalled 35.4 million tons, an increase of
10.4 million tons or 42 per cent over the 25 million tons exported
to the Community in 1975. The largest buyer of Soviet oil in the
EEC is Italy (almost one third of the Soviet oil exports to the
Community in 1976).

A comparison of the composition of the CMEA trade with
developed market economies to the structure of CMEA trade
with developing countries reveals an interesting dichotomy of
markets. The CMEA seems to have two different sets of comparative advantages, one for the developed, another for the
developing countries. In exporting to more developed countries, like the EEC, they concentrate on products in which they
can take advantage of their own cheaper labour. In exporting
to less developed countries, they concentrate in products which
are either technology intensive and/or subject to economies of
scale in their production. Table 7 gives a crude classification of
Western (not only EEC) exports and imports from Eastern
Europe by factor intensity. Chemicals and machinery were
considered technology intensive; textiles, processed foodstuffs,
other light industry and metal and wood products were classified
as labour intensive, and the rest as resource intensive. Over the
decade 1965–74, on average 60 per cent of Western imports from
the CMEA were resource intensive products and another 26 per
cent labour intensive. Conversely, 46–51 per cent of the Western
exports to the CMEA were technology intensive products.

The composition of CMEA trade has led many observers to
the conclusion that over the longer run the growth prospects

of East–West trade are bleak. However, as incomes per capita rise in the CMEA area, changes in factor supplies will take place which in their turn will produce systematic shifts in comparative advantages. Thus with changes in the level of economic development there will be changes in factor endowment. Such changes will come about from the increase in the capital stock per worker, the further reaping of economies of scale and the increase in skills and education. As the development of the CMEA countries proceeds, new demand patterns emerge which will permit the state industrial enterprises to familiarize themselves with the production of new products that could become exportables in the future. Fears of stagnation in East–West trade based on the drawbacks of the composition of the current trade of the CMEA with the West are not well founded.

2

The accumulation of huge trade deficits by the CMEA countries led within a very short period of time to an enormous growth of the indebtedness of the Eastern European countries to the West. Estimates of the precise amount of the CMEA debt to the West differ since not all details of Eastern European lending operations are publicized. The Chase Manhattan Bank put the figure for the end of 1975 at $24 000–28 000 million – a rather conservative estimate. The Union Bank of Switzerland estimated that the total CMEA debt to its ten major trading partners in the West could have reached a total somewhere between $25 000 and $40 000 million at the end of 1975. A more recent study by one of the contributors to this volume[8] estimates that the gross debt (i.e. the debt before allowances are made for CMEA deposits with Western banks) reached $41 000 million at the end of 1976 from an amount of $8300 million at the end of 1970. If account is taken of CMEA deposits with Western banks then the size of the *net* debt to the West was about $35 000 million at the end of 1976. The sheer size of this debt has raised fears about the future of East–West trade in general. The ability of the Eastern European countries to repay their debts

8   Richard Portes, 'East Europe's debt to the West: interdependence is a two-way street', *Foreign Affairs* (July 1977), pp. 750–82.

should be judged by reference to their economic potential. Furthermore the debts of some of the CMEA countries are still relatively small by comparison to some other non-socialist countries. For example, the debt of Hungary is half that of Denmark and the debt of the Soviet Union half that of Brazil. Most of the CMEA countries can cope without much difficulty with their present level of foreign (Western) indebtedness. Their planned economies can deal more effectively than market economies can with import restrictions. Perhaps it is considerations like these that explain the willingness of Western banks to go on lending to the CMEA countries, plus of course the unblemished repayment record of Eastern Europe and the belief that Russian gold ultimately guarantees every loan.

Of the total CMEA debt to the West, the Soviet Union accounts for about one third. But it is not the Soviet Union that raises problems. Countries like Poland and Bulgaria are the main candidates for concern. Thus although in 1975 the end year net debt ratio to hard-currency export earnings was 1.5 on the average for the whole of the CMEA, it was 2.1 for Poland and 3.2 for Bulgaria.[9] Despite this situation there are reasons – additional to those already discussed – why Western banks will continue to lend to the CMEA countries and facilitate in this way the smooth expansion of East–West trade. The CMEA countries are less affected than are market economies by world recessions. During the last recession they continued to grow at about 5 per cent a year on average. This steadiness in their rate of economic expansion affects favourably their creditworthiness in the international capital markets. It is no surprise, therefore, that they manage – despite their worsening debt position – to obtain extremely good terms and make the most of declining interest rates in the Eurocurrency markets.

In order to improve their ability to borrow, Eastern European countries are now prepared to provide Western banks with more information, with appropriate documentation and details of their debt repayments schedule. There is also a tendency to tie selected loans strictly to development of particular projects.

Foreign indebtedness does not constitute at present a serious

9 *Ibid.*; see also Wilczynski's estimates in chapter 7 below (p. 194).

impediment to the orderly expansion of EEC–CMEA trade. More serious obstacles are the dependence of this trade on planners' preferences and not on market forces, the lack of currency convertibility and of an elementary integration of Eastern Europe in the international monetary system, the slow expansion of the Western economies and the delays in devising an appropriate institutional framework for a constructive dialogue on trade and commercial policy matters between the EEC and CMEA.

Socialist foreign trade is guided by the preferences of central planners rather than market forces. Changes in world prices do not affect the plans of the state industrial enterprises working for exports or with imported inputs since such plans are not determined on the basis of profitability. Thus there are not automatic expansion forces at work which could have produced increases or decreases in the supply of exported goods or in the demand for imported products. Therefore the size of the foreign trade sector in a socialist economy would diverge from what it would have been in a market economy with similar relative factor endowments.

The CMEA can make their payments deficits with the EEC and the West more manageable if they are prepared to go ahead with monetary reforms to make their currencies convertible. Currency convertibility, however, will expose the Eastern European economies to the world markets and will oblige them to introduce a flexible pricing system. Such reform, therefore, will run contrary to the principle of the supremacy of the planners' preferences. Yet Hungary has already taken steps for the creation of a unified exchange rate for the florint which no doubt will facilitate its convertibility in the future.

In the meantime two other solutions have been put forward to break away from the present cumbersome system. The first is the idea of extending the transferable ruble to third countries that trade with the CMEA. The transferable ruble is already used as a unit of account for intra-CMEA trade. Most of the dealings in transferable rubles are handled by the International Bank for Economic Cooperation (IBEC) – a CMEA bank. In principle it was possible to use transferable rubles to settle trade outside the CMEA after 1972. The refusal of non-CMEA countries to use this method led to a change of the rules early in 1977. It is no longer obligatory for organizations using transferable rubles to plan in advance how accounts are to be settled. Moreover, IBEC is permitted to advance transferable ruble credits to cover 100 per cent, instead of a portion, of agreed payments. However, the holder still cannot cash his transferable rubles holdings for hard currency. Transfers of such holdings are permitted only if the recipients also have accounts with IBEC. It is obvious that the use of transferable rubles by organizations outside the CMEA is a rather hazardous transaction. Only very large companies who have the human resources and the know-how in setting up barter or counter-purchase deals may contemplate settling in transferable rubles.

In view of these difficulties a second solution has been proposed – the introduction of an 'externally convertible ruble' (ECR). The ECR would be guaranteed by the CMEA countries as a whole with foreign exchange and gold. In such a case the ECR, unlike the transferable ruble, would be convertible to hard currency rather than to goods only. It must be admitted, however, that as long as the Western Banks are prepared to lend to the CMEA countries so they can face their obligations in hard currencies, no Western organization will show any willingness to settle trade in ECR or other half-way solutions. Moreover, the growing importance of compensation agreements or 'buyback' deals helps to by-pass the hard-currency shortages and in this way further postpones currency convertibility. According to the UN Economic Commission for Europe, compensation agreements accounted for between 20 and 25 per cent of the total East–West trade in 1976, and in the short time between July 1975 and July 1976 300 new inter-company cooperation agreements were signed. Indeed, special organizations are now being set up in the EEC and elsewhere in the West to handle products involved in such deals.

Despite their recent growth, 'buyback' deals also have their problems. One of these problems is the safeguarding of the suppliers' profit in such a long-term transaction. One solution that has been suggested is to include in the price at which the equipment is sold the profit derived from the part of the market that will be supplied in the future by the CMEA enterprise. The

TABLE 8   Average industrial weekly wages (£) (mid-1975)

Bulgaria	30	Poland	36
Czechoslovakia	43	Romania	25
East Germany	45	USSR	35
Hungary	34	UK	52

Source: *The Financial Times* (18 October 1976), p. 4.

conditions of competition are such that in most cases it is difficult to adopt such a pricing procedure.

Apart from the difficulties stemming from the lack of currency convertibility, the orderly expansion of EEC–CMEA trade is threatened by the prolonged recession in Western Europe. The obstacles are more numerous than the mere reduction in the rate of growth of imports in general as a result of the slow growth in incomes. The slow growth of demand in the EEC makes the competition for the maintenance of existing market shares more intense and cultivates fears of dumping by foreign competitors. Dumping allegations are more easily levelled against CMEA imports, despite the fact that the Eastern European market share involved is usually very small. But the artificial price and currency systems prevailing in the CMEA countries make cost comparisons meaningless: the Western value of a pair of shoes manufactured in an Eastern European country could vary widely depending on the exchange rate used (the so-called commercial or the black market one). If demand continues to stagnate in the EEC then the development of a 'cold war' against CMEA imports should not be excluded. Evidence from the UK Department of Trade shows that in 1976 more than half of the dumping allegations considered or investigated involved at least one CMEA country. Whilst in the past there have been successful anti-dumping cases brought against East European goods the fact remains that cheaper labour is one of the competitive advantages enjoyed by the CMEA countries, as table 8 indicates. One way to get out of this tangle of dumping charges and countercharges is to develop more structured trade relations between the EEC and Eastern Europe.

The institutionalization of the economic relations between the

EEC and the Eastern European countries has proved to be a difficult undertaking. The relations with the planned economies of Eastern Europe are far more complex than are commercial relations with market economies to be regulated by simple policy instruments like the Common External Tariff (CET). The lack of a comprehensive *Ostpolitik* at the Community level did not help in the elaboration of a common approach regarding economic cooperation with Eastern Europe.[10] Things improved, however, in the early 1970s when as a result of the Russian initiative to convene the Conference on European Security and Cooperation, an external impulse was given to elaborate a common stand on issues relating to cooperation with Eastern Europe. Another difficulty – as is explained in detail in another part of this book – came from the refusal of the CMEA countries to accept the legality of the departures stipulated in Article 24 of the GATT regarding customs unions, free trade areas and regional integration schemes. This in effect meant Eastern European refusal to recognize the EEC officially. The common stand of the CMEA was broken when Romania, in order to benefit from the Community's scheme of generalized preferences, decided to establish direct relations with the EEC in 1972. Despite the Brezhnev speech of 20 March 1972, which implied Russian preparation to drop their hostility towards the EEC, the coordinated EEC approach to trade with the East is hampered by the fact that the Commission considers the Russian offer of talks on an organization-to-organization basis not an appropriate framework for negotiations. While the formal reason for the Commission's standing is the lack of supranationality by the CMEA and its competence to negotiate on behalf of its members, in pursuing this line Brussels is careful to avoid initiatives which may 'promote a process of consolidation of hegemonial structures on the other side through or during the negotiations'[11] on a bloc-to-bloc basis. The dialogue between the EEC and the CMEA is still in the phase of 'talks about talks'. The EEC Commission's reluctance to move into real talks on an

10 John Pinder, 'A Community policy towards Eastern Europe', *The World Today*, vol. 30, no. 3 (March 1974).

11 Ralph Darendorf, 'The Foreign Policy of the EEC', *The World Today*, vol. 29, no. 2 (February 1973).

organization-to-organization basis may prove wise at the end. Following Romania, Hungary and Poland are now ready to negotiate separately, within the framework of GATT, textile agreements with the Commission of the EEC.[12]

3

The economic relations between the two 'integration blocs' in Europe are becoming more complex with the growing interdependence between them. These complex interrelationships and the implications of growing interdependence are examined in a detailed and systematic way in the contributions included in this volume. The contributions that follow focus on the development of trade and cooperation, on the opportunities for further growth, on the financial and institutional constraints which impede this growth and on the consequences of closer relations for both sides. Special attention is paid to the industrial cooperation agreements which have come to play such a prominent part in East–West economic relations.

As the CMEA converges on the EEC, changes in the attitudes of its member states towards the EEC and East–West cooperation can be traced. The developments are examined in chapter 2 where Peter Marsh analyses the qualitative change which has taken place in EEC–CMEA relations in the mid-1970s by focussing on two major factors. The first factor is the attitude of the CMEA states towards East–West economic cooperation. The second factor is the degree of advantage to be gained by the EEC member states from collective action towards the Soviet Union and Eastern Europe. With regard to the former he traces in detail the shift in the Soviet attitude from ideological condemnation and hostility towards the EEC to a more pragmatic acceptance of the necessity for economic cooperation – a shift which culminated in the CMEA's recognition of and dialogue with the EEC. With regard to the latter, he examines the internal and external developments which converged to persuade the nine countries that the advantages of a collective approach to East–West economic relations outweighed the advantages of independent national policies; and the progress made

12 *The Economist* (27 August 1977).

by the EEC Commission in acquiring the authority to coordinate and regulate the economic relations of the member states with Eastern Europe. But while consolidating its own authority to act on behalf of the nine countries, the Commission has studiously avoided bloc-to-bloc negotiations by denying that the CMEA is a comparable organization and endeavouring to deal directly with individual East European countries. The irony is that in the earlier period antagonism had been caused by the refusal of the CMEA states to recognize the EEC. Now, as these states have adopted a much more flexible and accommodating position, the EEC's reluctance to accept the equal status of the CMEA is creating a stumbling block to the compromises necessary for a constructive dialogue between the two organizations.

The chapter by Peter Wiles and Alan Smith traces the convergence of the CMEA on the EEC. The move to adopt the supranationality goal by the CMEA started in 1962 following complaints by the industrialized members of the bloc about the lack of specialization. This move by Khrushchev was initially blocked by Romania. Subsequent events showed that the imitation of the EEC – albeit within the constraints of a very different system – is still a goal for the Soviet planners. Recent developments in the technical, commodity and credit fields point to more centralized planning within the CMEA.

Chapter 4 by John Pinder is essentially a complement to chapter 2. Only with a clear understanding of the Soviet thinking on integration, and in particular Western European integration, can we explain the changing attitudes towards the EEC.

Soviet definitions of integration tend to vagueness – perhaps wisely, as they must be used to support such diverse propositions as the inapplicability of integration to relations between the United States and Western Europe, and the necessity of integration between the Soviet Union and Eastern Europe. With respect to Western Europe, one of the principal tasks of the Soviet analysts has been to reconcile the continued existence of the Community institutions with the traditional assumptions about capitalist contradictions. This has led them to distinguish two integration processes: private-monopoly integration and state-monopoly integration. Private-monopoly integration is the cross-frontier activity of big firms. State-monopoly integration requires coordination of economic management in order to keep the system of capitalism going.

Unfortunately, Soviet analysts cannot give an objective view as to whether the EEC and its member states will evolve a new economic management that will deal effectively with the problems of inflation, unemployment and currency crises. But most of the books and articles published so far do not assume an early breakdown of the capitalist system; and their arguments do not constitute an obstacle to 'business-like relations' or to negotiations between the European Community and the East Europeans.

The subject of industrial cooperation is discussed in two chapters, 5 and 6, by Philip Hanson and Richard Portes. Hanson argues that the Eastern countries are probably trying to emulate the Japanese experiment over the period 1950–67 of a policy of planned and active technological borrowing without inflows of foreign direct investment. The author doubts whether the Eastern European experiment will be as successful as the Japanese one. The capacity of the administrative economic systems of Eastern Europe is inadequately adapted to absorb rapidly major technological innovations, and generally to facilitate the diffusion of innovations at high speed.

The question of the costs and benefits of Western investment in Eastern Europe is discussed in the contribution by Richard Portes. He points to some dangers stemming from the precarious balance of payments position and the growing indebtedness of the Eastern European countries. He emphasizes the limited leverage of the EEC in securing fulfilment of the planned debt repayment schedules. The paper concludes by presenting a set of policy prescriptions which would guide future policy on industrial cooperation with the Eastern European countries.

J. Wilczynski examines in chapter 7 the problems that arise in the fields of monetary and financial relations. He examines not only the issues raised through the lack of coordination of export credit policies but also the new problems resulting from the turmoil in the currency markets. The financial dealings between the two 'integration blocs' have accelerated, especially since the early 1970s. At least seventeen EEC-based banks have opened twenty-four representative offices in the CMEA region and more than forty bank offices, branches, affiliates and independent banks have been established by the CMEA countries within the borders of the EEC. The CMEA countries have benefitted from large credits and other forms of finance obtained from official and private sources for a variety of purposes and on generous terms. In this, the Euromoney and Eurobond markets have played a prominent part.

Capitalist and socialist partners have also entered into various types of financial operations, extending even to third countries. In spite of a number of problems the financial dealings across the largely disintegrated financial curtain have proved of considerable benefit to both sides, bringing the two economic groupings closer together.

The chapter by Friedemann Müller attempts to measure the extent of the economic interdependence between the EEC and the CMEA by means of a series of appropriate indicators. The author emphasizes the extent of the import dependence of the CMEA countries. He finds that such dependence is particularly high for certain technology-intensive products. Thus import dependence in this instance implies also a high degree of technological dependence. It is this high technological dependence that explains the growing interest of Eastern Europe in industrial cooperation agreements with Western European enterprises. Industrial cooperation is desired as a vehicle for the transfer of technology.

The last chapter in this volume deals with institutional issues. Since the onset of détente in the late 1960s, a gradual but marked change has taken place in the attitude of the CMEA countries towards West European and international economic organizations. Their relative isolation gave way to intensified attempts to gain acceptance and play an active part in the Western-dominated international economic order. Baumer and Jacobsen trace this change to the desire of the smaller East European countries to enhance their economic freedom of action by reducing their dependence on the Soviet Union and developing alternative options. The Soviet Union while conscious of the potentially adverse effects of this interaction for the stability of the 'socialist' economic and political order and hence anxious to retain control over her allies' relations with the West and with Western institutions, has permitted these closer contacts because of the direct and indirect benefits she perceives for herself from improved CMEA access to the European market. The position of the CMEA countries in relation to the EEC, the European Commission for Europe, GATT, IMF and UNCTAD is analysed in the light of these divergent interests. The conclusion is that if, as seems likely, the existing framework proves inadequate for the institutional regulation of East–West economic relations, a solution would have to be sought in a New International Economic Order.

2

The Development of Relations between the EEC and the CMEA

PETER MARSH

Writing in 1972, Ralph Dahrendorf pinpointed the central issue arising from the development of the EEC. This was that, long before full political union had been achieved, the EEC had become an operative force in world politics. As he put it, 'for many countries in the world, including the most powerful and most important, the European Communities are not only an economic but also a political reality.'[1] To Dahrendorf the evidence for this assertion was to be found in the fact that other states and organizations had to take the EEC's existence into account when framing policy, and that the member states of the EEC themselves were gradually losing the fight to retain national control of crucial areas of foreign policy.

An examination of the development of the EEC's relations with the member states of the Council for Mutual Economic Assistance (CMEA) would seem to confirm the essential truth of Dahrendorf's proposition, although Community competence in this sphere has only recently been acknowledged and has yet to be consolidated. What can be said is that in the period from 1974 to 1977 political and economic forces have gathered momentum to produce an increase in the authority and relevance of the Community in foreign economic policy and to effect the beginning of a qualitative change in EEC–CMEA relations.[2]

1 R. Dahrendorf, 'Possibilities and limits of a European Community Foreign Policy' in S. Warnecke (ed.), *The European Community in the 1970s* (New York, 1972), p. 115.
2 Throughout the study, the term 'CMEA' will be interpreted as covering not just the Council for Mutual Economic Assistance but also its individual members, namely the Soviet Union and the Eastern European states. Until late 1974, the EEC had no official

These forces have caused changes in the two major factors governing EEC–CMEA relations which are:

(1) The attitude of the CMEA states towards the EEC and East–West economic cooperation.

(2) The degree of advantage to be gained by the EEC member states from collective action towards the Soviet Union and Eastern Europe.

In order to understand the new developments in relations between the two organizations and to appreciate their real significance, it is necessary first of all to analyse these factors in detail.

1. Changes in the Attitude of the CMEA States Towards the EEC and East–West Economic Cooperation

From its inception, the EEC has always aroused considerable interest amongst the communist states. Initially this interest took the form of hostile condemnation of the EEC as an organ of West European monopoly capitalism doomed to inevitable destruction because of its internal contradictions. This attitude remained important in Soviet and Eastern European ideology throughout the period from 1957 to 1972 and was used to justify the policy of non-recognition. It also reflected the sense of 'threat' that the success of the EEC created amongst the communist states.[3]

However, alongside the brusque condemnation of the EEC as a 'knot of imperialist contradictions' there developed a more practical analysis of the Community which recognized its growing reality. This reappraisal took place from 1962 to 1972 and coincided with the EEC's consolidation and with changes in the political and economic climate in Eastern Europe. Whilst

contact with the CMEA but was actively forming a policy towards the individual states.

3 As late as August 1972 *Pravda* repeated the familiar attack on the EEC by stating: 'Events show that isolation of West European states is not a quest for co-operation but a manoeuvre by the monopolies of West European countries to strengthen their positions in competition with the trusts of other countries, the U.S. and Japan.' *Pravda* (25 August 1972).

continuing to denounce the economic motives behind the EEC, the CMEA states began also to examine its experience in relation to their own and to move gradually away from the policy of non-recognition. Three developments in particular served to alter Soviet and Eastern European attitudes to the EEC: the drive towards CMEA integration; the development of domestic economic reform; and the invasion of Czechoslovakia in 1968.

The reappraisal of the EEC began in 1962 with the publication of the Soviet Union's 'Thirty-Two theses on the Common Market' and Khrushchev's speech on 'Vital questions of the development of the world socialist system'. Both these texts recognized the EEC as 'an economic and political reality' and marked the growing dissatisfaction in Soviet and East European circles with the essentially negative approach of earlier ideological statements on the EEC.[4] At this stage, however, the new approach to the EEC was designed more for fulfilling Soviet purposes in the CMEA and persuading the Eastern European states of the benefits of closer integration. Thus Khrushchev's speech closely identified the emergence of a strong European Community with the need to improve the CMEA's functioning and to introduce supranational planning. To this end he declared:

We take cognisance of the objective tendencies towards internationalisation of production which operate in the capitalist world and we design our policy accordingly. In this connection the question arises of the possibility of economic co-operation and peaceful economic competition not only between individual states with different social systems but also between their economic federations.[5]

Khrushchev's shrewd and perceptive speech was used to back up his attempts to improve the CMEA. As such it indicated the powerful 'demonstration' effect that the EEC was already beginning to have on the CMEA, throwing light on its slow progress towards integration and displaying the advantages, in terms of economic growth and rising standards of living, that

4   C. Ransom, *The European Community and Eastern Europe* (London, 1973), p. 24.
5   N. S. Khrushchev, 'Vital questions of the development of the world socialist system', *Kommunist*, no. 12 (August 1962).

integration was bringing to Western Europe. Unfortunately, the long-term benefits of integration for the smaller states of Eastern Europe were not sufficient compensation for the short-term loss of sovereignty and independence that Khrushchev's proposals for integration by supranational plan implied. The prospects for CMEA integration and the future cooperation of 'rival economic federations' therefore foundered on the rocks of small state intransigence in the form of Romania's sabotage of Khrushchev's proposals.[6]

Desires for an increase in CMEA integration were at the heart, therefore, of the initial modification of the rigid ideological attitude to the EEC in 1962. Similarly in the period from 1968 to 1974, moves towards strengthening the CMEA coincided with a decisive change in attitude and policy towards the EEC. By this time, however, the whole domestic and foreign policy conceptions of the communist states had been drastically revised under the impact of economic reform and the Czechoslovakian crisis. These developments made it far more likely that a move towards further CMEA integration would lead to the abandonment of the policy of non-recognition and the beginning of a new stage in East–West economic and political cooperation.

Economic reform was the fundamental cause of the major policy changes of the period 1968–74. Its rationale was to increase the productive efficiency of the Soviet and Eastern European economies by incorporating new techniques and introducing 'market forces' into their systems of economic management.[7] To this end it encouraged a search for advanced

6 For details see M. Kaser, *Comecon: Integration Problems of the Planned Economies* (London, 1967). For a theoretical analysis of the problems of CMEA integration, see K. Kaiser, 'The interaction of regional subsystems, *World Politics*, no. 1 (1968).

7 In the period 1965–8, most of the CMEA states carried out reforms which decentralized economic decision-making, loosened the foreign trade monopoly and placed a greater emphasis on efficiency and profitability. Notable developments were in Hungary, the GDR, Poland and Czechoslovakia. The decade 1960–70 also produced a faster increase in trade with the capitalist states than in intra-CMEA trade. During this period, the share of developed capitalist countries in the CMEA's total exports rose from 21.4% in 1960 to 24.4% in 1970 and in total imports from

technology, more sophisticated management techniques and additional sources of investment. This automatically led to a new emphasis on foreign trade and economic cooperation with the Western capitalist states in order to draw on their reserves of financial credit and technological expertise to the full. In addition it placed a greater emphasis on the export performance of Soviet and Eastern European enterprises, which now had to try to penetrate Western markets and achieve 'world market standards' in production.

In the sphere of economic policy, the question of relations with the Western capitalist states and the use of market techniques seriously challenged traditional ideological considerations. The spread of capitalist management techniques, the 'joint venture' deals with Western corporations and the influx of Western consumer goods into the CMEA states meant that ideological flexibility would be called for on the part of the ruling elites of the individual states. Only by being flexible could the ruling elites justify the tremendous changes in their economic systems and reap the benefits of intensified economic growth without having their power undermined. Although the impact of changes in domestic and foreign economic policy was not such as to reduce immediately the authority of the traditional political elites, economic reform did produce a technocratic orientation that in the long term could have had such an effect. In particular it challenged orthodox views on the nature of socialist economies and on economic relations with capitalist states.[8] Moreover eco-

22.9% to 27.9%. For detailed figures see GATT, *International Trade 1970* (Geneva, 1971), and 'Prospects of economic integration in Comecon', research report prepared by East–West Advisory Service (Brussels, November 1971), p. 18. This trend alarmed the Soviet Union, whose own trade with Eastern Europe began to suffer. Soviet concern was expressed in *Soviet Foreign Trade*, nos. 7 and 8 (1967), nos. 4 and 8 (1968), no. 1 (1969).

8　In East–West economic relations, the spread of 'industrial cooperation' agreements and co-production schemes were the key feature of the late 1960s rather than conventional trade. These agreements usually provided for the participation of Western corporations in major projects in the CMEA states or for the sale of technology and 'know-how'. Major examples were Fiat's deal with the Soviet Union to supply investment, equipment,

nomic reform did more than anything else to widen the differences within the CMEA and to create tension between the Soviet Union and the more advanced Eastern European states. The most dramatic result in this respect was the Czechoslovakian crisis in 1968, but a more fundamental consequence of economic reform was the Soviet Union's reappraisal of its relations with Eastern Europe and with the West after the crisis. This reappraisal proved to be a turning-point for the CMEA and for its relations with the EEC.

The most extreme example of the disintegrative effect of economic reform occurred in Czechoslovakia, where economic reform produced a major social and political upheaval and a reassessment of foreign economic policy. The Czech press openly criticized Czechoslovakia's trade relations with the Soviet Union and with the CMEA and advocated a return to Czechoslovakia's pre-war connections with the West European economies. At the same time, West German business interests were warmly welcomed with promises of massive export opportunities and a relaxation of price discrimination against Western manufactured goods on the Czech domestic market.[9] Even without the precarious political situation, the Soviet Union could no doubt have found grounds for alarm in these economic

technology and skilled personnel for the build-up of the Soviet automobile industry in 1965; British Leyland's deal with Poland to manufacture diesel motors in Poland for home and export use; Mannesman's deal to supply large diameter steel pipe to the Soviet Union in return for Soviet natural gas. A major role in these agreements was played by Western financial credit usually backed by Government. By 1973 there were roughly 600 cooperation agreements in force. For more details see UN ECE, *Analytical Report on Industrial Co-operation among E.C.E. Countries* (Geneva, 1973).

9 The changes in foreign economic policy were contained in Ota Sik's proposals for economic reform. For details of the criticisms of CMEA trade see *Summary of World Broadcasts (Eastern Europe)* (2 December 1969) and P. Marsh, 'The politics of economic integration in Eastern Europe with special reference to East Germany', unpublished MA thesis (University of Manchester, 1973). The Soviet Union responded after the invasion by increasing raw materials supplies to Czechoslovakia and offering her a large financial credit.

developments and ultimately stepped in to halt the process of change in foreign economic policy. Although not opposed to increased trade with the West and 'cooperation deals' with Western corporations, the likely scale of developments in Czechoslovakia and the political friction they were causing in one of the Soviet Union's major trading partners made intervention a regrettable necessity.

Intervention, however, was only the short-term remedy to the crisis produced in Soviet–East European relations by the Czechoslovak situation. In the long term the Soviet Union had to tackle the more fundamental question of how, in the light of the impact of economic reform, it would redefine its relationship with the Eastern European states. This meant ensuring that they were transformed into a coherent regional group working for and not against Soviet economic and political interests. To solve this problem, the Soviet Union had to recognize the specific interests of the Eastern European states in domestic and foreign policy and to incorporate those interests in a new Soviet foreign policy centred on the revival of the CMEA and the building of a constructive East–West détente. Only in this way could it avoid the possibility of another disastrous blow to its prestige and to its control of Eastern Europe in the future.

Factors at work in the domestic sphere coupled with the situation in Eastern Europe ensured that the Soviet Union produced such a policy in the period from 1968 to 1974. The Soviet Union itself was faced with the problem of a stagnant economy and badly needed to improve the material living standard of its population, both for prestige reasons and in order to preserve the power of the ruling bureaucracy. To achieve this it had to rely on the provision of Western technology and long-term financial credits, which in turn required a harmonious international situation and improved relations with the major capitalist states. This therefore gave the Soviet Union common grounds with the other CMEA states who also wanted better economic and political relations with the West.

The Soviet Union was consequently able to offer the Eastern European states a 'package deal' of benefits with conditions attached. It would launch a major foreign policy initiative to improve economic and political relations with the West in return for greater cohesion amongst the Eastern European states and a strengthening of their relationship with Moscow. This new cohesion would be centred on the revival of the CMEA and the launching of 'socialist economic integration', which would ensure that increased contacts with the West would not have a disruptive influence on the functioning of the Eastern European states and their economic and political relations with the Soviet Union.

The Eastern European states were prepared to accept the 'package deal', not just because they were intimidated by Soviet power but because they too saw the benefit of united action in a world that was increasingly being dominated by large economic and political blocs. As their major concern was to expand foreign trade and gain access to world markets, they were perhaps conscious of their relative lack of leverage when acting individually. Moreover the majority of the industrialized member states were also enthusiastic about the revival of CMEA integration because they had definite interests in expanding cooperation and specialization of production amongst themselves, so as to take advantage of economies of scale. They therefore fell into line with the Soviet proposals but prepared also to articulate their own positions on integration and foreign economic policy, and to preserve their interests in crucial areas against those of the Soviet Union.

It was the revival of discussion on CMEA integration after 1968 which inevitably raised the question of the EEC once again. During the course of the debate the EEC was examined as a successful example of integration and the question of future relations between a strengthened CMEA and the EEC was discussed. The result was that the discussion of CMEA integration engendered by economic reform and its impact on Soviet–East European relations in turn produced a new attitude towards the EEC and thus set in motion the process whereby EEC–CMEA relations became an important issue for the communist states.

Despite the fact that the Soviet Union launched the drive towards CMEA integration in 1968 which culminated in the adoption of the 'complex programme of socialist economic integration' in August 1971, it was the industrially developed states of Eastern Europe which had the major say in the preparatory stages of the debate.[10] These states were concerned to ensure that any integration scheme adopted should reflect the emphasis on 'market forces' embodied in their domestic economic reforms, rather than be based on supranational planning. From this position they took issue with Soviet concepts of integration by supranational plan and advocated integration through enterprise amalgamation, the creation of a convertible CMEA currency, and a uniform price system in harmony with world prices. It was in this context that they first introduced a more realistic appraisal of developments in the EEC as evidence for the efficiency of integration by spontaneous market forces.

Thus in January 1970, D. Nemes, then a member of the Hungarian Party Politburo, frankly drew an unfavourable comparison between CMEA and the EEC when he stated:

Unlike the countries of the European Common Market which have made considerable progress in economic integration the C.M.E.A. countries are lagging behind in specialization or production cooperation even at the lowest level. How is one to explain that the Common Market countries which are divided by capitalist contradictions have forged ahead in integration whereas the C.M.E.A. countries which share common interests have only recently decided...to take the necessary steps in this direction?[11]

A satisfactory explanation was not readily forthcoming but prominent spokesmen of the reform economies repeatedly used the EEC as an example to back up their demands for a greater role for 'market forces' in CMEA integration. Inevitably such statements acted as a solvent on the extreme ideological position

10 For details on the formation of the 'Complex programme', see Marsh, 'The politics of economic integration', and H. Schaefer, *Comecon and the Politics of Integration* (New York, 1972). For the text of the Programme see *Die Wirtschaft*, no. 32 (11 August 1971).

11 D. Nemes, 'Leninism and the development of the world socialist system', *World Marxist Review* (January 1970). Two years earlier another Hungarian spokesman had declared, 'The Common Market is a fact and we, who are always realists have to acknowledge the existence...If our trade relations required us to call on some of the Brussels offices...we would not consider this step a renunciation of our principles.' J. Fock, 24 February 1968, quoted in F. Alting von Geusau, *Beyond the European Community* (Leyden, 1969), p. 149.

adopted by the communist states towards the EEC and created a more favourable climate for a *modus vivendi*. This could only take place after agreement on the basic preconditions for CMEA integration and the build up of the organization as a prospective partner for the EEC. Nevertheless, despite the hesitant progress towards CMEA integration and the low key nature of the 'Complex programme' (primarily due to the difficulty of compromise between 'plan' and 'market' approaches to integration, and to Romanian nationalistic intransigence), some sources in Eastern Europe were not afraid to point the way forward.

Commenting in August 1971 on the publication of the 'Complex programme', a Polish journal numbered amongst the major factors influencing integration in Eastern Europe 'the processes of economic unification within the EEC'. It went on to draw the following significant conclusion:

This means that a speeding up of the rate of our integration is not only in the interests of the socialist countries alone but also in the interest of economic equilibrium in Europe as a whole, so that the two large community areas should develop more or less side by side and could establish between each other, natural and even necessary ties of trade and co-operation.[12]

Faced with this type of thinking amongst the Eastern European states, it was not long before the Soviet Union began to rethink its attitude towards the EEC. From about 1967, the Soviet leadership had been trying to offer a more positive criticism of the EEC, as was evident in Kosygin's comment during a visit to Britain in 1967 that 'The very name Common Market is a drawback in that it is not "common" because not all countries are free to join. Markets of this kind should be open to co-operation of all the nations of Europe on an equal footing.'[13] After 1968 this criticism developed into a positive alternative policy centred on the holding of a European Security Conference and the possible creation of all-European institutions to foster East–West economic and political cooperation. The Soviet Union seemed initially to be offering all-European cooperation

12 Slowo Powszechne, 9 August 1971, in *Summary of World Broadcasts* (11 August 1971).
13 A. Kosygin, at the London Press Conference, 1967, quoted in W. Feld, *The European Common Market and the World* (New Jersey, 1967), p. 158.

as an alternative to closer West European integration and using the Economic Commission for Europe as an example of fruitful East–West collaboration. Nevertheless it soon became clear that this policy was unrealistic and that any East–West cooperation would have to be based on the continued existence and growth of the EEC.[14] This made it all the more necessary to build up the CMEA as a potential partner in the future détente.

A major indication of the new orientation of Soviet foreign policy came with Brezhnev's by now famous reference to the EEC in a speech in 1972. In his speech Brezhnev declared that 'The Soviet Union is far from ignoring the actually existing situation in Western Europe, including the existence of such an economic grouping of capitalist countries as the European Common Market and its evolution.'[15]

More importantly he went on to indicate that Soviet relations with the Community were dependent on it too, recognizing 'the realities existing in the socialist part of Europe, specifically the interests of the member countries of the C.M.E.A.' In conclusion he called for equality in economic relations and criticized trade discrimination.

Brezhnev's remarks were cautious and measured, saying nothing of actual Soviet and East European recognition of the EEC.[16] Nevertheless they did indicate an eventual adjustment of Soviet and Eastern European policy towards the EEC which was to take place from 1973. Moreover they represented the outcome of a fundamental foreign policy reappraisal undertaken by the Soviet Union under pressure from the economic demands of the Eastern European states, the political threat of the Czech crisis, and its own economic weakness. Henceforward CMEA integration would be the basis of proposals for an EEC–CMEA dialogue made necessary by the successful development of the EEC.

In order for this dialogue to develop, however, the EEC had

14 The prospective enlargement of the EEC from 1970 together with its greater coordination of foreign policy in preparation for a European Security Conference were major factors in the Soviet Union's changed attitude.

15 L. Brezhnev, speech to the 15th Congress of Soviet Trade Unions, quoted in *The Times* (21 March 1972).

16 As Charles Ransom notes in *The European Community*, p. 89.

to define its attitude to the Soviet Union's new initiative, to the future pattern of East–West economic and political relations, and to the CMEA as a potential organizational partner. By the early 1970s forces were at work within Western Europe that would ensure a positive EEC response despite the long period of inactivity on the question of a common policy towards the CMEA states. In order to understand the emergence of the new EEC–CMEA relationship, therefore, it is necessary to examine why the EEC member states were able to perceive advantages from a collective approach to East–West economic and political cooperation when hitherto they had preferred to pursue independent policies.

2. The Development of Collective Action by the EEC Member States

In his theoretical study of the process of integration, J. S. Nye has observed that one of the factors motivating states towards closer integration is the extent to which they develop a common perception of the external situation. Nye hypothesizes that 'It is the common definition of the nature of the external situation and the measures to be taken to deal or not deal with it that constitutes the favourable condition for an integrative response to the process mechanisms.'[17] If this hypothesis is applied to the analysis of the EEC's policy towards the CMEA states, it helps to explain why, in the period after 1970, the EEC began to move perceptively towards the formation of a common policy and to a new relationship with the communist states. What happened was that changes in the 'external situation' both in Europe and the world as a whole made the advantages of individual policies towards the communist states less and less obvious, and the prospect of collective community action more and more attractive. Amongst these changes the most important was the growing crisis of the international economy and the consequent increase in competition for world markets.

One result of this factor was the enlargement of the EEC from

17 J. S. Nye, 'Comparing Common Markets – a revised neo-functionalist Model' in L. Lindberg and S. Scheingold (eds.), *Regional Integration – Theory and Research* (Harvard, 1969), p. 216.

six members to nine in 1973 and an increase in the enlarged Community's awareness of its particular economic and political interests in relation to those of its two major rivals, Japan and the USA. This process was only tentative but it was sufficient to give a new impetus to the evolution of Community policy towards the CMEA states and to ensure that the changes made in Soviet policy after 1968 would meet with a positive, if cautious, response.

Before examining how these changes initiated a new stage in Community policy towards the CMEA states, it is necessary to give a brief history of the EEC's policy in this sphere. Since 1957, the EEC had had a vague commitment to the introduction of a common commercial policy set down in Article 113 of the Treaty of Rome. For several reasons, however, the activation of this commitment with regard to state trading countries was continually postponed and member states were able to pursue foreign economic policies largely independent of each other. In the early years of the EEC's existence, trade with the Soviet Union and Eastern Europe was of little economic importance in the total trade of the member states. It was not surprising, therefore, that little was done to speed up the formulation of a common commercial policy. It was really only in the late 1960s that East–West trade began to develop considerably and it was from this point that the European Commission, as the EEC body most concerned with the implementation of the Treaty of Rome, began to take initiatives on the question of harmonizing member states' policies.[18]

At this time, however, trade was beginning to take on forms that the Treaty of Rome could not possibly have envisaged. Increasingly, the exchange of goods between East and West was becoming dependent on the availability of Western financial

18 A procedure for prior consultation on trade agreements between member states and state trading countries had been instituted as early as 1961 and trade agreements were to be limited to the end of the transition period of the Treaty (1969). These moves did not, however, appreciably alter the individual approach of the member states to the communist states. For details see Ransom, *The European Community*, pp. 37–50 and Feld, *The European Common Market*, chapter 8.

credits to compensate for the shortage of convertible currency in the communist states. In addition, the Soviet Union and the Eastern European states were becoming more interested in the import of technology and sophisticated plant so as to modernize their industry and make its products more competitive on world markets. This meant that the communist states wanted 'co-operation agreements', rather than straightforward trade, in which Western companies backed by their governments entered into long-term commitments with communist economic bodies to supply plant, technology, managerial skills and marketing networks. Thus instead of a simple exchange of products, East–West trade now began to centre on 'joint-venture' deals in which a Western company supplied technology, 'know-how', and capital, and the communist states supplied labour and back-up services. The end product of deals of this kind could either be marketed in the East or the West or even in third countries.

The gradual substitution of 'economic cooperation' for conventional exchange was both cause and consequence of the growth in East–West trade in the decade from 1964 to 1974. During these years the Western European states actively vied with each other for a share in this trade and in doing so made it more difficult for a common EEC commercial policy to emerge. In what can only be described as a scramble to enter the communist market, most Western European governments adopted export promotion policies using state credit guarantees to foster increased trade with the East. They were aided in their penetration of the Eastern market by the absence of America and Japan, who until the early seventies were still restrained by Cold War attitudes towards trade with communist states.

After British action in guaranteeing a fifteen-year credit to the Soviet Union (for the purchase of a fibre plant from Courtaulds in 1964) had broken the five-year maximum of the Berne Union agreement on credits, the way was open for unrestricted competition of the Western European states in Eastern trade. France under De Gaulle led the way in launching new economic and political contacts with the communist states, but by the late 1960s West Germany and Italy were also challenging. Faced with an apparent free-for-all the Commission vainly attempted to coordinate the credit policies of its members, but not until

October 1970 was it able to produce a clear policy statement. Then, the Council of Ministers adopted two directives providing for common standards on insurance for medium and long-term credits, a small gesture towards solving what was a major issue for the future success of a Community commercial policy.[19]

In the meantime the Commission continued to put greater emphasis on securing authority over the conventional trade activities of the Community's member states despite the fact that issues such as import quotas, tariffs and most-favoured-nation treatment, the standard weapons of trade diplomacy, were being increasingly replaced by long-term cooperation agreements and credits. From 1964 a timetable was laid down that would see a gradual transition to a Community policy towards state trading countries over five years. This was put off further by a Council of Ministers' decision of 1969, which extended the deadline to 1 January 1973, later to be postponed once again to the beginning of 1974.

This activity on the part of the Commission did little to alter the methods used by members to pursue economic relations with the CMEA states or the self-interested nature of the process.[20] Only changes in the economic situation of a long-term nature could hope to do that. By the late 1960s and early seventies, however, these changes were beginning to take place. The growing crisis of the Western economy during this period increased the pressure on individual states to maintain their expanding economies. The most dramatic example of the

19 For more details see Ransom, *The European Community*, p. 49, who points out: 'It is evident that the majority of the member states were not convinced that solid commercial advantages could be gained by hastening the establishment even of common procedures in dealing with Eastern Europe: otherwise the course of events might have been different.'

20 An American observer of the EEC member states' policies commented, 'Export Promotion is undoubtedly a form of competition between the member states with the goal of securing the greatest possible share of the imports of the Eastern block.' I. Walter, 'Die Einstellung der Vereinigten Staaten Zum Ost–West Handel und deren Implikationen für Westeuropa', *Aussenwirtschaft* (journal of the St Gallen College of Economic and Social Science), vol. 29 (March 1974), p. 94.

vulnerability of the Western states to the crisis came with the changes in American economic policy after 1968 which indirectly stimulated Western Europe into a course of collective action towards the CMEA states.

Under the pressure of increased Western European and Japanese competition in foreign and domestic markets, the United States responded with increased protectionism at home and a search for new economic outlets abroad. This led it to reappraise its economic and political attitudes towards the communist states and, with Japan, to emerge as a new and significant factor in East–West trade and cooperation in the early 1970s. Evidence of the new American and Japanese interest in the communist world mounted during this period. American and Japanese corporations began to seek out major deals with the Soviet Union involving the export of technology in return for Soviet raw materials. In doing so they received much more enthusiastic backing from their respective governments than hitherto and with this aid they were able to challenge the West European states' dominance of East–West trade. Japanese companies agreed to participate in the development of Siberian raw materials deposits and were allowed to set up branch offices in Moscow to facilitate business negotiations. In addition, Japan granted the Soviet Union a $1000 million credit in 1973. Similarly, American corporations such as IBM and Occidental Petroleum concluded major contracts with the Soviet Union and were given permission to open offices in Moscow. In May 1972 the Nixon–Brezhnev summit meeting in Moscow led to the signing of a trade agreement and the promise of Export–Import Bank credits for the Soviet Union, conditional upon Congress's consent to a new Trade Bill. Despite the breakdown of this measure in early 1975 due to American attempts to link increased trade with easier emigration for Soviet Jews, American–Soviet trade appeared from 1972 to be on a steadily upwards swing.[21]

21 Since 1971 the United States trade with the Soviet Union and Eastern Europe has increased seven-fold and US exports reached around $2.5 billion in 1973. This, however, was still only a fraction of Western Europe's trade with the East but it did indicate a real potential threat. Japanese penetration of the Eastern market in

Faced with this alteration in the external situation, the states of Western Europe slowly began to realize that advantages might be gained from closer collaboration so as to present a united front to the United States and Japan and to the Soviet Union and Eastern European states also. By coordinating their actions the Western European states could hope to avoid damaging competition amongst themselves and prevent the Soviet Union from playing one state off against another to obtain the most favourable terms of trade. Moreover, with major initiatives such as the European Security Conference in the air it became more and more vital to develop a Community policy on the possible direction of East–West economic cooperation in the future, rather than let the Soviet Union and United States monopolize the discussions. Naturally the transformation from a common definition of the external situation to actually taking measures to deal with it would have to take place over a long period of time. By 1973–4, however, the process which would lead to the creation of a common policy towards the CMEA had begun. Criticisms of the Commission's focus on conventional trade policy and its neglect of problems of economic cooperation and harmonization of credits formed the first stage. Positive action to formulate a new Community policy constituted the second. Together they represented a qualitative change in the EEC's position on relations with the Soviet Union and Eastern Europe which interacted with the new approach of the communist states to alter the course of EEC–CMEA relations from 1974.

Before analysing the concrete developments in EEC–CMEA relations it is useful to examine how the Community began to perceive changes in East–West economic relations and prepare the ground for a new policy that would combine the short-term interests of its member states with long-term concerns dictated by external developments. During the course of this re-evaluation of East–West relations, the Community's institutions and spokesmen, by stressing the benefits to be derived from collective action, came to champion Western Europe's future

the 1970s was more immediately threatening. By 1974 Japan had become the Soviet Union's second major capitalist trading partner. For details see W. Krause and F. Mathis, 'The U.S. policy shift on East–West trade', *Journal of International Affairs*, no. 1 (1974).

policy. It only remained for the individual member states to develop the political will to provide for its implementation.

Initially, dissatisfaction with the individualist approach to economic relations with the East was expressed by prominent business organizations within the EEC and then taken up by Community organizations and spokesmen. As early as 1966 UNICE, the organization representing industrial companies at the community level, had passed a motion deploring what it called 'the increased disadvantages resulting from the disparity of member states' commercial policies, particularly in respect of the Eastern Bloc'.[22] As a remedy it proposed greater coordination of national policies at the EEC level. By 1971, under the influence of the increasing competitiveness of Eastern European trade, European spokesmen were echoing this concern. An Italian member of the European Parliament declared that 'Without a doubt a new policy towards the state-trading countries is called for from the Community.'[23] The Community institutions themselves began to study the new conditions in which East–West trade was conducted and produced some outline recommendations which highlighted the increase that would be necessary in the Community's role if it were to assume control of East–West economic relations in the future.

Significantly a Community information document of June 1971 pointed to the key problem of finance and credit policy which would require a major shift from the national to the European level if a dynamic Eastern policy for the 1970s and beyond was to be constructed. The document stressed:

It is essential to be in a position to undertake investments in common. For the purposes of an active commercial policy, a financial establishment is needed comparable to the Export–Import Bank in the United States. This role could perhaps be entrusted to the European Investment Bank, on which it would fall to seek or develop the most appropriate means for co-operation between private firms in the Community in their quest for new markets abroad: and those of Eastern Europe could be particularly interesting.[24]

22 Cited in Feld, *The European Common Market*, p. 156.
23 D. Angelini, quoted in A. Masnata, *East–West Economic Co-operation* (London, 1974), p. 76.
24 *European Community Information Bulletin* on 'The E.E.C. and East–West Relations' (June 1971), quoted in Masnata, *Economic Co-operation*, p. 115.

At that point, such a policy suggestion went far beyond the narrow horizons of national decision-makers. Nor had the point been reached where the disadvantages of individual action in the sphere of credit policy would begin to outweigh the advantages. This point only began to be reached around 1973 when American and Japanese competition had intensified the struggle for Eastern Trade and when the Western European states were furiously undercutting each other on Eastern European markets. The absurdity of this situation when the EEC had the machinery to implement coordination of Western European credit policy for mutual advantage was highlighted by a member of the European Parliament in 1973. Supporting his plea for a more active Community policy on economic cooperation agreements with Eastern Europe, Mr Jahn, a German member, declared: 'The situation should not arise where a German delegation arrives in Moscow and is told "What do you mean by credit? We have 6% from the French and you want 9%, there is no point in any further discussion." This is what happened to us a few weeks ago with a delegation from Parliament.'[25] Anxieties of this kind were building up in 1973 and adding impetus to the Commission's attempt to implement the common commercial policy towards the state trading countries and to broaden its scope to meet the changed conditions of East–West trade. Already in October 1973, the Commission had sent a communication to the Council of Ministers proposing a regular information and consultation procedure on member states' cooperation agreements with the communist states.[26] It remained to be seen how far the national interests which predominated in the Council responded to this move to widen the commercial policy.

By 1973 and early 1974, therefore, a definite change had taken place in the Community's attitude to economic relations with the communist states. This change coincided with the end of the deadline for the establishment of the common commercial policy, the new foreign policy initiative of the CMEA states and the holding of the European Security Conference. The outcome of the interaction of these various developments was to produce

25 *Debates of the European Parliament*, no. 167 (18 October 1973).
26 *Bulletin of the European Communities*, no. 10 (1973).

significant progress towards a new stage in EEC–CMEA relations during the year of 1974. Nevertheless, observers of the EEC as it approached the deadline for the implementation of the common commercial policy towards the CMEA states could justifiably be critical of the hesitant movement towards collective action on the part of the member states. In particular many academic commentators warned of the short-sightedness of those elements within the EEC who continued to believe that cooperation agreements should be exclusively the concern of national governments. John Pinder, writing in March 1974, commented, 'The Commission's long march down the route outlined in the Treaty of Rome will soon reach its destination, and it looks as if on arrival not much will be found'.[27] This he attributed to the Community's failure to wrest the initiative from member governments on the vital questions of trade policy – credits and cooperation agreements. Shortly afterwards, however, the Commission took positive steps towards establishing a common commercial policy that in the long term was designed to extend its area of competence beyond that of conventional trade matters. The fact that it was able to even begin challenging the authority of the member states on questions such as credit policy and cooperation agreements seemed to indicate that changes in the external situation had started to erode the advantages of individual action in these matters.

How fast the progress would be towards a realistic community policy being put into operation with regard to the communist states was, of course, another matter. What was made clear by events in 1974, though, was that there were positive forces at work strengthening the Community's hand in the area of East–West relations and making collective action more attractive to the individual member states. Not least of these were the increasing competition of America and Japan for Eastern trade and the surprise decision by the CMEA states to approach the Community as a body for discussions on matters of common interest. How these external changes affected the formation of the EEC's policy on relations with the communist states will now be analysed.

27 J. Pinder, 'A Community policy towards Eastern Europe', *World Today* (March 1974).

3. The Development of EEC–CMEA Relations, 1974–7

In its communication to the Council of Ministers of 8 October 1973 proposing a consultation procedure for cooperation agreements, the Commission stated, 'it is important that the Community should dispose in the years ahead of efficient intervention and co-ordination instruments enabling it to sustain the competition of its other trading partners in the markets of Eastern countries in particular.'[28] The acquisition of these 'intervention and co-ordination instruments' came one step nearer realization in 1974 due to two developments – the holding of the European Security Conference and the CMEA approach to the Community requesting cooperation. In a sense the second development was a logical consequence of the first. For it was the united front on economic matters presented by the Community member states at the committee stage of the Conference that prompted the communist states to approach the Community institutions with new respect. This in turn gave an added impetus to the Commission's desire to implement an effective common commercial policy and to coordinate the actions of the member states on credit policy and economic cooperation against the competition of the USA and Japan.

More than anything else, perhaps, the experience of the European Security Conference persuaded the member states of the immediate advantages of collective action and in doing so gave a strong internal boost to the process of forming a common West European policy towards the CMEA states. The CMEA approach of 1974 merely altered the context in which the EEC policy-making process was operating.

As early as 1972 the EEC had begun to organize coordination of member states' activities in preparation for the European Security Conference. The key organs for coordination were the Davignon Committee (composed of the Political Directors of the Foreign Ministries of the member states) and two specially created groups, the Sub-group (dealing mainly with political aspects) and the Ad-Hoc group (concentrating on economic questions and including representatives of the Commission). These groups did much of the groundwork for the initial

28   *Bulletin of the European Communities*, no. 10 (1973).

meeting of the Conference and enabled the Community to speak with a united voice on the major issues raised by the Soviet Union.[29] At the second stage of the Conference, the detailed discussions held in Geneva on security, economic and human welfare matters, the Community was again active, particularly in the committee dealing with East–West economic cooperation. At this stage the Commission maintained permanent representation in the Committee's discussions although delegates sat as representatives of nation-states. The Commission coordinated activity through the Ad-Hoc group, and ensured that on detailed matters national delegations were well briefed on any agreed Community viewpoint.[30]

As a result the Community developed a definite identity during the discussion on East–West economic cooperation that helped to convince both its own members and the member states of the CMEA of its relevance to future developments in this sphere. Coming at a time when the Commission was launching its common commercial policy towards the state trading countries, the experience of the Security Conference could only have improved the prospects of the policy's success.

As the policy-making process was set in motion during 1974, four major issues came to the fore: the Community's role in economic cooperation agreements; Community acquisition of control over orthodox trade matters – tariffs, import quotas and most-favoured-nation treatment; the outline of a draft common policy; and the future relations between the EEC and the CMEA as institutions. It was not until the autumn of 1974 that solutions appeared to be in sight on these questions.

The Community's role in economic cooperation agreements was undoubtedly one of the key issues in the construction of the common commercial policy, for in this sphere the Treaty of Rome appeared to give no official sanction to the extension of Community authority. France in particular contested the right

29 For details see M. Palmer, 'The European Community and a Security Conference', *World Today* (July 1972).

30 M. Noel of the Commission commented favourably on the Commission's role in the second stage of the Conference in an address to the University of Manchester Seminar on the EEC's External Relations, 1974. See also Pinder, 'A Community policy'.

of the Commission to have jurisdiction over this field, arguing that cooperation agreements were not conventional trade and therefore did not fall under Article 113 of the Rome Treaty. Nevertheless, despite misgivings, most member states by 1974 were becoming convinced of the need for a *minimum* Community policy on cooperation agreements for reasons already stated. They were thus prepared to accept the Commission's role as a coordinator and harmonizer of the conditions offered by Community members to state trading countries, because it had tangible advantages in the long term. This in effect was the aim of the Commission proposals which emerged during 1974. In October 1973, the Commission had presented its proposals on cooperation agreements to the Council, arguing for a regular 'information and consultation procedure' prior to the conclusion of agreements between individual member states and state trading countries. It made clear that this was the first step in the direction of Community control over such agreements but that this would only take place with the completion of full economic and monetary union.[31]

On the basis of the Commission's proposals and after intensive discussion within the Council and the European Parliament the Council formally decided on 22 July 1974 to introduce a 'notification and consultation procedure'. The procedure was to apply to agreements with state trading and oil producing countries and was designed to stop what the EEC Bulletin called the 'escalation in credit terms offered to non-member countries in co-operation agreements'.[32] The Council's decision set up a system whereby members were to provide information to each other and to the Commission on the substance of cooperation agreements and the commitments they would involve.[33] This information would be monitored by the Commission through a Select Committee which would ensure that cooperation agreements did not violate the conditions of the common commercial policy. It would also be given the more positive task of co-ordinating member states' policies towards third countries and might eventually aid the formation of EEC consortia to tackle

31   *Bulletin of the European Communities*, no. 10 (1973).
32   *Bulletin of the European Communities*, no. 7/8 (1974).
33   *Ibid.*

projects, particularly in the Soviet Union, which were too large for the resources of national companies and their governments.[34] These latter implications of the 'consultation procedure' were clearly envisaged for the long term. In the short term the coordination and exchange of information by the Commission was the main aim. It was not until the autumn that the newly created Select or 'Restricted' Committee first met and its powers were more clearly defined. Member states were to notify the Commission of agreements already concluded and to give prior notification of future ones. If the Commission or another member state objected to any particular aspect within eight days, consultation was to take place in the Restricted Committee to try and reach a settlement of the grievance and if possible to promote cooperative action.[35]

This, then, was a small but important step in the direction of real collective action by the member states of the EEC towards the CMEA states. The first meeting of the Committee coincided with a general acceleration in the progress towards a common commercial policy that took place in the autumn of 1974 and as such laid the basis for future collective actions towards the Soviet Union and Eastern Europe. Moreover, it formed part of a general increase in the Commission's role in the complex field of international trade and credit at a time when Western Europe most needed to be united on such questions if it was to survive the growing crisis in the world economy. This crisis therefore played a major part in the member states' acceptance of a gradual increase in the Commission's role as a coordinator of foreign economic policies.[36]

34   *Ibid.*
35   For details of the first meeting see the report in *Europe* (*Agence Internationale D'Information pour la Presse*) (Brussels, 2 October 1974) (hereinafter referred to as *Europe*). The Commission's reply to a question in the European Parliament on 10 December 1974 confirmed that France and Germany had respected the procedure before signing agreements with the Soviet Union and stressed that consultation was only the first step in the direction of a more developed Community policy. For details see *Europe* (13 December 1974).
36   The EEC states had also begun in 1974 to coordinate their actions on credit policy in negotiations with America and Japan on a

Whilst moving towards greater control of economic cooperation agreements, the Commission was also moving towards
increasing Community control over the less contentious aspects
of commercial policy affecting the Communist states, namely
import quotas, tariffs and most-favoured-nation status. In this
area the Commission's problem was essentially to achieve a basis
for harmonization. In the event this basis turned out to be the
very lowest of common denominators acceptable to all the
member states. But the Commission's apparent satisfaction with
this state of affairs perhaps indicated its awareness that conventional trade questions were no longer the factor most affecting East–West economic relations. Accordingly it put a lower
priority on controlling this area than it did on economic
cooperation and credit policy. On 7 May 1974 the Council
reiterated the fact that from January 1975 all trade negotiations
should be conducted through the Community, and on 17 September it agreed to speed up the work on the evolution of a
common commercial policy. During the course of working out
this policy, however, the Commission found that the policies of
member states were drastically out of line and that there was
little to be gained at that stage in forcing common conditions
on them. In the interests of furthering progress on more important issues of East–West economic relations, therefore, the
Commission decided to recommend the endorsement of the
status quo.

'gentleman's agreement' to stop ruinous competition for world
trade. Meetings were arranged after July 1974 and some progress
was made at a meeting on 12 September 1974. The EEC states
defined their position in common in April, holding out for a
longer period of repayment than the US and Japan, particularly
for credits to state trading countries, and for lower interest rates.
At these talks, the Commission participated alongside the member
states and coordinated their position, which was based on an
informal agreement between the larger members about uniform
interest rates and periods of repayment. The talks continued with
the EEC presenting a united bargaining position to the US and
Japan. See *Europe* (12 September 1974; 4 November 1974).
However, in 1975 Britain, France, Italy and West Germany began
to negotiate independently of the Commission, in the OECD and
at the Rambouillet summit in November, a fact which indicated
the tenuous nature of the Commission's control of credit policy.

Rather than harmonize the varying conditions operating in the member states on trade with the Soviet Union and Eastern Europe, the Commission simply decided to incorporate them *en bloc* into a new common commercial policy. Thus the different import restrictions imposed by the member states on Soviet and Eastern European goods would form the basis of the new Community policy. They would be gradually harmonized over time as states such as Italy, France and Britain with high restrictive quotas became more prepared to moderate them. Until then, however, the Community proposed merely to 'photograph' the existing situation. In addition the common commercial policy would contain special safeguards for steel and textiles against Soviet and Eastern European 'dumping'.[37]

When the third major issue arose, therefore, of formulating the actual draft policy towards the state trading countries, the Commission proposed two lines of action: firstly the creation of a 'specimen agreement' between the EEC and the countries in question, and secondly the definition of an 'autonomous' policy which would be applied immediately and would simply put a Community label on existing national trade legislation.[38] These two lines of action together with the already agreed procedure for consultation on cooperation agreements would constitute the Community's policy towards the communist states for the future.

Inevitably, the construction of a specimen cooperation agreement between the EEC and individual state trading countries caused the most difficulty. In the first place, the agreement had to be formulated without consultation with the communist states themselves, who at that point were not prepared to commit themselves to recognition of the EEC by entering into negotiations individually. In the second place, the idea of a specimen agreement encroached most seriously on the powers of the member states and tested the strength of their desire for collective action towards the CMEA states. As envisaged by the Commission, the specimen agreement would further the member states' main objectives in East–West economic relations

37 Report of the Commission's proposals in *Europe* (18 September 1975).
38 *Ibid.*

by providing mechanisms for bringing the full power of the Community to bear on the state trading countries. The Commission defined the Community's main objectives in East–West relations as being two-fold: the development of the Community's exports and the continuity of its supply of basic raw materials. In its view a specimen agreement would best be able to achieve these objectives if it was long term (five to ten years), was watched over by a joint committee of representatives of the EEC and the state concerned, and provided for reciprocal trade liberalization measures.[39] In addition, the Commission proposed that the specimen agreement should also include the potential for developing economic and technical cooperation with the individual state trading countries, thus putting the Community agreement on a par with current economic cooperation agreements formulated at the national level.

This latter point was clearly the most controversial. The Commission formally sent its proposals to the Council on 3 October 1974, and the Council considered them on 15 October. It was authoritatively reported that the question of the inclusion of provisions on economic cooperation in the specimen agreement was the major point of discussion.

France was initially opposed to their inclusion on the grounds that economic cooperation lay within national competencies. However, a compromise appeared to be reached in the Council whereby the agreement might contain provisions on economic cooperation if the communist state concerned requested them. Moreover the proposal for the acquisition by the Community of powers over economic cooperation was moderated to imply that this would occur over a period of time rather than immediately.[40] On this basis the Council adopted the Commission's proposals on the specimen agreement at its 15 October session, subject to the finalization of the documents by the Committee of Permanent Representatives. The finalization was completed by 29 October and the basis of the new Community policy laid.

The specimen agreement took the following form. It was to incorporate the liberalization of quotas, respect for the prin-

39 *Europe* (18 September 1974).
40 For details see *Europe* (14 October 1974; 16 October 1974).

ciples and mechanisms of the Common Agricultural Policy and ad-hoc provisions for payment and financing of trade. More importantly an 'evolutive clause' in the agreement provided for communist states to proceed to economic cooperation rather than trade with the Community as soon as it acquired powers in that direction. Finally the agreement was to be administered by a 'joint committee'.[41]

The specimen agreement having been finalized it remained for the Commission to offer it to the state trading countries. In the absence of Soviet and East European diplomatic representation to the Community, the Commission agreed to forward the agreement, together with an *aide mémoire* inviting the opening of negotiations, to their diplomatic missions located in Brussels. In the meantime, whilst waiting for the communist states to respond, the Commission would apply the straightforward 'autonomous policy' endorsing the status quo.[42]

Thus by the end of 1974 the common commercial policy had taken shape. The method of employing it, however, was to rely exclusively on the establishment of relations between the EEC and individual communist states. There was no question of approaching the CMEA as a parallel organization to the EEC for trade negotiations. The fourth major issue of 1974, namely the nature of future EEC–CMEA relations, arose largely from initiatives made by the communist economic organization to which the EEC was forced to reply.

The reasons for the revival in the CMEA's activity have been examined in a preceding section where it was made clear that the CMEA's revitalization was in fact a response to the success of the EEC and also a preliminary to the construction of a new EEC–CMEA relationship. The CMEA states, led by the Soviet Union, saw definite benefits in collective action towards the EEC

41 *Europe* (28/29 October 1974).
42 The autonomous policy was ratified by the Council of Ministers on 12 November 1974. *Europe* (12 November 1974). It merely gave Community sanction to the different policies of member states in conventional trade matters. The specimen agreement though only existing on paper was the most important half of the new policy because it vastly increased the potential power of the Community over trade relations in the long term.

which would prevent them being isolated in negotiations with the full might of the Community. Obviously Soviet pressure was a key factor in the adoption of collective action, but the interests of the Eastern European states in relation to the EEC were quite consistent with such a course.

The promotion of the CMEA as the natural negotiating partner for the EEC during 1973 and 1974 was, therefore, a logical development from the changes in Soviet–East European relations and Soviet foreign policy. It had the effect of creating a united front amongst the member states in preparation for the expected launching of a Community commercial policy. It also aimed to check the opportunistic policies of some of the Eastern European states who were entering into private negotiations with Brussels. Hungary, Poland and Bulgaria were reported to have made informal contacts in order to raise problems concerning the Common Agricultural Policy, whilst Romania had actually gone as far as joining the Community's Generalized Preferences scheme for developing countries.[43]

Unofficial contacts with the Community were made in late 1973 by the CMEA's Russian secretary, Mr Fadeyev, who approached the Danish Government with a proposal for talks with the EEC.[44] The reply given by the Council of Ministers through Danish diplomatic channels was that under the terms of the Treaty of Rome the Commission dealt with all relations with international organizations, and that the CMEA secretary should therefore approach the Commission. This was the start of a delicate diplomatic game whereby the CMEA states tried to reconcile their continued official reluctance to recognize Community institutions with the question of how to initiate talks with the Community. By first approaching the Community through the diplomatic channels of national governments who had key representatives on Community institutions, the com-

---

43   The Romanian request was made in February 1972 and granted in June 1973. R. W. Dean, *West German Trade with the East: The Political Dimension* (New York, 1974), pp. 241–2.

44   The President of the Council of Ministers was at this time a Dane. *European Community Information Bulletin* (April 1974). The June 1973 meeting of the CMEA sanctioned the initiative. See Dean, *West German Trade*.

munist states were preserving the policy of non-recognition. The EEC, on the other hand, was equally determined that the approach should go through official channels and thus force the communist states into *de facto* recognition of the Commission. The diplomatic shadow-boxing dragged on for almost a year, during which time the EEC concentrated on constructing a common commercial policy aimed at the individual communist states rather than the CMEA. Only when it became clear what the outlines of the policy were did the CMEA make a reluctant and circumspect move to renew its earlier initiative. At the end of July, a Russian official of the CMEA who just happened to be on holiday in Brussels called in at the Commission's offices and had talks with EEC officials as an 'interested tourist'. This absurd incident marked the beginning of a new stage in the relationship between the two organizations.

On 20 September 1974, Fadeyev discussed EEC–CMEA relations with the French *chargé d'affaires* in Moscow. Following this talk, in which the necessity of approaching the Commission was stressed, a letter arrived at the Commission's headquarters on 24 September. The letter arrived by normal delivery, post-marked Moscow, and was nearly mislaid in the day-to-day mail. Inside the letter was an invitation to M. Ortoli, the President of the Commission, to visit Fadeyev in Moscow in order to open EEC–CMEA talks.[45] The Commission duly passed on the request to the Council of Ministers which was in the process of accepting the final outlines of the common commercial policy. The CMEA proposals clearly emphasized that for the Soviet and Eastern European states, contacts between the two economic organizations were going to play a major part in future East–West economic relations. This of course ran completely counter to the EEC's evolving policy which was aimed directly at individual communist states.

The EEC was therefore forced to mount a cautious defence of its own approach whilst at the same time responding to the CMEA initiative. This took the form of playing down the

45 This farcical series of incidents was described by a member of the
    Commission in the Seminar on the External Relations of the
    European Community held at Manchester University, 1974–5. For
    details see *Europe* (25 September 1974).

importance of the CMEA in East–West relations and denying
it the position of strength that the communist states were trying
to claim in future bargaining between East and West. In the
Commission's view the CMEA was not a parallel organization
to the Community because it only had coordinating, secretarial
duties, whereas the Community had extensive powers of management and initiative, and was truly supranational. Relations
with the CMEA should consequently be seen only as a 'complement' to relations with the individual states in question and
should not replace in any way these direct relations. This somewhat derisory view of the CMEA put forward by the Commission did not, however, preclude the opening of contacts. It was
proposed that talks should begin on general questions such as
the economic situation, environmental problems, and exchanges of statistics, and that these should be conducted at the level
of leading officials. A meeting between Ortoli and Fadeyev
would perhaps take place in the future if common ground was
found at the preliminary talks.[46] The EEC–CMEA talks finally
took place in February 1975 when a delegation led by Wellenstein, a Director General in the Commission's section on External Relations, visited CMEA headquarters for three days.[47]
Nothing really emerged from the visit except a proposal for
CMEA representatives to visit Brussels for further talks. It
seemed that the CMEA representatives had expected the meeting to prepare the way for an Ortoli–Fadeyev summit. The EEC
delegation, however, had stuck firmly to its brief of sounding
out the communist side on technical matters and of finding out
in detail what an EEC–CMEA dialogue could offer that relations
with the individual states could not. As a result they refused to
subscribe to the CMEA's optimism on future relations and were
unable to agree on a joint communiqué due to differences of

46   For the Commission's position see *Europe* 21 September 1974; 18
     October 1974). The Council of Ministers endorsed the
     Commission's position on 15 October.
47   Prior to this meeting the first formal contact between an EEC
     institution and the CMEA had taken place in December when a
     delegation from the CMEA Investment Bank called unannounced
     at the Luxemburg headquarters of the European Investment
     Bank. *European Community Information Bulletin* (December 1974).

approach.[48] A Tass statement of 9 February declared that the two sides 'had made progress in the drawing up of proposals concerning the next meeting of the leaders of these two bodies'. If this was the case then it was surely very minimal 'progress', and the explanation lay not in the lack of preparedness of the CMEA delegation but in the fundamentally different policies of the two organizations.

Whereas the Soviet Union and the Eastern European states wanted to elevate the CMEA to a status of parity with the EEC and saw an Ortoli–Fadeyev summit as a major step in this process, the EEC wanted negotiations to remain in the first instance essentially low key. The main thrust of the Community's common commercial policy was undoubtedly directed towards establishing relations with the individual communist states. Clearly any recognition of the CMEA's equality of status with the EEC would undermine that policy and lead to less favourable circumstances for the pursuit of Western European objectives.

Despite all the Community's rhetoric about the need for more detailed talks with the CMEA and for greater information about its powers, the basic reason for the EEC's reluctance to establish relations was that such relations might assist in the creation of a countervailing power in the East capable of thwarting the EEC's economic and political strategies in that area. Only when this fundamental difference of interest between the Communist states and the Community is realized can the halting development of the relationship be understood, and the seemingly endless diplomatic manoeuvres of both sides since the first abortive meeting of early 1975 be placed in their real political and economic context.

Nevertheless, after the talks the Commission was still at pains to point out that it was ready at all times to enter into negotiations with individual communist states, and that it saw no reason why the CMEA should claim the right to represent its members in

48 For detailed press comment on the meeting see *Europe* (8 February 1975; 10 February 1975), *Guardian* (8 and 10 February 1975). Wellenstein cited two main reasons for the failure of the meeting: (1) a fundamental difference of approach, (2) the unpreparedness of the CMEA to discuss detailed questions.

negotiations with the EEC when it did not claim the same right of supervision over their trade negotiations with countries such as Japan and the United States.[49] Behind this viewpoint lurked a certain wounded pride that the communist states had still not recognized the EEC and had made their approaches through the Council of Ministers and not the Commission. More importantly, the Commission's motivation in stressing its readiness to deal with individual communist states was perhaps to entice one or more of the smaller CMEA states to break ranks and approach Brussels on some specific area of concern. To make the success of such a strategy more likely, however, the Commission had to show that its influence over East–West trade and payments was increasing. Unfortunately the propensity of the Community's own members to break ranks in this area cast a cloud of uncertainty over the Commission's gambit.

The Commission was thus faced from 1975 with managing two complicated policies with regard to East–West economic relations – increasing the scope of its authority over the vital question of credit policy, and securing the tacit recognition of its authority by one or more of the communist states. Obviously a successful pursuit of the first policy would make success in the second area more likely, as would further accretions of power to the Community in areas such as import quotas and fisheries policy, which would force the communist states to negotiate with the Commission. From 1975 to 1977, therefore, it was developments in these ad-hoc areas of credit policy, import quotas and fisheries policy which determined the progress of EEC–CMEA relations, and not the continued desire of some of the communist states for a formal linkage of the two economic organizations. Despite some setbacks, the initiative, after two years, still lay with the Community rather than with the CMEA.

Ironically the setbacks to the Commission's strategy of increasing its power and relevance in East–West trade came largely from the actions of EEC member states in the crucial area of export credits. The Commission made determined attempts to assert its authority in this field, for example by proposing the

49 This was the line taken by Commission officials questioned by the author in 1976.

creation of a European Export Credit Bank to support the activities of Community consortia formed to win large export contracts. It was argued that such a bank would help eliminate the 'ridiculous competition' between member states for large export contracts and provide uniform interest rates and repayment terms for such contracts. In doing so it would gradually wrest all the initiative away from national credit institutions and place it in the hands of Brussels.[50]

Not surprisingly, the Community member states were lukewarm about the idea. Although they had moved further towards the principle of a collective approach to export credits and cooperation agreements since 1973, in practice the pressures of competition still dictated the attitudes of national governments towards trade and exports. Earlier in 1975, Britain had proved this to be true by offering a £950 million line of credit to the Soviet Union at an interest rate of 7½ per cent without consulting the Commission or other member states. According to press reports, Commission officials were furious at this unilateral action which allowed the Soviet Union to play off one EEC member state against another.[51] Nevertheless there was little that could be done without creating a serious confrontation between the Commission and the individual states who were pursuing their own national economic interests.

Later in 1975, however, the Commission appeared to be prepared to risk such a confrontation in an effort to bring the member states into line on the question of credit policy. The provocation which spurred the Commission into asserting itself took the form of unilateral action on credit policy by Britain, France, West Germany and Italy in the Organization for Economic Cooperation and Development (OECD) and at the Rambouillet economic summit in November. In these forums, the leading member states showed themselves willing to ignore the Community framework and negotiate with Japan and the United States on concluding a 'gentleman's agreement' on credit terms in international trade. The Rambouillet summit in fact laid down this willingness in the joint declaration agreed

50 For details of this proposal see the *Guardian* (26 July 1976).
51 *Guardian* (24 May 1975).

on by the participants. Point ten stated that 'We look to an orderly and fruitful increase in our economic relations with Socialist countries. . . We will also intensify our efforts to achieve a prompt conclusion of the negotiations now under way concerning export credits.'[52]

Such independent action, which had been well in evidence before the summit, testified to the determination of the leading industrial states to do their own bargaining on the sensitive question of export credit guidelines. The Commission concluded, however, that enough was enough and that the unilateral search for a 'gentleman's agreement' involved the leading member states in behaviour that was considered ungentlemanly from the Commission's point of view. In late November 1975, therefore, the Commission took its courage in both hands and went to the Court of Justice for an opinion as to the rights of member states to conduct export credit policy. The Court found in the Commission's favour and defined Article 113 of the Rome Treaty as indeed giving the Community control over export credit policy. The member states had no right to control such matters and in fact were endangering the Community by preventing 'the latter from fulfilling its task in the defence of the common interest'.[53] With right on their side, the Commission thus prepared to confront the member states with their sins.

Unfortunately the leading member states failed to be shocked into admitting the error of their ways and repenting. They continued to offer tempting credits to prospective buyers of their goods and to work through the mechanism of the 'summits', from which the Commission was excluded, for the creation of international credit guidelines. It was all very well for the Court of Justice to pronounce and for members of the Commission to talk about the advantages of common action in trade negotiations.[54] The question remained, who was really in control of export credits? The answer came in June 1976 when the four leading EEC states announced their adherence to a set

52 *Guardian* (18 November 1975).
53 *Bulletin of the European Communities*, no. 11 (1975), para. 2308.
54 As Mr Wellenstein did in a speech to the European Movement in Oslo, where he spoke on behalf of Mr Soames, Commissioner for External Relations. See the *Guardian* (4 November 1975).

of loose guidelines on export credits agreed at the Puerto Rico economic summit.[55] Along with America and Japan, the four leading EEC states unilaterally declared that they would be bound by the guidelines for an experimental period. The Commission was left to contemplate the degree of respect that member states had for the Treaty of Rome and its guardian the Court of Justice.

In July 1976, the Commission appeared to be prepared to challenge the right of the states concerned to agree to credit guidelines independent of the Community. The Commission announced that it was intending to invoke Article 169 of the Treaty against the four states concerned, and to ask for explanations of why they had defied the Treaty and the Court of Justice's ruling by concluding an agreement on export credits outside the Community framework. Letters were sent to the four offending states but at the last moment the Commission appeared to draw back from the confrontation. Influenced by a Council of Ministers meeting in March 1977, at which the smaller member states decided to join with the 'big four' and endorse the guidelines, the Commission backed down and withdrew its infraction proceedings. Although still critical of the guidelines as too loose and open to violation, the Commission now recognized that they at least constituted an initial step towards collective action. Consequently they were endorsed as EEC policy until such time as the Commission and the member states could work out a more comprehensive arrangement.[56]

Thus, in the field of credit policy, the actions of its own member states prevented the Commission from consolidating its hold over commercial policy and using this hold to persuade

55 The export credit guidelines set down minimum rates of interest, maximum credit periods and the percentage of down payment to be made by the buyer. These terms were, however, to vary according to whether or not a buyer country was classified as rich, poor or intermediate. Each of the seven states who agreed to the guidelines (the four major EEC states plus the US, Japan and Canada) made unilateral declarations of support for the principles although they were not to be mandatory. For details see *Press Bulletin of the Moscow Narodny Bank* (16 June 1976), and *Bulletin of the European Communities*, no. 3 (1977).

56 *Bulletin of the European Communities*, no. 3 (1977).

the CMEA states to enter into official negotiations with Brussels. As long as Community control over credit policy remained loose and ineffective, a key inducement for the communist states to focus their economic diplomacy on Brussels was missing. This was all the more regrettable from the Commission's point of view because in other fields, notably those of import quotas and fisheries policy, the Commission's hand in East–West economic relations was being strengthened. In the case of import quotas the growing impact of the Community's protectionist agricultural policies was forcing some of the smaller CMEA states to approach Brussels informally to protest for example about the ban on beef imports imposed by the Community in 1975. Romania also found itself unable to subscribe completely to the CMEA line of 'inter-organizational links' as early as June 1975, when the Romanian Prime Minister, Manescu, told a CMEA meeting that 'There are and will continue to be problems in relations with the Common Market which will have to be directly solved by each C.M.E.A. member country.'[57]

Predictably, therefore, it was Romania who shortly afterwards broke CMEA ranks by entering into negotiations with the Commission on the question of textile import quotas. These negotiations began in March 1976 and were concluded three or four months later with an agreement that provided for quotas on Romanian clothing imports, agreement on basic price levels and the opening of Romania to EEC textile exports. The negotiations were justified by Romania as arising from common participation with the EEC in the GATT Multi-Fibre Arrangement covering textiles.[58] A similar justification was made some months later when in January 1977 Poland began talks with the Commission about textile exports to the Community.[59] Such technicalities did not hide the fact that there were the beginnings of cracks in the CMEA's united front and that the Commission's role in East–West trade negotiations was being enhanced.

However, it was the decision by the Community to adopt a Common Fisheries Policy in 1977 which lured the biggest fish

57 *Guardian* (8 August 1975).
58 *Bulletin of the European Communities*, no. 7/8 (1976).
59 *Guardian* (11 January 1977).

of all, the Soviet Union, into the Commission's net. The adoption of a 200-mile fishing limit round Community coast lines from the beginning of 1977 vitally affected the large Soviet, Polish and East German fishing fleets. It also forced the respective communist governments to realize that the Commission was the prospective partner in any negotiations they might have to enter into to preserve their fishing rights in EEC waters. In January 1977, the Council of Ministers made it clear that the Community was united on this point by issuing an ultimatum to the communist states that either they notify Brussels of their fishing fleets in EEC waters and begin discussions on fish quotas and ship numbers, or they be expelled from EEC waters.[60] In February came the answer when the Soviet Union, breaking all precedents, entered into negotiations on a fishing agreement with a Community delegation composed of members of the Council and of the Commission.[61]

Although the chief Soviet spokesman played down the significance of the talks and stressed that they did not amount to Soviet recognition of the EEC, there was no doubt that the Commission saw the talks as a breakthrough in its attempts to force the Soviet Union and other East European states into acknowledging the Community's growing competence in trade and economic matters. Mr Jenkins, the new President of the Commission, described the talks as 'a great achievement', and it was clear that although the Soviet delegation preferred to think that they were negotiating with the individual states, led by Britain who occupied the Presidency of the Council, the Commission regarded the victory as theirs.[62] Further evidence of this came as the talks progressed and the Soviet delegation realized that they would ultimately have to sign a reciprocal fishing agreement with the Community itself. Mr Ishkov, the Fisheries Minister leading the Soviet side, declared that he had instructions only to sign an agreement with the various member states and that recognition of the Community could not be discussed in the forum of the fishing negotiations. By March

60 *Guardian* (19 January 1977).
61 *Guardian* (17 February 1977).
62 *Guardian* (19 February 1977).

1977 the talks had stalled on this matter, with the Commission pressing for an official agreement between the Soviet Union and the Community, and the Soviet delegation trying to avoid committing themselves to such a significant step in the direction of recognition.[63]

The reason for the Soviet reluctance was that it was waiting for some result from a separate CMEA initiative towards the EEC begun in 1975, of which it was the main supporter. Against the Commission's strategy of aiming its commercial policy at the individual CMEA states and relying on its increased authority in various fields to force the CMEA states to break ranks, the Soviet Union was trying to maintain a unified CMEA response. This Soviet strategy was aimed at maintaining Soviet control over East–West economic contacts, securing EEC recognition of the CMEA as an equal negotiating body, and improving the bargaining position of the communist states against the industrially more powerful EEC states. For the last two aims the Soviet Union had a fair degree of support from the smaller Eastern European states.

Unfortunately the developments of the period from 1975 to 1977 had undermined this policy and shifted the balance in favour of the Commission's ad-hoc accretion of influence over East–West economic relations. After the failure of the EEC–CMEA talks in February 1975, the CMEA had persisted with its search for an official agreement with the EEC despite the latter's coolness. At a CMEA meeting in November 1975, a further approach to the EEC was authorized and this culminated in the meeting of Gerhard Weiss, the East German Chairman of the CMEA Executive Committee, with his opposite number, M. Thorn, President of the Council of Ministers, in February 1976.[64] At this meeting Herr Weiss presented a draft proposal for a 'framework agreement' between the two organizations which would allow individual member states on both sides some freedom of action on detailed trade and cooperation negotiations.

The framework agreement proposal was taken back to the Community for consideration by the Commission and the Coun-

63 *Guardian* (11 March 1977).
64 *Guardian* (3 November 1975; 16 February 1976).

cil. The Commission was clearly lukewarm to the idea because it attempted to set up the CMEA as an equal to the EEC. More importantly, however, the framework agreement cut across the Commission's strategy of aiming commercial policy at the individual communist countries. As details emerged it appeared that Weiss's proposal was intended to lay down a set of general rules governing trade and cooperation between the two blocs which the EEC and CMEA would use to regulate individual exchanges between respective member states. The framework agreement also attempted to present a joint CMEA approach to EEC agricultural policies and their effect on communist agricultural exports, called for an end to trade discrimination through quotas, and requested EEC help in securing credit on favourable terms from the West. In return it promised to investigate the possibility of convertibility of currencies between the two sides and to expand trade opportunities for the EEC member states.[65]

After consideration by the Council of Ministers at its meeting on 29 March 1976 the framework agreement was passed to the Commission for further detailed study and the preparation of a response. After that very little was heard of it and it appeared to have been buried in the Brussels bureaucracy whilst the Commission concentrated on pursuing its ad-hoc initiatives on credit policy, import quotas and fisheries policy.

As the amount of Soviet involvement in the latter question became more and more evident, the Soviet Union's need for a definite response to the CMEA proposal was all the more urgent in an effort to save itself from a humiliating *de facto* agreement with the Community on fishing rights. It seemed as though the Soviet Union was waiting for some kind of concession from the EEC on the question of the framework agreement and had in fact entered into negotiations on fishing rights in the confident expectation of progress towards an official EEC–CMEA relationship. Whether this was true or not, the EEC showed no sign of hurrying the matter and although the question of EEC–CMEA relations was scheduled for discussion at the Council of

65 *Guardian* (3 March 1976; 29 March 1976).

Ministers meeting of 21 May, no firm proposals for an agreement between the two bodies had emerged by mid-1977.[66]

However, a CMEA delegation led by Mr Marinescu, the Chairman of the Executive Committee, visited Brussels on 21 September in order to revive the prospect of an EEC–CMEA agreement. Although being greeted officially by M. Simonet, the President of the Council of Ministers, the CMEA delegation showed themselves quite prepared to sit down and negotiate with a delegation from the Commission led by Wilhelm Haferkamp, the Commissioner for External Relations. This was perhaps the furthest the CMEA had gone in the direction of recognition of the Commission's right to conduct external trade policy. It was therefore indicative of the socialist side's desire to conclude a framework agreement covering issues such as credits, tariffs and import quotas as soon as possible. On the other hand the EEC showed no signs of altering its position that talks between the two organizations be restricted to general areas such as the exchange of economic information, and studies of European transport and environmental problems. Although it was decided to begin negotiations early in 1978 on a possible agreement between the two organizations, no new grounds emerged from the talks in Brussels for believing that this would be accomplished quickly. The EEC continued to believe that the individual socialist states were the legitimate targets for its trade policy and not the CMEA. The gap between the positions of the two sides thus remained as great as ever despite the apparent progress represented by the resumption of official negotiations.[67]

The reasons for this, of course, were rooted in the conflicting strategies of the EEC and the CMEA which had evolved in response to the basic needs and interests of the member states of the respective organizations. By 1977, EEC–CMEA relations had developed considerably from their previous antagonistic

---

66 Confirmation that the EEC Council was discussing EEC–CMEA relations at its next meeting was given by the British Foreign Secretary in reply to a Parliamentary question. See *Hansard* (4 May 1977).

67 *European Intelligence* (6 October 1977), p. 4.

state, but were stalled by the EEC's reluctance to recognize the CMEA as an equal negotiating partner and its determination to direct its policy towards the individual communist states. The success of that policy from 1975 to 1977, based on the extension of the Community's power in important economic fields affecting the communist states (despite the setback on credit policy), ensured that the initiative in EEC–CMEA relations still lay with Brussels. The situation was ironic in that the previous period of antagonism had been caused by the refusal of the CMEA states to recognize the EEC. Now, as these states showed signs of moderating their position, the EEC's reluctance to accept the equal status of the CMEA was creating a stumbling block to the compromise necessary for a lasting dialogue between the two organizations.

Conclusions

The reasons for the current hiatus in EEC–CMEA relations are ultimately to be found in the differences of economic and political interest between Eastern and Western Europe and in the nature of the EEC's economic and political power. If it is accepted that the primary interest of the Soviet and Eastern European states in seeking improved relations with the West is to attract technology and investment, and the primary interest of the EEC member states is to maximize their export opportunities and increase their access to raw materials (as the Commission stated), then the underlying conflict between Eastern and Western Europe is self evident. Obviously the Eastern European states need to combine to strengthen their bargaining position in negotiations with the West. Equally obviously the Western European states have recognized that they too can benefit from collective action. It follows from this that each side seeks to strengthen the basis of its own collective action and to try to undermine the basis of the other side's.

Thus EEC–CMEA relations have evolved on the basis of conflicting economic and political interests and at the current stage appear to be beset by the contradictions arising from those interests. Whether or not this will limit the development of EEC–CMEA relations permanently is another matter and depends ultimately on the real nature of the EEC's economic and political power as it assumes greater control over foreign economic policy. Without briefly analysing that power, observations about the future prospect of EEC–CMEA relations are academic.

The majority of Western commentators on the EEC and on East–West relations in general accept the argument that the real stumbling block to peaceful East–West cooperation is the Soviet Union. Accordingly they welcome the EEC's increase in power as a useful counter-weight to the assertion of Soviet power, and view the CMEA as merely a respectable cover for Soviet economic and political control of Eastern Europe. From this point of view they are suspicious of the CMEA's claim to speak for the interests of the Eastern European states, and they support the EEC's policy of attempting to deal with individual communist states in isolation and free from the pernicious influence of the Soviet Union. Not surprisingly they see no contradiction between EEC policy and the fundamental interests of the Eastern European states, which are separate from those of the Soviet Union. Looked at from this point of view the impact of the EEC on Eastern Europe can only be seen as benevolent – providing technology and investment to modernize the economies of Eastern Europe, creating mutually profitable trade and acting as a political counter-weight to the Soviet Union. Any attempts to interfere with that process can only be the result of Soviet attempts to retain authoritarian control over its sphere of influence.

However, some observers of the Community take a rather different view of the nature of the Community's power, and in doing so offer an alternative perspective from which to view the current state and future prospects of East–West relations. For Johan Galtung in particular, the EEC approximates more to an 'embryonic superpower' seeking to spread its political and economic influence over other areas of the world and in doing so attempting to create the conditions most favourable to West European penetration and dominance.[68] For Galtung, the EEC's relationship with the CMEA states is an example of its general

68   J. Galtung, *The European Community: A Superpower in the Making* (Oslo, 1973), chapter 7.

predisposition towards creating areas of dependence where it can best exert its influence. He portrays trade between Eastern and Western Europe as basically 'colonial', seeing the transfer of technology and investment from West to East through cooperation agreements as a means of expanding Western economic and political power in Eastern Europe. At the same time bourgeois life patterns and consumer habits are carried into Eastern Europe, eroding the ideological separateness of the communist states. Such developments says Galtung, are sanctioned by the Soviet Union because of the economic weakness of the Soviet state and the pragmatism of the Soviet leadership who mobilize 'great flexibility in marxist thinking to justify co-operation with capitalist firms'.[69] Galtung's conclusion on relations between the EEC and the CMEA states is that the relationship is one of exploitation and that 'it is difficult to see how the net result can be anything but dependence on Western technology'.[70]

Whilst the majority of Western analysts would dismiss Galtung's claims as mere speculation, support for his interpretation of the EEC's power would be more forthcoming in the CMEA states. From their standpoint it is difficult not to see the current stage of EEC policy towards the CMEA states as the pursuit of a strategy designed to increase the Community's economic and political influence in Eastern Europe and to maximize the advantages that can be gained from improved East–West relations. The EEC's treatment of the CMEA, regardless of the actual status and power of the organization, can really only be understood by recognizing that it is primarily in the interests of the Community that the CMEA states remain disunited. Moreover the EEC's attitude to the CMEA is scarcely consistent with its own traditions and, as Michael Kaser has pointed out, 'the enlarged Community would hardly be true to its European ideal if, for narrow economic advantage or in misplaced political expectation, it seeks to force individual negotiations upon C.M.E.A. members'.[71]

Thus, in a sense, EEC–CMEA relations are a testing ground

69   *Ibid.*
70   *Ibid.*
71   M. Kaser quoted in Palmer, 'A Security Conference'.

for rival theories about the nature of the EEC's economic and political power. The decision on the part of the communist states to put forward the CMEA as a bargaining weapon against the EEC was itself an acknowledgement of an increase in the Community's power and the product of genuine fears amongst the Eastern European states (not just Soviet pressure) about how that power might be used. Only by recognizing the CMEA's position as a potential bargaining partner, therefore, can the EEC begin to allay those fears and disprove those critics who see the new Community policy towards Eastern Europe as an attempt to increase the penetration and dominance of Western economic interests. The future prospects of EEC–CMEA relations will be conditioned by the developing outline of Community foreign economic policy and the motives underlying it. It is to be hoped that those motives do not stem from considerations of mere short-term economic and political gain but are the product of a genuine desire to contribute to a lasting East–West economic and political détente. Only then will the atmosphere of mutual trust be created in which a real EEC–CMEA dialogue can take place. At the moment the Community holds the key to the nature of this relationship; it remains to be seen whether or not it will use its power in this area constructively.

3

The Convergence of the CMEA on the EEC

PETER WILES AND ALAN SMITH

1. The Original Nature of the CMEA

The CMEA and the EEC were conceived as very different organizations, but their structure and powers have (allowing for the very different economic systems they administer) substantially converged. This is because we observe today in both of them a will towards supranational status formerly quite missing in the CMEA. This will is an objective necessity of the situation in which the CMEA now finds itself.

The CMEA was formed before the EEC (1957) and even before its precursor, the European Coal and Steel Community (1952). It is more to be regarded as an economic Cominform. There is no harm in being literal-minded. The Cominform (founded September 1947, dissolved April 1956) existed to keep its members mutually informed in political matters, so the Council for Mutual Economic Aid (founded January 1949) enabled them to render economic aid to each other! Both bodies had small powers and low pretensions, because both were formed by Stalin, who was paranoid about the possibility that his new satellites should combine against him. In 1947 he had just vetoed a federation of them all.[1] He himself required no more supranational powers than his occupying army and his all-pervasive 'advisors' gave him. He saw a supranational CMEA

---

[1] Indeed during the war Stalin had characteristically vetoed the proffered accession to the USSR of parts of Yugoslavia. S. Clissold, *Whirlwind* (London, 1948), pp. 82, 240; E. R. Goodman, *The Soviet Design for a World State* (New York, 1960), pp. 328–32. If he did not want his satellites to form one strong country over against him, neither did he want to incorporate their security problems within his borders.

as a potential rival, with the advantages of formality and inter-national law.[2]

Moreover there was a point of international commercial law that argued against a strong CMEA. The USSR had not, and still has not, most-favoured-nation (MFN) status[3] with several advanced capitalist countries, notably the USA. But in order to obtain this ardently desired non-discriminatory privilege the USSR must herself eschew discrimination. This issue goes back to the origins of Bolshevik power, and there is no more tradition-bound government than that of the Soviet Union. Hence many passionate denials that CMEA members give each other any trade preference, whether by tariff or by administrative fiat. The onerous and binding annual bilateral trade protocols, which used to swallow up 80 per cent of each member's foreign trade with the world, were allegedly based on pure commercial convenience. Moreover there was no CMEA rule about them, and they were not – and for the most part still are not – settled under CMEA auspices.

If there is to be a Western parallel for that early CMEA, we should rather look to the Organization for European Economic Cooperation (OEEC).[4] For this too is more of an 'Informburo' than anything else. It was founded in April 1948 in order to administer Marshall Aid, and the CMEA was precisely Stalin's reaction to this event, and his previous rejection of Marshall Aid itself. But after the Marshall years the OECD has continued more as a club: a recommender of policies and a conductor of quasi-official research. Meanwhile whatever major influence the USA wished to exercise on its allies was exercised directly or bilaterally: so that the OECD was, just like the CMEA, less important than it looked.

An amusing further resemblance is that the OEEC, becoming

2 Zhdanov and Voznesenski, however, wanted a strong Cominform and CMEA. The latter even wanted monetary reform so as to give CMEA a rational base. Cf. P. J. D. Wiles, *Communist International Economics* (Oxford, 1968), p. 313.

3 If A has MFN status with B, B cannot make a tariff concession to C without also making it to A.

4 In December 1960 this became the 'Organization for Economic Cooperation and Development', to give us the OECD we know today.

the OECD, dropped its place-name 'European'. Expanding to include Japan and Australia (it had always uncomfortably included USA and Canada), the OECD came to represent not Western Europe but advanced capitalism. Meanwhile the CMEA has come to include Cuba (July 1972) and now Vietnam, North Korea, Laos and even Angola are teetering on the brink: it represents not Eastern Europe but Soviet-type communism.[5]

2. The EEC was Always Supranational

The EEC was and is an attempt at political and military unification by way of economic integration. Those who, for example during the accession of Britain, pretended the Community was only economic were consciously perverting the truth; ultimately the members are meant to volunteer to lay aside their veto and to submerge their whole sovereignty. This is at no point clearer than now, as the threatened fledgling democracies of the Mediterranean shore try to join. For them the Community is indeed a source of funds, but above all a political protection for the newly chosen form of government. Nor is the Community itself behindhand since it has many of the trappings of sovereignty. Its senior officials have diplomatic status as they travel among the member countries; its parliament will shortly be directly elected; many countries including non-members send it ambassadors, and so on.

Small wonder that when the EEC got under way the Russians held it to be an ontological impossibility: capitalism was meant to lead to war between capitalist states, yet here it was striding forward into political union, while communism had just saddled itself with an organ strictly based on national sovereignty. The French Communist Party even wrote a letter to the Community addressed c/o NATO. The long Soviet refusal of diplomatic recognition is only now crumbling.

5 Mongolia (June 1962) forms part of the continuous land-mass, and so is 'excusable'. But it was first necessary to excise the word 'European' from Article 11/2. Yugoslavia had already split before the CMEA was founded. Albania was excluded in December 1961. In Berlin (July 1976), Vietnam, North Korea and Laos sent 'delegations': an apparently superior status to that of Angola, the 'observer'. L. Nikolaev and A. Sokolov in *Mirovaya Ekonomika i Mezhdunarodniye Otnosheniya* (September 1976).

The trappings must not, of course, be confused with the reality. Our definition of supranationality lies not in the colour of certain officials' passports but in the possibility of overriding a member country's veto. This possibility will shortly exist for minor matters in the EEC – naturally the power will reside in the Council of Ministers, as befits a group of democratic societies (each minister is appointed by the government of a member country). The possibility does not exist in the CMEA. Although there are now ministers-resident, the corresponding organ in a group of communist countries would be a regular meeting of delegates from Party Politburos. There are such meetings, but there are no Politburo members-resident, and in any case they cannot override the treaty so they are not supranational. Only Soviet invasions and embargoes are that.

3. The CMEA's 1962 Crisis of Supranationality

The EEC, then, has had a single aim, though a very long-run one. We examine below the extent of its success. If the CMEA had no aim under Stalin, the unwillingness of Khrushchev to take sides openly in the dispute between the more and the less industrialized members prevented it from acquiring one until 1962.[6] The issue turned on the reconciliation of bloc and national interests which could only be decided in favour of the former by the acquisition of supranational powers. The industrialized members were particularly aggrieved by the practice of bilateral balancing of trade and the lack of specialization and cooperation which restricted the market for machinery and equipment, and hindered the development of plants of sufficient size to benefit from economies of scale. Furthermore a shortage of iron ore threatened the steel industries of those countries. Romania's plans to expand her own iron and steel industry as a step to the development of a machine building industry threatened further to limit the potential of this market while creating additional demands for raw materials. For Romania, however, the establishment of a form of industrial independence based on a policy of 'many-sided' industrialization (industrialization over a broad

6   The period 1953–62 was one of numerous bilateral agreements, many not even under the 'auspices' of the CMEA. But what is an auspice?! Cf. Wiles, *Communist International Economics*, pp. 315–19.

spectrum of commodities) had been a major policy goal of her Communist Party since 1945, whilst the desire not to remain a predominantly agricultural nation was an article of Romanian nationalist faith with pre-communist antecedents. The problem could, therefore, only be resolved in favour of the industrialized members by supranational intervention in Romania's internal investment plans.

In 1962 Khrushchev came out openly for the industrialized countries. At the June CMEA meeting he proposed ministers-resident at CMEA headquarters, and the admission of Mongolia. He *seems* to have carried these points formally, but the matter is curiously doubtful.[7] In September 1962 he spoke of the diseconomies of small-scale production, condemning the principle of 'having everything of your own, regardless of the cost'[8] and spoke of the need to 'go in for planning at the level of the CMEA'.[9] On 19 November 1962 at the plenum of the Central Committee of the Communist Party of the Soviet Union he went a considerable step further and proposed the establishment of a common planning organ (*Obshchii edinii planovy organ*) composed of representatives who would be 'empowered to compose common plans and resolve organisational questions in order to coordinate the development of the economies of the countries of the socialist system'.[10]

The threat of a 'Common planning organ' combined with Khrushchev's denunciation of 'metal-eaters'[11] at the same plenum must have given a final indication to Romania that her heavy industrialization plans, based on anticipated Soviet cooperation in the construction of a steel works at Galaţi (the focal point of the dispute) were doomed. A special plenum of

---

7 M. Kaser, *Comecon*, 2nd edn (Oxford, 1967), pp. 245–6.
8 N. S. Khrushchev in *World Marxist Review* (September 1962), p. 11.
9 *Ibid.*, pp. 8–9.
10 *Ibid.* p. 111. This view has subsequently been strengthened by a Lenin quotation: 'A world economy as a whole, under a common plan.'
11 N. S. Khrushchev, *Razvitie Ekonomiki SSSR i Partiinoe Rukovodstvo Narodnim Khozyaistvom* (Moscow, 1962), p. 55. A major part of Khrushchev's speech was devoted to an attack on the overproduction of steel whilst indicating the economies that could be obtained by replacing steel products with chemical substitutes. He had given similar indications whilst visiting Romania in August 1962.

the Romanian Central Committee was convened on 21–23 November, and on 25 November it was announced that the construction of the Galaţi steel works would proceed with the assistance of an Anglo-French consortium.[12]

The CMEA's only possible aim was thus revealed – to its own members. This aim was, and could only have been, supranationality: the imitation of the EEC within the constraints of a very different system. Romania has kept out of many co-operative schemes, from that day to this, as is her perfect treaty right. But she won a more important victory: she stopped the movement towards supranationality. No legal move of this kind has been possible since she refuses to amend the treaty. Above all, central planners consult often, but no all-CMEA plan has emerged, even informally.

Apart from the low ambitions and modest constitution with which it started, why did the CMEA make so little headway from 1962 to 1969, and why has subsequent progress been so slow?

(i)   Romania is a tougher obstacle than any EEC member.
(ii) The USSR has not really made an issue of these things. Her most senior and able people do not work for the CMEA. Only 3–4 per cent of her national income is exported to these countries.
(iii) The member states have very serious enmities, especially because of frontier disputes which have been only formally settled (Hungary–Romania, USSR–Romania, USSR–Poland, Poland–GDR). There are no such enmities in Western Europe.
(iv) Planning *governments* are far more difficult to integrate than market *economies*. There is nothing automatic or impersonal about such integration; it is a sustained and direct attack on sovereignty.
(v)   The technological pull of the West is extremely strong, and is exercised on each member individually (see section 8 below).
(vi) There is in any case no fundamental agreement on whether to integrate through planning or through the market.

12 S. Fischer-Galati, *The New Rumania* (Cambridge, Mass., 1967), pp. 90–1. At the same plenum Birladeanu, Romania's CMEA representative in Moscow, was promoted to the Politburo.

4. An Excursus on Irrational Integration

Point (vi) above claims our longer attention. Western writers nearly all make the facile assumption that the CMEA *cannot* integrate its member economies without a proper inter-member market in goods and currency, and that this presupposes a rather thorough 'marketization' of each domestic economy in turn. But this is to lay far too much weight on optimal micro-allocation. It is quite correct that until detailed central planning has been very greatly improved it will not come as close to such optimality as a free market, even a quite imperfect one. But the Soviet-type system offers substantial compensations for this disadvantage, in stable prices, full employment, equal distribution, etc. – a well-worn theme upon which we shall not here enlarge.[13] But what is true of each domestic economy is true also of the group of them. They cannot, notably, exploit the international division of labour properly but they can avoid major balance of payments crises.

In particular sub-optimal integration, through supranational detailed planning, is entirely feasible, and will probably bring *some* benefit. To elaborate our own crude and elementary example,[14] let there be two commodities 1 and 2, both produced in two Soviet-type economies A and B. Let small letters stand for quantities, and large letters for unit costs in the two home currencies. Then

total cost used to be: $a_1 A_1 + a_2 A_2 + b_1 B_1 + b_2 B_2$.

It is now decided to specialize each country, whether by supranational planning or by bilateral agreement. A takes 1 and B takes 2. Total cost after specialization is

$$a_1 w A_1 + b_1 w A_1 + a_2 x B_2 + b_2 x B_2;$$

where b_1 is now produced in A and a_2 in B, and $w, x < 1$ are the ratios of the unit cost after enjoying economies of scale to the unit cost under autarky. Moreover, for simplicity, there is 'marginal bilateral balance', so that the specialization scheme

13 Cf. e.g. A. Nove, *The Soviet Economy* (London, 1961), chapter 12; P. J. D. Wiles, *Economic Institutions Compared* (Oxford, 1977), *passim*.

14 Wiles, *Communist International Economics*, p. 332.

does not affect the balance of payments. In other words $b_1 = pa_2$, where p is the relative international price in the clearing unit of account (e.g. the transferable ruble). Input prices and quantities of output are assumed constant throughout.

Now clearly

$$a_1 wA_1 < a_1 A_1, \quad b_2 xB_2 < b_2 B_2,$$

but if our international and domestic price systems are sufficiently bad this circumstance may only lull both parties into supposing they have improved their situation. For the relations of $b_1 wA_1$ to $b_1 B_1$, and of $a_2 xB_2$ to $a_2 A_2$, are anyone's guess, until we have agreed on a truthful purchasing power parity for the two countries in respect of the relevant inputs. Let a unit of B currency be worth π units of A currency in this sense. We distinguish several cases.

(i) *Loss all round.* Despite the economies of scale, the new costs may so far exceed the old (e.g. $b_1 wA_1 > b_1 B_1$) as to outweigh in each country the saving on the production that has not been reallocated. Then

$$b_1 wA_1 > b_1 \pi B_1 \quad \text{and} \quad a_2 x \pi B_2 > a_2 A_2, \tag{1}$$

so that A pays more in domestic factors to make b_1 for export than it used to when it made a_2 as an import substitute, and *mutatis mutandis* similarly B. In this case total domestic cost has risen in each country, and everyone is worse off. Yet even so we should still be forced to say that the two countries had been integrated. There would have been *an intensified international division of labour to everyone's disadvantage*: a perfectly possible thing to which theory has paid far too little attention.

(ii) *Sub-optimal gain all round.* Both countries may gain, but less than they might, because the wrong scheme of specialization has been chosen. In this case

$$b_1 wA_1 < b_1 \pi B_1, \quad a_2 x \pi B_2 < a_2 A_2$$

(factor inputs are reduced in both countries) but the other specialization

$$a_2 yA_2 + b_2 yA_2 + a_1 zB_1 + b_1 zB_1$$

(where $y, z < 1$ are the ratios of cost reduction as before) would have yielded a better result, or

$$b_1 \pi B_1 - b_1 wA_1 + a_2 A_2$$
$$- a_2 x \pi B_2 < b_2 \pi B_2 - b_2 yA_2 + a_1 A_1 - a_1 z \pi B_1. \qquad (2)$$

Note that cases (i) and (ii) are virtually the same. For if (1) holds, the left hand side of (2) is actually negative.

(iii) *One gain, one loss.* For instance A may gain (productivity, not income) while B loses, in that $b_1 wA_1 < b_1 \pi B_1$, but $a_2 A_2 < a_2 x \pi B_2$; and vice versa. Note that in this case B can still easily be compensated by a change in p, and the two countries together can still gain.[15]

This is not the place for an exhaustive analysis. It is clearly more likely that costs in domestic currency are saved whether A specializes in 1 and B in 2 as shown, or vice versa. *Any* intensified international division of labour is likely to bring *some* benefit, at least to both countries taken together. The next possibility is that it should benefit each country separately: but if both specialization schemes achieved also this we could still easily be sub-optimal. If there were rational prices expressible in one currency via a rational π we could also know, without a free market or convertibility, which of the two specialization schemes best exploited comparative cost opportunities. Many say specialization in the CMEA will yield nothing until the institutions are different, not until the prices are right. But they are wrong: we have already shown it will yield something, even with wrong prices (and with the right prices it will yield everything). We agree of course that Soviet-type institutions are more likely to yield wrong prices; but to assert their total incapacity to integrate is to confuse the international division of labour – a very general concept – with its optimal variant, division according to comparative costs. And rightly or wrongly communists hesitate to believe in comparative costs.[16]

There is therefore no absolute need for:

(*a*) uniform relative prices among the member countries;

15 But then, since $b_1 = pa_2$, a new p will disturb the balance of payments. Note that if we reverse the specialization we may also need a new p to re-establish balance.
16 M. Senin, *Socialist Integration* (Moscow, 1973), pp. 232–4.

(*b*) rational relative prices anywhere (see the above example);
(*c*) a commodity-convertible international currency (for of course commodity-convertibility contradicts command planning);[17]
(*d*) a purely-financially-convertible international currency, for the instant settlement of bilateral balances (since administrative transferability, as at present, or settlement in some 'fungible' raw material, will do as a *pis aller*).

It is on the contrary quite feasible, and absolutely consonant with Soviet traditions, to impose an aggregated supranational plan on the plans of CMEA members, whose central planning offices would then become the slightly more disaggregated *second* stage in the development of detailed command plans at enterprise level.

An all-CMEA plan would of course be a Soviet plan, and another nail in the coffin of satellite sovereignty. No-one outside the USSR wants this to happen. Therefore intellectual confusion about its feasibility is a good thing. If clever people in Warsaw and Budapest can convince slower thinkers in Moscow that a free internal Soviet market is necessary before there is integration, more power to them, but it is unlikely that they will succeed. Moreover such a market isn't necessary, it is merely desirable.

It is also improbable. For since 1971 (Brezhnev replaces Kosygin as the industrial spokesman), or at any rate 1973 (large associations of enterprises take over many of the powers of enterprises), the internal Soviet trend has been anti-market. This implies that the next steps in CMEA integration will also be of a non-market type; the trend could not go one way in the USSR and the other in the CMEA.

5. The Renewed Drive towards Supranationality in the CMEA

Recent experience confirms Soviet preference for integration of the non-market type. Kosygin[18] told the 23rd (Special) CMEA

---

17 For a detailed discussion see P. J. D. Wiles, 'On purely financial convertibility', *Banking, Money and Credit in Eastern Europe* (NATO Directorate of Economic Affairs, Brussels, 1975).

18 A. N. Kosygin, *Izbrannye Stat'i i Rechi* (Moscow, 1974), pp. 430–57.

Session in April 1969 that 'The Planning Principle must be the basis of co-operation of socialist countries. Through this a more effective use of monetary levers will lead not to a lessening of the role of planning but to its improvement.'[19] Though firm, he was also much more moderate than Khrushchev:

We have not in view the coordination of national economic plans as a whole, or combined indicators for such plans. But we are deeply convinced that the mutual involvement of many plan indicators and of a number of products and mutually dependent branches of production on the basis of perspective scientific–technical prognoses is the true and hopeful path of economic collaboration between our countries.[20]

This speech may be considered as the start of the current phase of integration measures. It clearly indicated that the use of money and credit levers was to be subordinated to planned commodity flows, a view that is still held by Soviet economists specializing in CMEA affairs[21] but has met opposition from Hungarian and Polish economists who have placed greater emphasis on decentralized (price) criteria. Although the 'Complex programme', approved at the 25th (1971) CMEA Session, contained many compromise proposals it still put greater emphasis on integration through plan coordination, with a subsidiary role for the use of monetary levers.[22]

---

19 *Ibid.* p. 451.   20 *Ibid.* p. 443.

21 E.g. 'Practice indicates that the decision of such problems as the development of a system of multilateral accounts in transferable roubles, multilateral long term credits etc., depends in the final analysis on establishing cooperation in the field of planning activity, in the first place by coordinating national economic plans.' Yu. Shiraev in *Mirovaya Ekonomika i Mezhdunarodniye Otnosheniya*, no. 6 (1976), p. 25. Cf. J. Belayev and L. Semionova, *Sotsialisticheskaya Integratsiya i Mirovoe Khuzyaistvo* (Moscow, 1972), pp. 203–6.

22 Section 1 Article 4 of the 'Complex programme' states 'co-operation is based on...an organic combination of the co-ordination of plans, which is the basic method for organising co-operation, with a broader application of commodity–money relations'. Similarly the preamble to section 4 states 'The CMEA member countries consider co-operation in planning activities, especially the co-ordination of plans to be the main method for organising co-operation and extending the socialist division of labour.' Again section 7 on the Improvement of Monetary

Events since the 'Complex programme' indicate that 'integration through plan coordination' has gained the ascendancy, with the major integration proposals implemented since then, notably at the 1975 and 1976 Sessions, reflecting the proposals for improved cooperation in planning established in the 'Complex programme'. At the 1969 Session Kosygin[23] proposed that plan coordination should commence with joint activity in formulating long-term forecasts for economic development which would subsequently be the basis for cooperation in constructing members' five-year plans and would finally be introduced into annual plans. In particular there was to be improved joint planning activity in certain branches of production of joint interest to the members as a whole. These proposals were broadly reflected in the 'Complex programme' and considerable progress has since been made towards their implementation.

In 1973 (on Kosygin's initiative) work began on estimating an 'Agreed plan for multilateral integration measures' which was approved by the 29th (1975) Session. The 'Agreed plan' described as a 'new stage in the coordination of five-year plans' specifically provides for the construction of ten major projects of common interest to the bloc in the field of energy and raw materials to a value of 9 milliard rubles.[24] The provision of credits, supplies of capital and labour and repayments in the form of products will therefore be the result of physical plans with money flows passively following resource flows rather than determining them. Prices therefore will only affect the distribution of costs and benefits between countries rather than affecting or determining resource allocations. In addition the 'Agreed plan'

Relations refers to a 'more active role...in strengthening planned economic co-operation'. Although section 7 also refers to making the national currencies 'mutually convertible' this would not threaten the supremacy of planned flows unless the currencies were to be made 'commodity convertible' (our phrase). The 'Complex programme' has been reproduced in English in *The Multi-lateral Economic Co-operation of Socialist States* (Moscow, 1977), pp. 46–145.   23   Kosygin, *Izbrannye Stat'i*, p. 443.
24   Editorial, *Planovoye Khozyaistvo*, no. 4 (1977), p. 3. A milliard is a thousand million. 9 milliard is 2 per cent of Soviet investment in five years.

contains proposals for cooperation and specialization in production, joint research into technical problems, etc., all on the 'interested country' principle.

To implement the proposals, all CMEA members with the exception of Romania have introduced 'special sections' devoted to integration measures in their annual plans which specify the resource requirements of cooperation agreements and are subsequently coordinated with the other relevant sectors of the annual plan.[25] In this way coordination agreements are introduced in an *ex ante* and obligatory way into participating countries' plans. The special sections have been described by two Soviet economists as the 'basis for gradual agreement in the future for a methodology for compiling a system of planning and administration of the economy of the CMEA members as a whole'.[26] A special section has also been included in the USSR five-year plan for 1976–80 with the intention of making this a further method for strengthening the integration of five-year plans.

Finally a methodology for coordinating long-term perspective plans was approved at the 30th (1976) CMEA Session, consisting of five 'Long-term target programmes' for plan coordination and specialization over a period of fifteen years in fuel, energy and raw materials; machine construction; agriculture; transport; and industrial consumer goods. It is stated that one of the most important functions of the target programmes is to link them to members' perspective plans, while they will also form the basis of agreed five-year plans for the periods 1981–5 and 1986–90.[27] The major result of these measures should be that coordinated capital investment projects are reflected in participating countries' investment plans, as anticipated in the 'Complex programme'.

Many of the integration measures put into effect since 1969 are strongly reminiscent of Khrushchev's 1962 proposals. The proposals for plan coordination and in particular the 'Agreed plan' and the target programmes reflect Khrushchev's propo-

25 N. Faddeyev in *Planovoye Khozyaistvo*, no. 4 (1977), p. 9.
26 O. Rybakov and N. Khmelevski in *Planovoye Khozyaistvo*, no. 6 (1976), p. 36.
27 Faddeyev in *Planovoye Khozyaistvo*.

sals for the 'joint financing of industrial building, transport installations and other items of international significance...[but]...first of all in the raw material branches working for export',[28] whilst the foundation of the International Investment Bank is a more accurate expression of Khrushchev's proposal for the establishment of a joint bank for the provision of credits for jointly financed or specialized construction projects[29] than the IBEC which was established before his fall from power.

The significant difference between Khrushchev's proposals and current practice is the observation of the 'interested party' principle and the absence of any reference to supranational planning organs. Kosygin made this distinction quite clear in April 1969, as quoted above; but joint plans in certain sectors of the economy would be agreed between members who wished to participate, after which the required resource flows would be agreed and coordinated. The right to choose not to participate in various aspects of the 'Complex programme' was a basic principle of the programme itself, whilst it was also stressed that plan coordination would take place through the cooperation of national bodies rather than by the establishment of a supranational authority. Thus this is a far more limited but more realistic concept of integration than that proposed by Khrushchev, and has presumably been necessitated by Romania which does not participate in many of the joint construction proposals and does not include a section for integration measures in her national plan.

All this reminds one irresistibly of the debate on British entry into the EEC, and the 'sacrifice of sovereignty' issue. The Russians are not being candid any more than most of the supporters of British entry were candid. Sectoral plan coordination today will lead to overall plan coordination tomorrow, and that in turn will bring a single supranational plan the day after tomorrow. By saying now that he does not want the second stage, Kosygin is bringing the third stage nearer. Romania may possibly remain outside, but surely not the others.

28 Khrushchev in *World Marxist Review*, p. 13.
29 *Ibid.* p. 9.

6. The Sovereignty Barrier, East and West

We further asserted above that 'planning *governments* are far more difficult to integrate than market *economies*' (section 3, point iv). Now the founding fathers of the EEC conceived on the whole a natural progression from easy to difficult, a 'royal road to integration' from free commodity trade through free migration, a common commercial policy (CCP), and fiscal harmonization to fiscal and monetary union. They were right to expect difficulties at the other end! For eventually under state capitalism too the government claims sovereignty over the economy, if it be only in the setting of:

(*a*) tax rates as opposed to tax forms (we all use VAT, i.e. we are 'harmonized', but at quite different rates, i.e. we are not 'unitary'; we all use an income tax, but the balance between direct and indirect taxation is very various);

(*b*) budget surpluses and deficits;

(*c*) monetary policy;

(*d*) incomes policy;

(*e*) the rate of exchange.

When all else is integrated, these things come up for settlement, and the integrating body reaches its members' sovereignty barrier. We have already observed (point (iv) above) how soon that barrier is reached in the case of central planning; we now see how the EEC too is bumping up against it – much later, and after far more successes.

The sticking point for a sovereign state cannot be accurately located. Up to a point it will accept external authority on the grounds that the matter is unimportant, that the international community to which it belongs is 'only a treaty' (and we all sign treaties), that the proposal (let us say to adopt a foreign industrial standard) is of plain advantage, etc. Romania's actual sticking point was not the imminence of a supranational command plan – something at which every sovereign country would gag – but the very old-fashioned issue of permission to build a new steel mill: something bound to excite the passions of an underdeveloped country, though one can hardly imagine the GDR feeling so strongly.

Similarly one state-capitalist country will cheerfully accept to join the Snake where for another the proposal is stark ruin.

Broadly speaking, countries with reasonable trade unions are able to keep their price rises down to the West German level; and they find it advantageous to join the Snake whether or not they are members of the EEC.[30] On the other hand countries in which wage claims are uncontrollable could only join the Snake at the cost of extreme monetarist policies, leading to vast unemployment and probably a general strike or civil war. If the EEC were to impose the Snake on Britain or Italy, even France, it would have first to suspend the governments in those countries and govern in their stead.

Monetary union, then, is the 'sovereignty barrier' for most EEC members. Other things both great and small have given great offence: for example in Britain the admission of French lorries heavier than the previously allowed British maximum, and the threat to standardize beer; or in France the free entry of Italian wine. But either these threats have passed, or the members have knuckled under. Differential rates of cost inflation, however, even cost inflation of any kind, were not a problem perceived by the founding fathers of the EEC. Integration would be pursued along the 'royal road', in a world where no well-entrenched and passionate monopolies influenced the price level far more in one country than another.

Supranational planning would of course be an equal sticking point in the EEC, even of the loose French variety. There was such a suggestion in 1958, just after the Community's foundation: some Frenchmen wished to export their planning system to Brussels. But clearly not even France would have tolerated this for long, and mercifully for the Community the other members rejected the suggestion. In consequence France was obliged to modify her planning system so as to conform to the rules of the Community. There is, therefore, little left of the *économie concertée* or the 'democratically conceived input–output table'. French planners no longer really plan current outputs,

30 As this is written, West Germany, Belgium and the Netherlands are founder-members of the Snake. Switzerland, Austria, Norway and Sweden have a formal or an informal association. Currencies in the Snake are kept at a fairly exact parity with each other by means of central bank open-market operations. Thus the Snake is a 'gold standard' confined to its members.

as EEC rules would detect discrimination against imports. They only influence (indeed in very great detail) investment decisions: a practice curiously not forbidden by the Community. All this, then, is the mirror-image of the CMEA story.

7. The EEC's Common Special Policies and their CMEA Counterparts

Life is such that there are problems not located upon the 'royal road to integration' described above (free commodity trade, free migration, CCP, fiscal harmonization, monetary union). But the EEC is a serious body, and these problems must be tackled. So these special policies have concerned:

(i) agriculture. The Common Agricultural Policy (CAP) arose of course from the pre-existence of members' own agricultural policies. It is very like them: using price intervention not price control, i.e. stockpiling and import restriction. Since there is only one authority in these matters any more, the CAP could even be played down as a special kind of intra-Community free trade, and so not off the 'royal road' at all. It is also a prime example of thorough and successful integration without rationality![31] The CMEA members have no similar agricultural policies: in particular agricultural subsidies, though now large in the USSR, are not a traditional communist measure. Also their agricultural inter-trade is very small. The Council has an agricultural committee, but it does not remotely approach the strength and importance of its Western counterpart.

(ii) a regional development fund as a key instrument for redistributing income between member states. There are no subsidies to states as such, but some states have more poor regions than others! The fund is indeed so direct a system of international redistribution that it is a prime cause of membership applications from the Mediterranean, and a prime reason why existing members – rich or poor, all richer than they – hesitate to accept this rush. But the CAP is also redistributive: towards agriculture, and therefore,

---

31 The 'green currency' system even reproduces the communist system of disorderly cross-rates and multiple rates of exchange.

even among existing members, on the whole from rich to poor people[32] and countries. If it is adjusted to the support of sub-tropical agricultural products, it will become very redistributive indeed.

(iii) the discriminatory purchase of tropical agricultural products from certain countries. The Lomé Convention, 1975, includes most of Africa and a few other small countries. It arose out of the special privileges that France negotiated for francophone Africa already at the stage of the Treaty of Rome, 1957. Now that the USSR is trying to take over Africa she just might do the same thing; but it would be far from our present concerns to discuss this possibility here.

(iv) fuel. While the CMEA is for the present about autarkic with respect to energy supplies, the major fuel sources are located in the Asian sector of the USSR and involve rising marginal costs in their development and exploitation. Furthermore rapid industrial growth in Eastern Europe has resulted in demand growing faster than supply. Consequently the CMEA has been faced with the problems of the extent to which demand should be satisfied by internal and external sources, and of the allocation of the financial and physical costs of the development and transportation of internal sources between members. The problem is further complicated by the unwillingness of the USSR to commit a large proportion of its capital construction to developing fuel resources or to allow foreign ownership of capital in Soviet territory. We have seen (section 4 above) that the lack of rational price criteria and exchange rates hinders the development of *optimal* solutions to these problems, but it has proved to be an area that is conducive to joint-planning decisions. Thus the 'Agreed plan' provides for direct East European provision of materials, machinery and labour in the development of Soviet oil and gas reserves and pipeline construction in exchange for subsequent payment in products, whilst the target programme for energy is intended

32 I.e. subsidies raise the disposable personal income of poor farmers more than rich ones, even though farms with the highest gross turnover receive the highest absolute subsidies.

to establish perspective plans and long-term balances for fuel production and consumption. The Friendship pipe-line was of course established long ago (it links all European members except Romania).

Yom Kippur presented the USSR with the tremendous temptation to break her contracts and charge the new world price within the CMEA. She did not do so, but raised her price quite gradually, by a decent process of negotiation. The slow rise of the CMEA oil price, and the respect for contracts, show a sharp contrast between the OPEC–capitalist relation and the USSR–East Europe relation. As the dominant power, the USSR showed restraint. As the offended and fundamentally non-dominant powers, the OPEC countries showed none.

The EEC, a traditionally deficitary area, reacted with a *sauve qui peut*. Taken together, all members have a substantial monopsony power, but they did not use it. They preferred diplomacy and bilateral bargaining, mainly with offers of arms. The period after Yom Kippur has not been glorious for the EEC: if it is able to plan, if its members are brothers, what is it doing about oil imports? Indeed what about their own not negligible fuel supplies, notably but not only North Sea oil and gas? A committee exists in Brussels, but it has no powers. It is the opposite to the case of agriculture.

8. A Common Commercial Policy

The notion of a CCP raises many more questions. A frankly discriminatory block like the EEC is defined by, and rests upon, one great element of a CCP: the common external tariff. It is precisely upon not having this latter that the CMEA based its claim to be non-discriminatory. Hence its difficulty in introducing other elements like a common policy on foreign borrowing, foreign aid, etc. In all these respects CMEA members are genuinely independent, and they genuinely pursue different aims: compare Polish with Czechoslovak indebtedness, to take only the extreme example.

This is not to suggest that the CCP worked out in Brussels is greatly respected. But it has at least the merit of existing. It deals *inter alia* with dumping, the activities of export credit guarantee departments, commercial treaties with third countries and the principles of commerce with state trading countries and corporations. Evidently, the Lomé Convention is really a part of this concept. But the next most important thing after that is precisely, as we see from the above list, various East–West trade issues.

Today the CMEA is in urgent need of a CCP, and the subjects of this policy should be the acquisition of foreign technology and of the foreign capital to finance it. The bloc seems to have advanced into this new field without considering coordination, the use of its monopsony power, the specialization of members in branches, mutual guarantee of creditworthiness, the re-transfer of technology within the bloc, or indeed anything much.

Naturally supranational planning would take care of this as of everything else; for the plan would soon cover everything. But if that is vetoed there must be agreed policies, and these would be by definition openly discriminatory, whereas the myth of non-discrimination might possibly just survive the single plan. This is, then, a further difficulty, though surely a small one when we consider how many members already have MFN status with all important countries.

But how did the acquisition of foreign technology itself become so important? During the early 1960s the majority of CMEA countries experienced a slow-down in their rate of growth of industrial output and labour productivity which attracted the attention of Eastern and Western scholars.

Soviet economists[33] observed that although the rate of growth of labour productivity and industrial output was still higher in the socialist countries than in most industrially developed market economies, it had fallen in comparison with a decade earlier in the socialist countries, but had actually risen in the USA and certain West European economies.

Although Soviet and East European economists deny that the fall in the growth rate of industrial output was the prime or only reason for launching the economic reforms in Eastern Europe,

33 E.g. Senin, *Socialist Integration.*

they were becoming increasingly aware of the limitations of a growth strategy based mainly on increasing the quantity of industrial inputs (by maintaining high rates of investment and transferring labour from agriculture to industry, etc.) without paying sufficient attention to the efficient use of inputs and the quality of outputs. Formally, this awareness was reflected in the debate on the need to shift from extensive growth (i.e. increasing the quantity of inputs) to intensive growth (a more efficient use of inputs) which became the economic rationale for the reforms of the system of industrial management which took place in the European socialist economies in the 1960s.

An extreme advocate of a new economic model on the grounds that the old one hindered technical progress was, not surprisingly, Rezsö Nyers, the architect of the Hungarian reform, who in March 1964 wrote:

It is indisputable that during the first stages of the development of Socialism in our country, the pace of *technical development* was relatively slow. It was less than optimal, slower than conditions would have permitted. Why?...Objective conditions can hardly explain everything...one of the main reasons was that for six to eight years, technical development was not even given as much place in our economic policy as objective conditions would permit. *Economic dogmatism* has left a deep, negative mark on the level of our technical development...There is a relative 'lag' between technical development and economic effects – at least on the national level. The effects of our earlier efforts with technical development are largely just now becoming fully felt, and the effects of our current efforts will be realised in the future. If we have neglected technical development in the past, then it is today that we suffer its consequences, if we neglect our tasks today, then we must face the consequences in the future ...The fate of obsolete theories is the same as obsolete machines: we must discard them from our theoretical arsenal. The political economy of Socialism is a young, robust, lively science, and consequently we should not consider it surprising or damaging if from time to time we alter some of our earlier theories...During the *past* and in *some cases even today* the prospects for fully secure domestic markets and the belief that everything and anything can be passed along to the foreign sector have induced a 'drowsiness' in our Socialist firms...Under our conditions the demands of technical development express themselves along two planes: at the national and at the enterprise level...It would be incorrect to treat Socialist enterprises simply as the location for the execution of central divisions...For the sake of progress we must work simultaneously along both planes. From the centre must come the most encompassing global measures, from the enterprises we need as great a degree of initiative and mobility as possible...Enterprise productivity and efficiency are the mainsprings of technical development. How have we utilised these mainsprings in the past? Not sufficiently!...Our enterprises must spend more and more concentrated effort on the question of increasing productivity and efficiency. The best indicator of this activity is enterprise profits...and these profits will be used to the last forint for the cause of the people. Therefore this is the conclusion: we must pay greater attention to the growth of efficiency and profitability in order to provide a wider basis of support for the expansion of technological development.[34]

Nyers did also support consumer's sovereignty and the rational micro-allocation of resources, but his main motive was this one.

Furthermore other East European economists[35] argued that autarkic policies, combined with low levels of intra-CMEA cooperation and integration, acted as a bottleneck to industrial growth by limiting the size of the market and hindering the development of plants of an optimum size, to support the overheads associated with research and development and to benefit from modern technology. Indeed a major aim of Khrushchev's proposals in 1962 was to centralize production to bring about economies of scale. This problem was then most acute for the more industrial economies with a small domestic market, namely the GDR and Czechoslovakia, but was also starting to be felt in Poland and Hungary. These analyses became interrelated in the mid-1960s as the reforms of industrial management encompassed attempts to establish optimum-sized production associations in the CMEA countries, and discussions concerning improved intra-CMEA cooperation were initiated and work began on implementing specialization agreements, plan coordination and establishing jointly managed projects, etc., culminating in the adoption of the 'Comprehensive programme' at the 25th CMEA Session of 1971.

The attention of Western scholars to the retardation of the rate of growth of industrial output was primarily focussed on the USSR, concentrating on technological factors, and may be

34 R. Niyers, *Gazdaságpolitikánk és a Gazdasági Mechanizmus Reformja* (Budapest, 1968), pp. 38–41. We owe the reference and the translation to Dr Andrew Göllner.
35 E.g. Senin, *Socialist Integration*, chapter 3.

divided into three major types of study: firstly, production–function type analyses which, *inter alia*, attempt to assess from rather aggregated figures the contribution of technical progress and its diffusion to economic growth; secondly, attempts to estimate the Soviet level of technology industry by industry, in order to estimate the size of technological lags between Soviet and Western (however defined) industry; and thirdly, on the methods of international technology transfer.

Although there is general agreement from research of the second kind that significant technical gaps exist between Soviet and Western industry,[36] production–function analyses have produced a debate as to the causes of the slow down in the growth rate of industrial output. There is, however, agreement that there has been no equivalent slow down in the rate of growth of capital inputs and many studies have attributed the declining growth rate to a decline in technical progress.

Clearly if technical progress continues at its present low rate, but the authorities insist on rapid overall growth, they will have to increase simple capital accumulation continually. It has been calculated[37] that they may have actually to reduce the absolute (not to speak of the relative) volume of consumption. But domestic technical progress will so continue. For R and D are very inefficient in Soviet-type economies; this is one of the areas where capitalism shines in comparison. It has none of the security paranoia that lames the work of a Soviet researcher trying to travel or merely communicate with foreigners; little of the sense of hierarchy that makes the elderly Soviet boss such a bottleneck; and none of the 'planning' of research that wastes so much time in plan evasion. And when it comes to development the Soviet-type system is extremely rigid and slow in producing the prototypes required. Nor is it easy to persuade

36 See for example S. Wasowski (ed.), *East–West Trade and the Technology Gap* (New York, 1970), especially the article by R. W. Judy, 'The case of computer technology'. Further analysis of the existence of lags between Soviet and Western industry have been provided by R. Amann and R. W. Davies in a paper 'The technological level of Soviet industry', presented to the NASEES Conference, Cambridge, 1975.

37 A. Bergson in *Soviet Economic Growth* (Brussels, 1972).

ordinary managers to adopt new methods, since it puts their bonuses at risk and the planners will not relax the rules. Under these circumstances, importing technology embodied in machinery and equipment would serve the dual purpose of expanding the capital stock and enhancing technical progress.

There is now fairly general agreement that the whole movement for a European Security Conference and for so-called 'détente' was mainly based on a Soviet appreciation of this economic situation: either they used foreign R and D, and borrowed money accordingly, or they accepted a very low rate of growth, or they cut consumption or defence and substituted mere capital accumulation for R and D. Technology importation was the least bad alternative. But it is no longer, in modern conditions, simply a matter of buying machines. One must import a whole system, which is very expensive, and one must acquire the detailed, practical know-how, which means bringing in numerous foreign technical advisers. But the borrowing and the advisers imply political détente.

In addition Western European experience tends to indicate that technical (including managerial) progress was a major component of economic growth in the 1960s and that international transfer has in turn been a major source of technical progress.[38] Dunning has suggested that a country importing capital involves itself in the importation of two basic components – knowledge capital (taken in the widest sense to include managerial expertise) and money capital (involving in the short run a net transfer of resources).[39] Attention in the West has largely been focussed on the former as an agent in stimulating economic growth, and while it is difficult at the macro level to prove a causal relationship, it is clear that much foreign (particularly US) investment in Western Europe has been concentrated in industries with a considerable growth potential and

38 See for example J. H. Dunning in Charles Kindleberger (ed.), *The International Corporation* (Cambridge, Mass., 1970). A review of theories of technological innovation and transfer is contained in H. G. Johnson, *Technology and Economic Independence* (London, 1975), pp. 33–41.

39 J. H. Dunning in Geoffrey Denton (ed.), *Economic Integration in Europe* (London, 1969), pp. 246–7.

that investing firms are those with relatively high expenditure on research and development.[40] An explanation for this has been advanced by Vernon who argued that innovations tend to take place initially in countries with large markets where the overhead costs of research and development can be laid off over a large number of sales.[41] In the initial stage the innovating firm enjoys a monopoly which may make cost factors relatively unimportant in comparison to proximity to local scientists, banks, etc. One must add that large multinationals based on small countries also face large markets and are near-monopolists: they suffer very little from the smallness of their base. In the long run, however, production tends to be transferred to lower cost (but technically competent) areas, either in international investment through the establishment of subsidiaries, or by imitation, the sale of licences, the sale of complete installations, etc. Multinational corporations have probably tended to favour international investment, frequently for organizational reasons as much as on grounds of economic rationality – thus Dunning argues that multinational corporations are 'probably more responsible for the international dissemination of technological and managerial expertise in the last two decades than any other institution'.[42]

In Eastern Europe, however, the technologically more advanced countries possessed small domestic markets and were not the base of large multinationals such as flourish in Sweden and Switzerland, a factor that was compounded by the low level of CMEA integration; whilst the country of a size capable of sustaining large scale technical innovation was historically less developed in many branches of industry and had tended to concentrate research effort into the military sector. Furthermore, the institutional factors hindering Soviet R and D (above) had been spread to them. Thus, historical, geographical and institutional factors combined to make both the generation and the transfer of technical progress difficult within the CMEA bloc. In addition, however, autarkic policies together with the

40 *Ibid.* pp. 247–8.
41 R. Vernon, *Sovereignty at Bay* (Middlesex, 1971), pp. 71–82.
42 Dunning, *Economic Integration*, p. 247.

strategic embargo had prevented the CMEA nations from utilizing many Western gains in technology and managerial expertise, either embodied in the form of imported machinery and equipment or disembodied in the form of licences; furthermore the CMEA nations had been isolated from any technical transfer through the medium of multinational corporations.

CMEA countries' awareness of these problems were reflected in the measures referred to above to improve intra-CMEA specialization and cooperation, and in a series of measures taken in the late 1950s and early 1960s to overcome their technological isolation, involving the transfer of technology in disembodied form (monitoring foreign technology, licence purchases, agreements on technical cooperation, etc.) and embodied in the import of machinery and equipment. Later in the 1960s a greater interest was shown in industrial cooperation ventures, culminating in 1971 in the decisions to establish joint production ventures involving foreign minority capital participation on Hungarian and Romanian territory.

The first moves to import Western machinery and equipment were made in the late 1950s, but gathered momentum in the 1960s, with the result that by 1968 imports of machinery and equipment (SITC 7) from the West exceeded imports of basic manufacturers (SITC 6) and that Western European exports of machinery and equipment to the CMEA had grown from $350 million in 1958 to $2380 million in 1970, rising to $6360 million in 1974. Table 1 provides a further indication of the growing significance of machinery and equipment imports from the West in the first half of the 1970s. Due to CMEA foreign trade pricing procedures the proportion of Western machinery is probably considerably underestimated when measured in external prices. Hungarian sources indicate that the weight of Western machinery in total equipment investment from imported sources is approximately doubled when converted into internal prices (see row 7).

Although the use of CMEA currencies as the *numéraire* removes most of the effect of Western inflation (for these currencies have been appreciated), this effect has been slightly diminished as the prices of Western machinery and equipment have risen relatively to those charged in intra-CMEA trade. For

TABLE 1   CMEA imports of machinery and equipment

	1971	1972	1973	1974	1975
USSR					
(i) million rubles	945	1140	1445	1962	3645
(ii)	24.7	24.7	27.1	32.1	40.3
Poland					
(i) million zlotys	1302	2564	4274	6051	8102
(ii)	23.2	33.5	39.8	45.1	52.0
Hungary					
(i) million forints	1857	2126	1867	2595	NA
(ii) (external prices)	20.8	26.1	24.2	24.4	NA
(iii) (internal prices)	42.5	51.3	46.0	45.1	NA
Western exports of machinery to CMEA ($m)	2480	3310	4700	6360	NA

(i)   Imports of machinery and equipment from the West, evaluated according to CMEA trade nomenclature category 1.

(ii) Proportion of Western machinery in machinery and equipment imports evaluated at external prices (%).

(iii) Proportion of Western machinery in machinery and equipment imports evaluated at internal prices (%).

Note: Western exports are evaluated according to SITC category 7.

Sources: USSR: *Vneshnyaya Torgovlya* (various years); Poland: *Rocznik Statystyczny Handlu Zagranicznego* (1976); Hungary: *Statistical Yearbook* (various years); Western: *United Nations Statistical Yearbook* (1975).

the CMEA as a whole, however, mutual trade accounted for 62 per cent of machinery and equipment deliveries in 1975[43] whilst preliminary indications are that the high absolute level of Soviet machinery imports from the West in 1975 was maintained (or exceeded) in 1976 with CMEA supplies accounting for 54.8 per cent of her imports.[44]

The growing quantitative importance of Western machinery and equipment can be estimated from its weight in total investment in machinery. Although Hanson has demonstrated that only about 2 per cent of Soviet investment in machinery and equipment comes from the West,[45] this is largely due to high

43   At external prices: B. Ladygin and O. Rybakov in *Voprosy Ekonomiki*, no. 11 (1976).

44   V. Klochek in *Vneshnyaya Torgovlya*, no. 5 (1977), p. 10.

45   P. Hanson, 'The import of Western technology' in A. Brown and M. Kaser (eds.), *The Soviet Union Since the Fall of Khrushchev* (London, 1975), p. 31.

levels of investment from internal sources. But other CMEA countries have higher levels of investment from imports anyway, so that the expansion in trade with the West has resulted in a fairly significant weight of Western capital in machinery and equipment investment. Thus for Hungary the weight of Western machinery and equipment in total machinery and equipment investment can be calculated directly from primary statistical sources. We find that the weight grew from 8.5 per cent in 1961 to 19 per cent in 1967, reaching 27.3 per cent in 1972, and falling back to 23.7 per cent in 1974.[46] Calculations from secondary sources for Bulgaria and Romania, based on external prices, indicate that the weight of Western machinery rose in Bulgaria from 4–5 per cent in 1960 to 29 per cent in 1966 and in Romania from 5–6 per cent in 1960 to 22 per cent in 1967.[47] However, the valuation problems referred to above

46 Calculated from *Hungarian Statistical Yearbook* (various years).
47 The weight of imported machinery in total investment in machinery and equipment for Bulgaria can be calculated directly from the statistical handbooks for all years, but data for the estimation of the division of machinery from socialist and capitalist countries are not provided. It is, however, possible to make some approximations for this breakdown from scattered secondary Romanian sources. A. Puiu and O. Ciulea, *Probleme Economice*, no. 5 (1968) provide figures for the proportion of the West in total machinery and equipment imports for Bulgaria (41.7%) and Romania (45.8%) in 1966. Figures for the proportion of machinery and equipment imports from CMEA countries for various years provided by I. Perpegal, *Probleme Economice*, no. 12 (1971) and no. 2 (1968); and O. Ciulea and Rudareanu, *Lupta de Clasa*, no. 12 (1968), may permit an approximate estimate of the size of machinery and equipment imports from socialist countries. By multiplying the proportion of capitalist machinery imports by the proportion of imported machinery noted above, an estimate can be made of the importance of Western machinery. However, this assumes that the conversion factors of the values of foreign machinery imports into internal currencies are the same for both Eastern and Western sources. Similar calculations for Hungary reveal that this is not so and that a unit of machinery valued at x foreign currency units from the West may be several times more valuable in terms of internal currency than a unit of similar value in foreign currency units from the East. If this observation holds true for Bulgaria and Romania, the figures are a considerable underestimate.

mean that these figures are probably a substantial underestimate. A similar preliminary estimate, subject to the same reservations, for Poland would indicate that the proportion of Western machinery in 'total accumulation' expanded from about 8 per cent in 1971 to 30 per cent in 1975.[48]

Whilst importing technology embodied directly in the purchase of machinery and equipment enabled the CMEA countries to avoid many of the pitfalls associated with direct investment by multinational companies and may be ideologically more acceptable, it may also involve certain financial disadvantages resulting in balance of payments pressures. In this respect a parallel may be drawn between the growth strategy of the CMEA nations and certain aspects of Hirschman's analysis of the balance of payments problems faced by developing countries.[49] Furthermore the problem may be aggravated by specific East European institutional factors that tend to stifle the development of technically superior commodities, particularly where their development involves costs that would be external to a capitalist firm (by providing a competitive advantage), but which would be internalized by a Soviet industrial ministry.[50]

The essence of this argument is that balance of payments pressures may occur at specific stages of a growth sequence even in the absence of excess demand (although this may be present, and almost certainly is in the case of Poland in particular); they are due to a structural inability to produce commodities demanded in hard-currency markets, particularly if the processes transferred represent out of date technology the outputs of which may no longer be demanded in such markets. The problem is further aggravated in Eastern Europe by those institutional factors which result in time lags in implementing the new technology and in a lack of expertise in adapting and developing products to meet market needs. Thus in the absence of a growth in world demand the outputs of the imported technology will have to compete with existing producers in a

48 Based on similar calculations from *Rocznik Statystyczny Handlu Zegranicznego* (1976).

49 A. D. Hirschman, *The Strategy of Economic Development* (Yale, 1975), pp. 166–76.

50 This argument is also due to Hirschman, *Economic Development*, p. 61.

static market where price competition may be met by allegations of dumping and import controls. However, if economic growth does take place the nature of the technology transferred and the time lags in implementing it may make the products obsolescent in world markets. The problem is further compounded by the fact that the new processes developed will also require additional inputs of (imported) raw materials and by the CMEA countries' lack of expertise in marketing products in the West.

Under these circumstances these countries may find themselves faced with a structural inability to export which cannot be overcome purely by price changes.[51] If there are substantial positive externalities involved in the import of machinery and equipment via technical transfer (and if other imports are largely concentrated on raw materials) then the export bottleneck in turn becomes a constraint on economic growth and the export purely of 'value added' will be beneficial to the economy. Clearly this argument is more crucial for the East European CMEA nations which have no supplies of raw materials that can be relatively easily exported on world markets and in turn are faced by small domestic markets for manufactured outputs.

In the absence of windfall movements in the terms of trade, or increases in world demand for traditional exports at existing prices, the problem can only be overcome in the short run by a net transfer of resources from the technologically advanced countries combined with credit. In the long run there must be import-saving, particularly through the use of synthetic materials (where the home-produced value-added component may be high) and by adapting and developing technology to meet areas of high growth demand or by concentrating on sales to areas where technological obsolescence may not be so high.

To a certain extent direct foreign investment, particularly by multinationals, may help to overcome some of these problems. Initially the multinational may possess the financial resources

51 This argument has its parallel in the British debate on the efficacy of devaluation as a method of restoring equilibrium to the balance of payments.

and expertise to facilitate capital transfer without causing a corresponding import reduction elsewhere.[52] If the investing company's aim is to transfer production to lower cost areas, then by providing guaranteed outlets for the products of the plant it may make a positive contribution to the export of value added, and will possess a continuing interest in updating technology in order to ensure the marketability of outputs. However, it is also possible that under these circumstances many of the positive effects of technical transfer may be lost, particularly if the production transferred is in the form of components rather than finished products. In this case the only positive externalities to arise from the investment may be, as in Hirschman's analysis, reduced cost or profitable ancillary production either upstream or downstream from the original investment.

Thus although in the long run the multinational may intend from any specific investment to bring a net outflow of resources from the host country through the repatriation of profits, multinational investment overall may make a substantial contribution to the balance of payments over a development period if new investments outweigh repatriated profits or if exports of value added are increased.[53] Thus Dunning has shown that the EEC were net gainers of resources from 1950 to 1966 as a result of

52 This argument is not meant to imply that there are no costs to the host country resulting from multinational investment, or that investment is entirely rational from the host country's viewpoint, or that benefits necessarily outweigh costs to it, or that the USSR should permit multinational investment. It purely states the existence of benefits which are difficult to obtain without multinational investment.

53 Vernon, *Sovereignty at Bay*, p. 61, argues that import substitution and export promotion effects for the host country generally swamp balance of payments effects caused by profit remissions. In the case of Western European countries the size of the effect depends on whether one assumes that the host country would have imported the commodities concerned or started home production. In the CMEA countries the relevant opportunity cost (in balance of payments terms) of not allowing multinational investment for any specific investment would appear to be the capital cost of imported technology, less discounted profit remissions, plus forgone export markets.

US direct investment, primarily by private companies, the net gain being $1699 million between 1962 and 1965.[54]

Moreover the multinational is a definitive capitalist solution to the present problem of technology acquisition. Though of course such acquisition is a very old problem, it has recently made a quantum jump in intensity: it costs much more, it crops up much more often, and it requires much more personal contact. In this new form, communism has no adequate answer to it. Many serious objections can and should be made to multinationals, but they do at least do this job superbly well, and it is one of the world economy's main jobs.

It might be argued that the foregoing analysis is invalidated by Japanese experience where the inflow of technology has largely been of disembodied form in the post-war era and where exports have apparently grown to offset import requirements. However, geographic, historic and economic differences between Japan and Eastern Europe may tend to obscure certain similarities in their development. Firstly, Japan did experience balance of payments constraints in the 1950s and again in 1963 and 1964,[55] which were partially offset by windfall factors, notably US military expenditure and favourable movements in the terms of trade. Secondly, the ratio of imports to GNP is critically lower for Japan than for CMEA nations and has been concentrated on raw materials for which demand has grown slowly; so substantially lower exports have been needed. Thirdly, the standard pattern of Japanese product development has been import-led; initially a product is imported, followed by home production and subsequent exports. In many cases exports are initially directed to developing countries and only later to advanced industrial countries. Thus it would appear that the scale of the 'export problem' is substantially lower for Japan than for East (or West) European countries; but other basic differences are that Japan's defence effort is inferior and her development effort is superior to that of East European nations.

54 Dunning, *Economic Integration*, p. 272. This is *not* the net balance of payments effect.

55 This argument is based on A. Boltho, *Japan: An Economic Survey 1953–73* (Oxford, 1975), pp. 139–59.

This is consistent with our assumptions of the effect of East European institutions on product development. Furthermore, the existence of a state foreign trade monopoly may make it more difficult for central planners to estimate promptly commodities for which world demand is growing – a function that is served by imports in the Japanese case.

Arguments based on a similar analysis of the problems began to appear in Eastern Europe in the late 1960s[56] (although little reference was made to any beneficial effects of multinational corporations) and the CMEA nations initiated various policies to overcome some of the problems outlined without actually permitting direct investment in Eastern Europe. The most prominent policies were:

(a) to attract deliveries of machinery and equipment on credit and to raise finance in Western capital markets.

(b) to develop cooperative ventures with Western companies and organizations, in both research and industrial production, the latter to secure the delivery of machinery and equipment on credit against the future delivery of products; co-production agreements involving cooperation in the production of specific units by the communist country for assembly and sale in the West; production based on licence purchases to be repaid in products; commercial ventures for improving marketing in Western countries; and joint banking ventures to raise finance. Finally Hungary and Romania have since 1971 permitted minority equity capital participation within their territories.

(c) to remove tariffs and other barriers to exports through diplomatic initiatives towards Western countries and international organizations; whilst Poland, Romania and Hungary have become members of GATT and Romania of the IMF.

(d) to develop trade relations with developing countries to

---

56 For example, in Romania similar arguments have been advanced by A. Puiu, *Probleme Economice*, no. 12 (1969); A. Puiu and O. Ciulea, *Lupta de Clasa*, no. 8 (1967); C. Murgescu in *Eficienta Economica a Comertului* (Bucharest, 1967); and V. Aldea, *Lumea* (1 February 1973).

TABLE 2 Soviet and East European visible trade with industrialized capitalist nations (million rubles, f.o.b.:f.o.b.)

	1971	1972	1973	1974	1975	1971–5
Eastern Europe						
Exports	4 245	4 806	6 161	8 073	7 701	30 986
Imports	4 955	5 826	8 047	11 877	12 502	43 207
Balance	−701	−1 020	−1 886	−3 804	−4 801	−12 221
Soviet Union						
Exports	2 484	2 441	3 750	6 257	6 140	21 072
Imports	2 601	3 441	4 589	6 147	9 703	26 481
Balance	−117	−1 000	−839	+110	−3 563	−5 409
TOTAL BALANCE	−827	−2 020	−2 725	−3 694	−8 364	−17 630

Source: SEV (CMEA), *Yezhegodnik* (various years).

secure raw materials and to ensure export surpluses either for use in switch deals with Western countries or to obtain convertible currencies.

(*e*) to change the structure of exports in order to produce commodities for which demand is growing more rapidly in the West.

These policies have not been entirely successful. The quantitative significance of cooperative ventures is still low (accounting for about 4–5 per cent of East–West trade), and large deficits have been accumulated by the CMEA nations in their visible trade with the developed West. These have only partially been offset by surpluses on visible trade, notably tourism and transfer payments. Invisible surpluses have been rapidly eroded by the rising cost of debt servicing and licence purchase, as a result of which the CMEA as a whole may well be in deficit on invisible trade with the West by the late 1970s.

Structural causes of imbalance have been further compounded by a member of short-run factors in the early 1970s – raw material prices have moved substantially against Eastern Europe and Western recession has increased difficulties in marketing commodities in the West. Furthermore, poor harvests (combined with apparent changes in attitude on behalf of the Party leadership, notably in the USSR and Poland) have resulted in increased expenditure on imported foodstuffs.

The short-run factors have not affected the CMEA nations uniformly. The USSR, whilst suffering from poor harvests (1972 and 1974) benefited substantially in 1973 and 1974 from the increased price of raw materials (notably oil) and precious metals (gold, diamonds and platinum) of which she is a net exporter.

The problem of continuing deficits may prove to be more crucial for the East European countries which are net importers of fuel and raw materials. They may also find it difficult to insulate their internal price structure from the effect of relative changes in raw material prices without a loss of efficiency. These deficits may bear particularly hard on the less industrial nations which also face EEC restrictions on their predominantly agricultural exports. As a result the largest proportionate imbalances in trade with the industrial West have been incurred by Bulgaria, Poland and Romania, while Czechoslovakia and the GDR have succeeded in covering a greater proportion of their imports by exports.

A consequence of the indebtedness has been the need to develop new methods of financing current account imbalances. Partly as a result of the capital intensity of Western exports to the CMEA requiring long-term finance and the fact that commercial suppliers of long-term finance have largely restricted themselves to domestic markets, official credit support (OCS) was an important factor in East–West trade before indebtedness went so high. However, as CMEA borrowing has increased along with Soviet armaments and overseas expansion, the political and economic wisdom of OCS has been called into question in the West, and provision of credit has been viewed as a possible vehicle for political pressure.

Partly because of this and partly because of the sheer size and number of loans required, the USSR and East European countries have turned increasingly to commercial sources of credit and in particular to Eurocurrency markets. Furthermore, while loans negotiated through intergovernmental channels tie the purchaser to products from the country concerned, eurocurrency loans provide far greater flexibility – a factor that may be of considerable importance where high technology products are concerned. However, while CMEA countries have traditionally been regarded as highly creditworthy, due to their past repayments record and the state monopoly of foreign trade, the growing debt-to-hard-currency-earnings ratios and debt-service-to-export ratios have been a cause of growing concern in the West.

It may be time to assess the political and economic wisdom of continued Western credits to CMEA and their effect on CMEA cooperation. Here it is necessary to distinguish between the USSR and the East European nations.

The USSR's low import dependence, combined with her wealth in raw materials and precious metals, should mean that if she had the political will she could re-order priorities so as to divert resources to export markets or cut back hard-currency imports without too severe disruption of the domestic economy. Although it is unlikely that the East European countries intend to expand borrowing (or even maintain it at its current high levels) they could find that reduced credit facilities and the consequent reduction in imports could have considerable repercussions on their growth rates. A logical consequence of this would be to cause them to rely more on Soviet raw materials and to encourage them to participate in CMEA projects, particularly on Soviet terms. In the long run therefore East European inability to market commodities in the West may act as a spur to improved CMEA cooperation.

Thus the technical commodity and credit picture points in the same direction as Soviet institutions and ideology: to more centralized planning within the CMEA.

4

Soviet Views of Western Economic Integration*

JOHN PINDER

Since the early 1970s, a substantial body of writing has been produced in the Soviet Union on the subject of Western economic integration, and on the European Community in particular. The necessary resources have been allocated to this work because of the belief that 'a realistic and correct evaluation of capitalist integration is important for the policy of socialist countries'.[1] An understanding of the resulting literature is not without significance for those in the West who are concerned about the course of East–West relations and the relations between the 'two integration groups': the EEC and the CMEA. For Soviet policy is a major determinant of these relations; and the literature reflects not only the line of Soviet policy but also the thinking that goes into its formation.[2]

Other influences on Soviet policy towards the Community are doubtless weightier than the analyses of Western economic integration. The coincidence of ideology and traditional power politics as motives for the Soviet Union's hostile reactions to the

* The research on which this chapter is based was assisted by a grant from the Nuffield Foundation.

1 V. Martynov in *Materialy Mezhdunarodnovo Simpoziuma: Integratsionnye Protsessy v Sisteme Sovremennovo Kapitalizma* (Moscow: Institute of World Economy and International Relations (IMEMO), 1972), part 2, p. 230. In this, as in subsequent citations, the translation is mine.
2 For an evaluation of the role of IMEMO (which is the main source of this literature) in the formation of Soviet foreign policy, with particular reference to policy towards the European Community, see Eberhard Schulz, *Moskau und die Europäische Integration* (Munich: R. Oldenbourg Verlag for the Forschungsinstitut der Deutschen Gesellschaft für Auswärtige Politik, 1975), pp. 72–3.

establishment of the Community are clearly brought out by Schulz,[3] whose book provides a recent and comprehensive account of political and strategic as well as economic factors in Soviet policy towards the Community. The Soviet literature on economic integration itself, in line with the marxist belief in the indivisibility of economics from politics, deals with political issues that do not readily find a place in the literature of Western economics. The focus in this chapter is, however, on the Soviet view of economic integration, and political questions are raised only where they relate to that.

Nor are Soviet economic interests in relation to the Community evaluated here. It has been shown elsewhere[4] that, although the Soviet Union has a substantial interest in trade and economic cooperation with the Community countries, the commercial policy for which the Community itself carries responsibility on behalf of the member states is limited to matters (tariffs, quotas, import levies) which are of little interest to the Soviet Union, in view of the predominance of raw materials in Soviet exports to the Community. On the one occasion up to now when Community policy has affected a significant Soviet interest, in connection with fishing in the North Sea, the Soviet Union immediately overcame its political objections to negotiating with the Community institutions. But because, apart from this, Community policies have hardly touched Soviet economic interests, the Soviet Union has been able to decide its policy towards the Community largely on political and ideological grounds. So there has been more scope for Soviet conceptions of the significance of Western economic integration to influence Soviet policy than there would have been if material interests were more heavily involved.

3 *Ibid.*
4 In, for example, John and Pauline Pinder, *The European Community's Policy towards Eastern Europe* (London: Chatham House and PEP, 1975); and John Pinder, 'Economic integration and East–West trade: conflict of interests or comedy of errors?' in F. Alting von Geusau (ed.), *Uncertain Détente* (Alphen aan den Rijn: Sijthoff for John F. Kennedy Institute, 1978 forthcoming) and in *Journal of Common Market Studies* (Oxford, September 1977).

Soviet writings[5] on Western economic integration are of interest, as it happens, not only for the light they may throw on Soviet political behaviour towards the European Community, but also because they raise some questions about integration which are hardly considered in the Western literature. Although their answers are perforce constrained within ideological limits, they nevertheless contribute to an understanding of some vital aspects which have been largely neglected by Western economists; and some of their criticisms of the economics of integration as the subject now stands in the West are hard to gainsay.

The reason for this rather vigorous and effective intellectual response to the phenomenon of Western integration may have been the challenge presented by the failure of earlier marxist predictions about the Community and the capitalist economy as a whole. Instead of collapsing under the weight of its internal contradictions, the Community rapidly became one of the leading powers in the Western economy; and the initial Soviet reactions were revised to take account of the fact that the Community had evidently come to stay.[6] But the explanation

5 The Soviet works which are the subject of this chapter are M. M. Maximova, *Osnovnye Problemy Imperialisticheskoy Integratsii* (Moscow: Mysl, 1971); Y. V. Shishkov, *Obshchiy Rynok: Nadezhdy i Deistvitelnost* (Moscow: Mysl, 1972); *Materialy Mezhdunarodnovo Simpoziuma*; L. E. Glukharev (ed.), *Problemy Integratsii Proizvodstva pri Kapitalizme* (Moscow: Mysl, 1973); and a number of articles, most of which have appeared in *Mirovaya Ekonomika i Mezhdunarodnye Otnosheniya* (*MEIMO*), which is the journal of the Institute of World Economy and International Relations (IMEMO). There are also some relevant chapters by Soviet authors in the book of the Fourth World Congress of the International Economic Association, *Economic Integration: Worldwide, Regional, Sectoral* (London: Macmillan, 1976 and New York: Halsted Press, 1977). The works of authors of other East European countries are not dealt with unless they appear in Soviet symposia or are mentioned in the Soviet literature. It is remarkable how seldom the Soviet authors find occasion to refer to the works of Western marxists on this subject.

6 The first reactions were expressed in the '16 theses' produced by IMEMO and published in *MEIMO*, no. 1 (1957) and in *Kommunist*, Moscow, no. 9 (1957). This view was first revised in IMEMO's '32 theses', published in a special supplement to *MEIMO*, no. 9 (1962).

found for this single fact might have been relatively superficial, had it not been sought in the context of the much wider re-examination of Soviet thinking about modern capitalism, stimulated by the unexpected refusal of capitalism to behave like a doomed system should or of the 'imperialist' powers to come into serious conflict with each other during the post-war period. The theory of 'state monopoly capitalism', whereby the state works with the 'monopolies' (i.e. big companies) to maintain some stability in the modern capitalist economy through a measure of central regulation, had therefore been actively developed as a basis on which to build a theory of 'state monopoly integration', to help explain the durability of the European Community.

It was towards the end of the 1960s, 'when the problems of the development of socialist integration acquired particular actuality', that 'marxist science addressed itself to the analysis of integration as a world tendency'.[7] A strong Soviet interest in the economic integration of the CMEA had been aroused during the aftermath of the intervention in Czechoslovakia, an event which demonstrated the desirability of finding more convenient ways to maintain stability in the group. At the same time as the political advantages of such integration were perceived in the Soviet Union, the European Community was preparing another major advance in its own integration, in the form of the plan for economic and monetary union, with the prospect of enlargement to include Britain and other new members as well. The time was therefore ripe for the launching of studies in which the theory of 'state monopoly integration' was developed and publicized.

Just as 'state monopoly capitalism' is seen as an aspect of the modern capitalist economy, which does not remove its fatal contradictions but merely reduces their effects to a level that can be tolerated for a time and thus allow the system to last a bit longer, so 'state monopoly integration' is associated with 'private monopoly integration'.[8] Private monopoly integration

7 Maximova, *Osnovnye Problemy*, p. 125.
8 'State monopoly capitalism', 'private monopoly integration' and 'state monopoly integration' have been introduced in inverted commas, because they are terms used in Soviet writings, which I

comes first, and it is necessary first to know how the Soviet writers view this driving force of capitalist integration.

Private Monopoly Integration

There is no echo in the Soviet literature of the type of doubt expressed by some British economists, during the repeated debates about Britain's relationship with the European Community, as to whether a larger market is needed for the further development of a modern economy. It is an article of Soviet faith that the process of 'specialization, by its very nature, is endless – exactly as is also the development of technology... The progress of technology must bring with it the specialization of different branches of production, their socialization and, consequently, the enlargement of the market.'[9] Integration, which is a 'higher level of internationalization of production and of economic links, having defined qualitative features',[10] is therefore an 'objective phenomenon', rooted in the nature of technological and economic development rather than in the capitalist system as such; and the scope for it is endless.

Along with this robust faith in technological progress goes a healthy appreciation of the power of the big capitalist firms to promote it. The internationalization of the modern capitalist economy is described in terms not only of trade but also of cross-frontier mergers, investments and agreements among firms; and Maximova paints a most impressive picture of the strength and extent of this movement.[11] All this interlinking of firms is not the favourite subject of liberal economists, but it seems to fascinate the Soviet marxists. Doubtless Shishkov puts his finger on the reason when he cites from Lenin 'Forward

would not normally employ. Although the terms refer to real phenomena and can be helpful to the analysis of some aspects of the modern Western economy, the use of the word 'monopoly' seems to me tendentious, and reflects a Soviet attitude towards the Western economic system which I do not share. In order to avoid burdening the reader's eyes with an excess of inverted commas, however, they have been omitted in all subsequent use of the terms. But they remain there in the spirit, if not in the ink.

9   V. I. Lenin, quoted in Maximova, *Osnovnye Problemy*, p. 37.
10 Maximova, *Osnovnye Problemy*, p. 128.
11 *Ibid.* chapter 3.

through the trusts etc. and beyond them to socialism'.[12] The big firms would embody economic progress of the right sort if they did not happen to belong, for the time being, to the wrong people: to be in private, not public, ownership.

It is ironic that the achievements of capitalist firms, and in particular the multinationals, in weaving an international web of interlocking production should be so well brought out by the Soviet writers. For integrated production is precisely the aim of the CMEA's own integration: 'in contrast to West European integration, the primary aim of which is to establish a common market, the integration of the CMEA countries has from the outset been oriented toward joint efforts in tackling, above all, production and technological problems'.[13] Yet the achievements of the CMEA in integrating production seem far less impressive than the integration of production in the West, so vividly depicted by Soviet authors. The most plausible reason is clearly implicit in a Hungarian contribution to the symposium held in Moscow by the Institute of World Economy and International Relations (IMEMO) in 1972, as a focus for the new wave of studies of Western integration:

With the present level of knowledge of economic laws, there is not and cannot be a coordination of plans such as could encompass the whole circle of possible cooperation, precisely define all the details and foresee the powerful changes that will emerge in the course of time. All this demands significant economic independence of the participants in concrete cooperation, which can be guided in the desired channel with the help of various financial levers.[14]

But the stress in the CMEA is heavily on the coordination of plans, and the enterprises that 'participate in concrete cooperation' generally have too little independence: so it is not surprising that the integration of production proceeds too slowly.

That is not the concern of the Soviet analysts of Western

12 Quoted in Shishkov, *Obshchiy Rynok*, p. 253.
13 O. T. Bogomolov, 'International integration by market forces and through planning' in IEA, *Economic Integration*, p. 307.
14 F. Kozma, 'Osnovnye Razlichiya v Integratsionnikh Protsessokh Zapadnoy i Vostochnoy Evropy' in *Materialy Mezhdunarodnovo Simpoziuma*, p. 38.

integration, however. They point, rather, to the contradictions that arise in the course of private monopoly integration in the west.[15] The development of capitalist economies in general is 'spontaneous' and 'anarchic' because of the 'struggle for markets' and 'chase after profits' that are inherent in the system of 'monopoly capitalism'; and international economic competition adds another dimension to this, with the struggle between the capitalists of different countries and the 'economic inequality of states, exploitation of some nations by others, and unequal exchanges'.[16] There is, under capitalism, a 'law of uneven development', and this causes the big firms to benefit most from the process of integration, at the expense of small businesses, peasants and weak regions.[17] The unregulated market forces lead to inflation, unemployment and deficits.[18] The outcome is a further sharpening of class conflict.

'Bourgeois' (i.e. Western non-marxist) economists are criticized for concentrating on the trade effects of integration at the expense of the production and structural effects, failing to analyse integration in terms of the behaviour of big firms and ignoring its class content.[19] Western economists have, indeed, been overly attracted by complex and elegant calculations of the trade effects of tariff reductions, with results of negligible utility; and, with a few exceptions, they have failed to investigate the effects of integration on economic development. The trade calculations can be made with at least a good appearance of scientific accuracy, whereas the structural effects are, at least with the present state of knowledge, more speculative. But they are also much more important, and economists should address themselves to the important questions, even if they must set sail on rougher seas in search of the answers.

The Soviet economists, for their part, seem too ready to

15 A full account of these is given in Maximova, *Osnovnye Problemy*, part 3.

16 Maximova, *Osnovnye Problemy*, p. 173.

17 *Ibid.* p. 173.

18 *Ibid.* p. 293.

19 Critiques of the Western economic literature on integration are to be found in Maximova, *Osnovnye Problemy*, pp. 116–26 and 253–4, and in Y. V. Shishkov, 'Zapadnoevropeiskaya Integratsiya: Teoriyi i Realnost', *Voprosy Economiki*, no. 3 (1977).

content themselves with easy assumptions that the 'chase after profits' will disrupt the economy with damaging contradictions and that the 'anarchy' of Western markets is more important than their freedom. Having been accorded the status of articles of faith, such ideas are not subjected to sufficient criticism and verification. The tenor of the Soviet comments seems to imply that there are proven answers to the problem of managing a modern economy, which are embodied in the Soviet system. I have argued elsewhere that the straitjacket of excessive centralization in the Soviet system may be at least as damaging as the instability that results from the decentralization of economic decision-taking in the West.[20] The Soviet analyses of the Western economies would be more illuminating if they resorted less frequently to general propositions about the 'essence' of the system and gave more consideration to the form of economic management that would provide the desirable stability without sacrificing the flexibility and initiative that have made private monopoly integration, to take one example, such an impressive phenomenon. But the concept of state monopoly capitalism has, for all that, been developed into a powerful instrument for explaining the survival of the modern Western economies; and its extension into the theory of state monopoly integration lends a certain power to the Soviet analyses of integration in the European Community.

State Monopoly Integration

According to the theory of state monopoly capitalism, the Western countries have introduced enough central regulation into their economies to enable them to survive and even prosper during the post-war period. The forms of regulation comprise Keynesian economic management in a broad sense, including structural as well as conjunctural policies, together with the welfare state. This has prevented a reversion to the great depression of the 1930s and enabled workers to secure substantial increases in their real wages. But the government intervenes in the interests not of the working class but of the capitalist class (the significance of state monopoly capitalism being that the state

20 John Pinder, 'East–West economic competition', *Survey*, London, no. 3/4 (1976).

is working on behalf of the 'monopolies'), so there are contradictions which, among other things, prevent the interventions from ever being sufficient to solve the problems of the capitalist system.

Some of these contradictions have already been mentioned: between the big firms and small firms; among the big firms themselves; between strong and weak regions; and of course between the working and the capitalist class. But private monopoly integration brings a new contradiction that goes to the heart of our present subject: between the international market forces which private monopoly integration introduces into each national economy and the state monopoly capitalism which is trying to maintain national economic stability and growth.[21] It is to deal with this new contradiction that the governments of some capitalist countries have resorted to state monopoly integration.

State monopoly integration has two principal aims. The first is to liberalize trade and keep it liberalized. This liberalization is necessary for the efficient working of the big firms, which must, if they are to make full use of modern technology, develop the international links and exchanges that are the main element in private monopoly integration; and once the barriers at national frontiers have been removed they must stay removed, because modern technology demands that 'mutual economic relations between national economies adopt an ever more solid, stable, long-term character'.[22] An integrating group of countries must therefore control the tendency of their governments to use protection as an aid to the regulation of domestic economy.

The second aim of state monopoly integration is to enable the integrating group to deal jointly, through policies of the state monopoly capitalist type, with the market forces which are increasingly international in origin and scope.[23] Both cyclical and structural policies are required, and the integrating states

21 See Maximova, *Osnovnye Problemy*, pp. 179 *et seq*; and Y. V. Shishkov, 'Ekonomicheskiy Mekhanizm Gosudarstvenno-Monopolisticheskoy Integratsii i yevo Protivorechiya' in *Materialy Mezhdunarodnovo Simpoziuma*, p. 230.
22 Maximova, *Osnovnye Problemy*, p. 131.
23 *Ibid.* p. 190. See also A. Ciamaga, 'Sushchnot Ekonomicheskoy integratsii' in *Materialy Mezhdunarodnovo Simpoziuma*, pp. 107, 108.

are faced with the alternatives either of developing coordinated or common policies, or of reimposing their frontier controls and thus taking a step towards disintegration.[24] Disintegration of this sort would be regressive but not impossible. State monopoly integration is reversible, according to Shishkov, while private monopoly integration is not.[25] For the Polish economist Kamecki, 'contradictions can only slow the tempo and influence the direction and form of this integration, but cannot cut it short, still less evoke a process of disintegration'. A breaking of links among the Community countries would be a 'catastrophe'.[26]

In addition to its obvious achievements in internal trade liberalization, the European Community has introduced common regulation into the sectors of agriculture and external trade, a measure of common policies for other sectors such as coal and steel, and some other instruments of common policy such as the Regional Fund, the Social Fund and the Investment Bank. In view of the continued progress of private monopoly integration, however, which is bound to weaken the power of member governments to regulate their domestic economies, Soviet writers were not surprised at the appearance of the Community's proposals for an economic and monetary union, which would resolve one contradiction by transferring the main responsibility for conjunctural policy from the national governments to the Community. The logic of their analysis led Soviet writers to view the achievement of economic and monetary union as quite possible, though by no means inevitable.[27] Subsequent events have, as we shall see in the next section, caused them to become more sceptical. But the contradictions and obstacles in the way of state monopoly integration had always been stressed, so the Community's setback was not at all difficult for the Soviet analysts to explain.

Of the Community's policies to activate competition (through internal liberalization) and to restrain it (through common or

24 *Ibid.* p. 251.
25 Shishkov, *Obshchiy Rynok*, pp. 251–2 and 'Zapadnoevropeiskaya Integratsiya', p. 84.
26 Z. Kamecki, 'K Voprosu o Ponyatii Ekonomicheskoy Integratsii' in *Materialy Mezhdunarodnovo Simpoziuma*, p. 72.
27 See for example Shishkov, *Obshchiy Rynok*, pp. 251–2.

coordinated regulation), the latter had always been judged the weaker. If state monopoly capitalism was too weak, state monopoly integration was weaker still. Although the big firms provided the initial drive for integration, they also set limits to it because of their dislike of official regulation.[28] The interest of the big firms lies, indeed, basically in the customs union alone[29] rather than in more positive forms of integration. There would never be enough regulation, because intervention in the production process was not accepted by private business.[30] The problem lies 'in the nature of capitalism'.[31]

This gap between private monopoly integration and state monopoly integration is regarded as very damaging: even more damaging with respect to structural than to cyclical policy.[32] Capitalist integration leads to the increased 'socialization' of production (i.e. to greater interlocking of the different parts of the production process), with negative effects for the capitalist system[33] which is ill-equipped to deal with this aspect of the modern economy. Contradictions will therefore overtake state monopoly capitalism, perhaps before state monopoly integration is complete.[34]

If state monopoly integration was judged to be too weak in the European Community, it was weaker still in the wider Western economy. Here, state monopoly integration was more-or-less confined to measures relating to the liberalization of trade.[35] The contradictions between the countries of the European Community and the United States were said to be too great to allow them to venture beyond those limits;[36] it was a smaller number of countries with similar economic levels, such as the members of the European Community, that were able to move on to more positive forms of state monopoly integration.[37]

28 Maximova, *Osnovnye Problemy*, p. 195.
29 V. Fedorov, 'EEC i Nekotorye Aspekty Uchastiya FRG', *MEIMO*, no. 7 (1976), p. 70.
30 Shishkov, 'Ekonomicheskiy Mekhanizm', pp. 218–19.
31 Maximova, *Osnovnye Problemy*, p. 235.
32 *Ibid.* pp. 272–3.   33 *Ibid.* p. 251.
34 *Ibid.* p. 157.   35 *Ibid.* p. 190.
36 *Ibid.* p. 139.   37 *Ibid.* p. 151.

The Community clearly does have a more impressive array of common policies than the institutions of the wider Western economy as a whole. But it is as well to bear in mind that the Soviet Union may see a political interest in stressing this fact, as a source of divergence between Western Europe and the United States. Apart from the intense transatlantic integration in the private sector, with the interlocking production of the multinationals as well as trade and financial transactions, and the elaborate process of trade liberalization in the GATT, there is also the international monetary cooperation which is considerably more significant in the formal and informal procedures of wider Western collaboration than it is in the European Community.

When the major Soviet books on economic integration in the European Community were written, the proposals for economic and monetary union may have justified an expectation that the Community would go much farther in the monetary field as well. But since 1974, when the crisis of high inflation, unemployment and payments deficits hit the Western world, the plans for monetary union have been put on the shelf, and the centre of gravity of international economic management has moved towards the wider Western system in which the United States plays the leading role. Inevitably this has shifted the focus of interest for Soviet research about Western economic integration and the expectations of Soviet writers about the future of the European Community.

After 1973: A New Stage of Capitalism

The capitalist ills of inflation and unemployment did not go unmentioned by Soviet writers in the early 1970s, although for two decades they had not been very serious problems, at least in comparison with the inter-war years. They were explained by the usual capitalist contradictions and social conflicts, sharpened by the new contradictions that accompany economic integration.[38]

Explanations for the inflation, unemployment and other disequilibria that followed 1973 were therefore ready to hand.

38 Maximova, *Osnovnye Problemy*, pp. 352–3.

There was no need to develop new concepts, such as had been required when state monopoly capitalism and integration were introduced, to explain the failure of capitalist countries to collapse or to quarrel sufficiently with each other. But Soviet analysts were faced with the question whether this was the long-predicted 'final crisis of capitalism' or merely a 'new stage' of capitalism, which would stabilize itself and remain in business for some time ahead. The question was of the utmost practical importance, because if capitalism is keeling over the the last time, there is no little temptation for Soviet policy to help by giving it a push; and there were some signs within the Soviet hierarchy of a tendency to act in this way. But the principal writers on integration, like the top political leadership of the Soviet Union, firmly chose the 'new stage', with the implication of continuity for Soviet policy. The researchers at IMEMO expect a slow recovery for the Western economy through the remainder of the 1970s,[39] probably followed by a less violent recession than that of the mid-1970s. But although this is far from a final crisis, the contradictions and social conflicts are thought to be intensifying, with severe consequences for economic integration.

The growth of 'spontaneous' and 'anarchic' international market forces that follows from private monopoly integration had been expected to outstrip the capacity of state monopoly integration to control them; and this prediction was fulfilled – perhaps even overfulfilled – by the behaviour of international money, with some $250 billion awash in the eurocurrency markets, and of the world markets for energy and other primary products. While international control over these markets had not been achieved, the rapid growth of interdependence through private monopoly integration had eroded the ability of national governments to regulate their domestic economies in the face of these uncontrolled international forces.[40] Thus the Western countries have failed to develop state monopoly integ-

---

39 V. A. Martynov, 'Sovremennoye Polozheniye Kapitalisticheskoy Ekonomiki i Blizhayshiye Perspektivy yevo Razvitiya', *MEIMO*, no. 6 (1977), especially p. 116.
40 Y. V. Shishkov, 'Krizis Mekhanizma Ekonomicheskikh Otnoshenii Kapitalisticheskikh Stran', *MEIMO*, no. 1 (1977), p. 27.

ration enough to control private monopoly integration before the latter undermines state monopoly capitalism at home.

While this concerns the Western international economy as a whole, contradictions within the European Community itself have sharpened too. One that is new in degree, if not in kind, is the division between strong and weak countries.[41] The formation of common policies is impeded by divergences of both policies and conjunctures[42] – and, one might add, structures. There is more mention of a long period of stagnation for the Community, or even of its possible dissolution, and less thought of Community progress in state monopoly integration. Capitalism has failed to solve the problem of international economic management, and it is possible to pose the alternatives of a dash forward to Community regulation or a reversion to national regulation of the member countries' economies.[43] But the most settled prediction seems to be for the lengthy period of stagnation in Community policies.

As far as international policy-making in the West is concerned, attention has moved towards the wider system. This follows from the synchronization of economic cycles which became evident throughout the Western economy in the 1970s, and which calls for regulation of the system as a whole.[44] Yet only halting progress is made towards this. Competition among the United States, the Community and Japan has replaced American hegemony; the rules of the game are at a discount; and there is no clear view of the future.[45]

Although so much stress is laid on the difficulties in the Western economy and the deficiencies of international economic management, there are at the same time fears that too desperate a situation in the West could have unpleasant repercussions for the Soviet Union. The Western recession has

41 Y. V. Shishkov, 'Tupiki "Maloy Evropy"', *Mezhdunarodnaya Zhizn*, no. 2 (1977), p. 47. The position of West Germany in particular is analysed in Fedorov, 'Nekotorye Aspekty'.

42 Fedorov, 'Nekotorye Aspekty', p. 63.

43 Shishkov, 'Zapadnoevropeiskaya Integratsiya', pp. 83–4 and Shishkov, 'Tupiki "Maloy Evropy"', p. 51.

44 Shishkov, 'Tupiki "Maloy Evropy"', p. 43.

45 Shishkov, 'Krizis Mekhanizma', pp. 36–7.

already affected Soviet exports, and hence the capacity to import the technology that the Soviet economy so badly needs. Deeper recession would not only make this worse, but also raise the danger of right-wing coups in Western countries, after the Chilean pattern (an echo here of Italian communist views).

There is, therefore, no political inhibition against Soviet writers predicting that the capitalist countries will develop new instruments of state intervention to deal with the new difficulties that have arisen as a result of the 'development of productive forces and raising of the level of socialization of production'.[46] These advances in the capitalist economy were, after all, made possible by the new methods of state intervention that were introduced to prevent a recurrence of the deflationary crisis of the 1930s. The system has enough absorptive capacity to contain the present crisis and introduce new methods of intervention once again, in response to the problems of the more developed capitalist economies of today. But Soviet writers emphasize that this response will always be inadequate. The 'spontaneous market mechanism' and the 'state-monopoly intervention in the economy' are far from being of equal significance, and there is a constant struggle between them, leading to pronounced instability. The system will not collapse 'today or tomorrow', but neither can capitalism 'create an economic mechanism that answers to the level of the productive forces, which already long since outgrew the limits of capitalist production relations'.[47] Thus the inadequacy of state monopoly integration will remain as one major manifestation of the general inadequacy of state monopoly capitalism.

Conclusions for Soviet Policy

Soviet researchers have developed a flexible method of analysing Western economic integration which is well adapted to take account of new circumstances, such as the international economic crisis of the mid-1970s, or to justify new conclusions in the light of changing circumstances. Private monopoly integration is both the driving force of Western integration and the destabilizer, while state monopoly integration is the stabilizer,

46 *Ibid.* p. 26.   47 *Ibid.* p. 38.

albeit an inadequate one. Depending on the balance of power between the two, i.e. on the relative strength assigned to each at a given time, the Soviet analyst could predict stability or instability, progress (though not too much) or collapse. The same applies to the relationship between the market forces in the capitalist economies and the interventions of state monopoly capitalism within each economy as well as internationally.

Despite the opportunity to predict collapse that the condition of the Western economy in the 1970s has presented, the most influential Soviet specialists on the capitalist economic system have refrained from doing so, and have chosen instead to foresee, in the 'new stage' of capitalism, a period in which there is instability, but not so much as to prevent a moderate (if unsatisfactory) degree of economic progress, and in which state monopoly capitalism develops new instruments of intervention that may go some way towards dealing with the new problems. This is the general view of the Soviet political leadership, as expressed by Brezhnev at the 25th Party Congress in 1976: 'Communists are far from prognosticating the "automatic collapse" of capitalism. It still has considerable reserves.'[48]

This sober view of the medium-term future of capitalism does not necessarily preclude a more sensational view of the future of the European Community as such, for that particular example of state monopoly integration can be regarded as one of the weaker links in the system of state monopoly capitalism as a whole, in which the interventions by national governments are still far more important; and as we have seen, the possibility that the Community (as distinct from the private monopoly integration among the member countries) will break up has been mooted in recent Soviet writings on the subject. The implications for Soviet policy of a more pessimistic view of the Community's future could include a hardening of the negative attitude towards 'recognition' of the Community, in reversal of the recent trend to modify this line by moves towards some form of negotiation between the Community and the CMEA and by actual negotiation between the Community and the Soviet Union on fish. A further stage of hardening could lead to Soviet

48 Quoted in Shishkov, 'Krizis Mekhanizma', p. 38.

attempts to impede new developments within the Community, such as were evident in earlier stages of the Community's development.[49] Beyond that again, there could be an active policy to promote the dissolution of the Community.

The published references to a possible break-up of the Community have, however, taken the form of speculation about possible outcomes, rather than of predictions. The favoured line is that the Community will remain in being as a significant institution of state monopoly integration, even if its importance remains limited by an inability to construct new policies and the focus of interest moves to the management of the Western system as a whole. The policy analogue of this view is the more reassuring one of a continued, if slow, movement towards the establishment of normal relations with the Community, not a reversion to a more aggressively hostile stance.

Could the Soviet analysis be taken a step further so as to justify a policy of active cooperation with the Community? The Soviet Union could, it might be reasoned, tilt the balance of power in its direction by supporting the development of the Community and thus, perhaps, driving a wedge between Western Europe and America. But Soviet writers have not reasoned in this way,[50] nor has Soviet policy acted in this way; and if it did, the relationship with the Community would be inherently unstable, so long as the Soviet view of the Western economic system remained as basically hostile as it has been up to now.

Is there a possibility, then, that the Soviet view of the Western economic system could develop to the point where Western prosperity, together with the health of the institutions of international economic management that facilitate it, such as the European Community, would come to be regarded as a positive Soviet interest? There are elements in the Soviet writings on

49 An example of the intellectual support for such efforts in academic works is to be found in A. I. Shein, 'Angliiskiye Monopolii i Evropeyskoye Ekonomicheskoye So'obshchestvo' in Glukharev (ed.), *Problemy Integratsii*, pp. 207–13, where the line of the Communist Party of Great Britain towards Britain joining the Community was expounded.

50 See for example Maximova, *Osnovnye Problemy*, chapter 13, and Shishkov, *Obshchiy Rynok*, pp. 19–20.

Western integration that could, on the face of it, be thought to point in this direction. It is assumed that capitalism has sufficient 'reserves' and absorptive capacity to remain in being for some time ahead; and severe Western economic failure has been seen as inconvenient or even dangerous for the Soviet Union, in view of the effect on Soviet trade and the possibility of right-wing coups – not to mention the sacrifice of welfare for millions of workers, to whose advantage the Soviet system is supposed to operate. Would it not be logical to suggest that, if Western economic failure is for these reasons bad for the Soviet Union, Western prosperity might, for the opposite reasons, be good?

Why, moreover, if the coming of socialism is inevitable, should the Soviet Union oppose Western measures which put some of the elements needed for socialism already in place? It can be argued that some of the instruments of intervention introduced under state monopoly capitalism may be used as building blocks in constructing a socialist system. As Maximova says, the strength of working class organizations has substantially increased during the period of state monopoly capitalism,[51] which strengthens the social and political basis for socialism. Although the 'methods of central economic regulation' to which the Western governments must have recourse in order to deal with the now high level of 'socialization' (i.e. interlocking) of production 'are inherently alien to the nature of the capitalist economy and are borrowed from the succeeding historical formation – socialism',[52] these methods are nevertheless, to use Shishkov's vivid phrase, 'borrowed from the future'[53] and used as instruments of state monopoly capitalism. Why not encourage people who are borrowing from the future, if the future is where you want them to be?

This argument can be applied to the European Community in particular. Soviet writings accept that the Community has some 'progressive elements', such as nationalized enterprises, a degree of programming, regional policies, etc.[54] Its effect on workers could not be described in altogether negative terms, but

51 Maximova, *Osnovnye Problemy*, p. 77.
52 Shishkov, *Obshchiy Rynok*, p. 246.
53 *Ibid.* p. 246.
54 Maximova, *Osnovnye Problemy*, pp. 77, 337ff.

rather as 'complex and contradictory'.[55] The 'democratic alternative' regarded as a suitable aim for working-class organizations within the Community therefore includes the 'activity of the masses in the further development of state monopoly mechanisms of regulation of economic life in each of the integrating countries'; 'the development of the nationalized sector'; 'the development – in the interests of the workers – of the regulating basis in the activities of the integrating groups, and of economic programming on a democratic basis', for example by the 'active participation of the working class, its parties and organizations in the working out of long-term programmes of economic development'; and 'the democratization of the political structure of the integration mechanism, beginning with a fuller representation in the Community organs of anti-monopolist forces and ending with a review of the bases of the Rome Treaty in the interests of the broad masses of the people'.[56] Although there are other recommendations in a different vein, those quoted here seem compatible with the view that the institutions and policies of state monopoly capitalism can be improved, in the interests of the workers, by working in the existing system to bring about peaceful change: compatible, in fact, with the sort of policies pursued within the Community by the Italian Communist Party. Might one be justified in drawing the conclusion that Soviet policy could, accordingly, tend towards a policy of support for the Community in so far as it moves in such directions? Could this be one feature of a general 'historical compromise' between Soviet marxism and state monopoly capitalism?

Unfortunately, there is no sign of such a new approach on the Soviet side. Despite the possibilities that seem to be inherent in elements of their argument, many of the terms and concepts used by Soviet writers appear designed to preclude progress beyond the frame of reference of an adversary relationship. The literature abounds with assertions that capitalism must collapse and socialism triumph (with the implicit assumption that socialism is represented by the Soviet state), and that 'between the two there is no intermediate step'.[57] While terms such as

---

55 *Ibid.* p. 291.   56 *Ibid.* pp. 337–41.   57 *Ibid.* p. 251.

'collapse', 'triumph' and 'no intermediate step' can doubtless
be open to differing interpretations, it is hard to reconcile them
with the practical view of the development of state monopoly
capitalism referred to earlier. This general tenor of Soviet
writings, so long as it lasts, seems incompatible with progress
beyond a relatively superficial degree of cooperation.

Since many of the elements for a different approach, such as
the Italian communists have indeed adopted, seem to be present
in the Soviet literature, it appears reasonable to suppose that
the conclusions and the general tenor of the literature could
change accordingly, provided that the corresponding political
decisions were taken too. But however beneficial to both sides
this might seem to be, there is no evidence of any such political
developments.

The most realistic hope, then, is that Soviet policies towards
the Community will become less negative, rather than more
positive. The Community will probably have to put up with
Soviet unhelpfulness, if not hostility, for some time to come.
Despite the considerable merit in much of the Soviet writing on
the subject of Western integration, it does not seem likely that
the Soviet writers will be able to use their skills in the interests
of a much higher level of cooperation between the two groups.
Both sides certainly lose from this. But one source of loss on
the Western side will be reduced if we become more familiar
with the Soviet researchers' work and try to identify those
respects in which it can be usefully applied in our own analysis
of the problems of Western integration.

5

East–West Industrial Cooperation Agreements

PHILIP HANSON

1. Introduction

East–West industrial cooperation is an elusive subject. Its new-ness is one of its few reliably ascertainable characteristics. Usable statistics and firm conclusions about it are few and far between. One thing that is clear, however, is that the flows of goods and services directly affected by East–West industrial cooperation are small. It is not its present scale as an economic activity but its possible importance in the future that makes it an interesting subject.

A number of general surveys, notably the 1973 report by the UN Economic Commission for Europe (ECE),[1] discuss the definition, origins and extent of East–West industrial coopera-tion. The aim of this paper is to assess the East European interest in industrial cooperation as a vehicle for technology transfer, and to assess experience so far. I think it is necessary to begin, however, with some cautionary remarks. These con-cern the difficulties of identifying and measuring industrial cooperation and the dangers of exaggerating its present importance.

2. The Nature and Scale of East–West Industrial Cooperation

All definitions of East–West industrial cooperation attempt to distinguish it from 'ordinary' trade. They do this by stressing two considerations: time and interdependence. Ordinary trade

---

1 UN ECE, *Analytical Report on Industrial Cooperation Among ECE Countries* (with two addenda), E/ECE/844, 1973. Hereafter referred to as ECE, 1973.

is represented as a series of once-for-all transactions in which the contract specifies the goods and services to be sold and the payment to be made in return; these flows are then fixed, with only a small and often insurable risk that they will not materialize. Cooperation, by contrast, arises from contracts 'extending over a number of years' and requiring the partners to engage in 'a set of reciprocally matching operations'.[2]

These operations may be in one or more of the following: exchange of technical information; joint R and D; subcontracting by one partner to the other of component production or the manufacture of part of a product range; co-production (a two-way flow of components or final products as part of each partner's production programme); joint marketing in either or both home markets or in third markets; joint ventures in which each partner has an equity.

Many, though not all, such arrangements would be likely to include at least one of the following: licensing, know-how sales, engineering consultancy, training of labour, training of management, agreements on the use of brand marks and trade names. Cooperation often therefore involves the transfer of technology. For each partner the outcome may have a fair degree of uncertainty attached to it and will depend to some extent on the operations of the other partner.

It is easy to see that activities like this can have a duration and a character of continuing interdependence between contractual partners that are absent from, say, a contract to buy x million bushels of wheat. It is not so easy to distinguish sharply between cooperation agreements and supposedly once-for-all sales of whole plants and machinery. Contracts to sell capital goods frequently involve long delivery periods, cost-escalation and penalty clauses, associated consultancy services and know-how transactions, and so on. They can exhibit considerable *de facto* interdependence over a period of time so far as the eventual costs and benefits to both partners are concerned. This is especially true of turnkey projects, in which the contractor may undertake to provide training, to start up production and to hand over a plant that is shown to be fully operational.

2 ECE, 1973, p. 4.

Licence sales are another awkward category. Even so-called 'pure' licence deals (without associated know-how, consultancy or hardware transactions) commonly entail royalty payments over several years, related to the licensee's production; this introduces a measure of continuing interdependence. The EEC report handled this difficulty by treating licence sales as a form of industrial cooperation only if they were repaid wholly or partly with products from the licensed process or were part of a package deal combining other elements of industrial cooperation.

The logic of this distinction is that a turnkey project or licence deal acquires 'a cooperative aspect' if it 'includes provisions for inter-firm coordination of the future use of the productive assets transferred'. McMillan has argued persuasively that in an East–West, as in any other, context, inter-firm cooperation should be seen as an intermediate arrangement between market relations involving two separate business units and their merger as a single entity: it allows an element of direct, non-market (administrative) allocation of resources to occur in their joint operations; it creates complex property rights in respect of assets subject to cooperative activities, and these entail an interdependence that is 'qualitatively different from, if not quantitatively greater than, that generated through the market'.[3]

It may be impossible to decide whether a particular deal is an instance of industrial cooperation or ordinary trade if one does not know all the details of the contract. Bird-watchers, unable to distinguish arctic terns from common terns unless they have an extremely close view, have hit on the happy device of recording their sightings as comic terns. East–West trade-watchers are less willing to own up to their uncertainties. If the parties to a contract describe it as a cooperation agreement, the tendency is to take their word for it. Unfortunately, the parties to the contract may have an interest in describing an ordinary transaction as industrial cooperation.

3   Carl H. McMillan, 'Forms and dimensions of East–West inter-firm cooperation' in C. T. Saunders (ed.), *East–West Cooperation in Business: Inter-firm Studies* (Vienna: Springer Verlag, 1977), pp. 28–61. The quotations given here are from p. 29.

Furthermore, the figures usually quoted of numbers of cooperation deals include some agreements which may in practice be far less important to the partners involved than an ordinary sale of moderate size. These figures mostly come from East European government sources, and they cover all sorts of things. They may include, for example, the technological cooperation agreements between the Soviet State Committee for Science and Technology (SCST) and Western firms. By April 1975, there were reported to be 170 of these.[4] In many cases they have so far entailed nothing beyond assurances of mutual interest and perhaps some meetings to discuss information exchange. In late 1975 the judgement of the US Departments of State and of Commerce was that little substantive cooperation had so far occurred under the SCST agreements with US firms.[5] Many Western signatories to these agreements regard them chiefly as a goodwill exercise which they hope will provide them with advantages of status and access in dealing with Soviet government agencies. It looks as though many of these agreements, far from being a 'higher form' of commercial relations, are more like the traditional salesman's foot in the door. They are not considered further in this paper, but it should be noted that they may in several cases provide the 'umbrella' under which more operational agreements have been concluded.

There is no doubt that industrial cooperation in the ECE's general sense of the term exists and is growing between firms

4 K. Weisskopf, in London Chamber of Commerce and Industry, *Eastern Europe* (30 April 1975), p. 1. The ECE does not count these agreements as instances of industrial cooperation but Soviet sources are apt to do so. A thorough account of the organization, sectoral composition and initial results of these agreements (primarily those involving US companies) is given by Lawrence H. Theriot, 'US governmental and private industry cooperation with the Soviet Union in the fields of science and technology' in US Congress Joint Economic Committee, *Soviet Economy in a New Perspective* (Washington: US Government Printing Office, 1976), pp. 739–67. Theriot notes fifty-three agreements with US companies and at least fifty-two with other Western companies as of early 1976. (Several more have been signed since then.) Most are with large firms.

5 Theriot, 'US governmental and private industry cooperation', p. 752.

in the West and various agencies, foreign trade organizations, ministries, associations and enterprises in Eastern Europe. It is this micro-economic cooperation (as distinct from inter-governmental agreements) that is the subject of this paper. I shall deal mainly with the European CMEA countries, especially Hungary and the USSR, with only occasional reference to Yugo-slavia. I shall also confine myself to cooperation directly involving research, development and/or production within the borders of CMEA countries. The various joint East–West com-panies formed in the West to market CMEA products are a separate and older phenomenon, not closely related to tech-nology transfer, and will be ignored in what follows.[6]

Industrial cooperation in this sense is a newish activity. The ECE estimated that there were about 600 such agreements in force by mid-1972. Most had come into existence since 1965 and growth had been especially marked since about 1970. The ECE secretariat now keeps a register of agreements, based mainly on press reports. By August 1975, there were 376 agreements on this register, if those involving Yugoslavia are excluded. The secretariat put the total number in existence at that date, how-ever, in the region of 1000. Using a more restrictive definition, and on the basis of a survey of Western firms, McMillan has estimated that there were only about 425 agreements in force in early 1975. (As with the ECE figures, this excludes Yugoslavia and agreements of the Soviet State Committee type; it also excludes equity joint ventures in the West.)

Hungary and Poland were particularly active in promoting such projects in the early 1970s and appear to be still the front runners in 1977. Both the ECE register and the McMillan survey have shown that agreements are highly concentrated in the mechanical engineering, transport equipment and chemical industries. So far as the modes of cooperation are concerned, McMillan found, among the 198 non-equity, inter-firm agree-ments on which he obtained responses in his survey (excluding

6 They have recently been surveyed and described in a thorough manner in Carl H. McMillan, *Direct Soviet and East European Investment in the Industrialised Western Economies* (Ottawa: Carleton University Institute of Soviet and East European Studies, Working paper no. 7, 1977).

agreements with US partners), that technical assistance (know-how) was the commonest feature. It was present in 58.6 per cent of the agreements. Other features frequently found were the supplying of parts/components to the Eastern partner (54.0 per cent of agreements); the supply by the Eastern partner of parts/components to Western specifications for incorporation in the Western partner's product (49.0 per cent); training of Eastern personnel (47.5 per cent) and the provision of a licence (46.0 per cent). Co-production in the sense that both partners either produced the same end-product while exchanging components, or disposed of the same range of end-products through specialization and exchange within the product range was less common: it was reported in only 19.2 and 4.6 per cent of cases respectively.[7]

At present industrial cooperation agreements affect only a small portion of East–West trade – which is, in turn, only a very small portion (3.8 per cent in 1975) of OECD countries' total foreign trade turnover. There is only limited experience of how these agreements actually operate.

West German firms have probably entered into at least as many such agreements as those of any other Western country, yet the share of deliveries under cooperation agreements in 1972 was probably no more than 5–10 per cent of West Germany's trade turnover with CMEA countries, or around half a per cent

7   The 1972 figures are from ECE, 1973, The 1975 ECE data are from UN ECE, TRADE/R 320 (22 August 1975). Hereafter ECE, 1975. This is a secretariat note updating the statistical material of ECE, 1973. The data cited from the McMillan survey are from McMillan, 'Forms and dimensions', and relate to early 1975. On joint ventures, see section 4 below. The term 'East–West joint venture' should be reserved for enterprises in which both Eastern and Western partners have an equity stake. They have at the time of writing been established only in Hungary, Romania, Yugoslavia or outside the territory of CMEA countries. In 1976 Poland introduced legislation allowing joint ventures on Polish territory in some branches of the economy. (For details see *The Financial Times* (20 December 1976), p. 5.) Reports of joint ventures or of joint-venture legislation in other East European countries must be treated with care since there can be translation problems. For example, the Russian term *sovmestnyi proekt* is sometimes translated, even by Russians, as 'joint venture' when it is being used in the sense merely of 'cooperation agreement'.

of total West German foreign trade.[8] The ECE put cooperation-related trade, tentatively, at only some 4–5 per cent of total East–West trade in the mid-1970s. The share in Western machinery sales alone should be larger than this. A Soviet economist writing in 1976 put deliveries under industrial co-operation agreements at between 10 and 20 per cent of turn-over in machinery and equipment between CMEA and Western nations.[9]

East–West industrial cooperation, therefore, is small beer compared to the West–West industrial cooperation, joint ventures and direct investment that link a large part of industrial production in different Western countries. And it contains a strong element of West–East technology transfer and of Eastern sub-contracting for Western partners. By the same token, how-ever, it must be assumed that it could become much larger, and could also perhaps develop in the direction of more sophisticated roles for the Eastern partners.

3. Technology Transfer and Industrial Cooperation

It is not, I think, misleading to describe industrial cooperation with the West as an East European development strategy which attempts to emulate the technology-diffusing characteristics of Western multinational cooperations and joint ventures.

Whatever may be the full explanation of the rapid post-war growth of international business in the Western world, tech-nology seems to be a major part of it.[10] Eastern Europe mean-

8 P. Knirsch, 'Industrial cooperation between East and West: the FRG experience' in J. P. Hardt (ed.), *Tariff, Legal and Credit Constraints on East–West Commercial Relations* (Ottawa: Carleton University Institute of Soviet and East European Studies, 1975), p. 6.

9 The ECE estimate is from ECE, 1975, p. 7. The Soviet estimate is given by Margarita Maximova, 'Industrial cooperation between socialist and capitalist countries: forms, trends and problems' in Saunders (ed.), *East–West Cooperation*, pp. 15–28.

10 One argument usually put forward is that many post-World War Two technological developments have created lines of production for which the minimum threshold R and D costs are very high. This engenders economies of scale so large as to give advantages to firms operating on an international scale. Transport costs and

while has not allowed direct investment from the West for most of this period; has kept personal East–West contacts between scientists, technologists, managers or workers to a low level, and has remained a somewhat isolated trading bloc, recently conducting around 60 per cent of its members' total trade within the group. In addition, each member-state does rather less trade in total than Western countries of similar population size and development level have tended to do.[11]

Technology transfer from West to East has gone on, of course, but it has tended to rely rather heavily on what I have called 'non-negotiable' channels. These are mainly the traditional Soviet techniques of monitoring Western technical publications and small, once-off purchases of products which are then used as development prototypes; industrial espionage, too, may have made some contribution. These channels of technology transfer require a greater reliance on domestic adaptive R and D than does the outright commercial purchase of know-how and substantial quantities of hardware. For meeting a given investment and production programme, however, heavy reliance on non-negotiable technology transfer may not be the most efficient strategy.

> the footloose character of the key input of know-how favour the establishment of foreign subsidiaries or joint ventures rather than the concentration of production in one country. Hypotheses about the economic processes involved have been elaborated into the product-cycle theory. This sort of analysis may be a very incomplete explanation of the growth and branch distribution of multinational companies, but it does seem to be part of the story. It is also relevant to the growth of component, intra-industry and know-how trade. The role of licencing and know-how trade in promoting technical change in Western countries is documented in OECD, *Gaps in Technology* (Paris, 1970), where it is estimated (p. 185) that about three-fifths of 110 major industrial innovations after 1945 originated with US companies. J. H. Dunning, 'Technology, United States investment and European economic growth' in C. P. Kindleberger (ed.), *The International Corporation* (Cambridge, Mass.: MIT Press, 1970), pp. 141–79, provides evidence of the growth-inducing effects of US investment in Western Europe.
>
> 11 See S. Ausch, *Theory and Practice of CMEA Cooperation*, English edn (Budapest: Akademiai Kiado, 1972).

Evidence favouring other strategies has taken time to accumulate. Studies of science policy and the economic aspects of technology are no less recent in the East than in the West. The systemic weaknesses which seem to hamper innovation and diffusion in the Soviet Union, for example, may have existed for a long time, but few top-level policy-makers seem to have been aware of them, or much worried by them, before the early 1960s. The idea that machinery trade and direct personal contact are particularly effective forms of technology transfer is, as a widely held belief, fairly recent. It has naturally taken time for some of the most striking developments in the post-war capitalist world to suggest lessons for CMEA policy-makers: the growth of intra-industry trade in manufactures; the growth of international trade in components; the spread of multinational companies' operations; the rapid growth of trade in licences and know-how and Japan's success in benefitting from it.[12]

It also took time, of course, for Soviet policy-makers to appreciate that the 'catching-up and overtaking' of the West was not going as well as Khrushchev had foreseen in the Twenty-Year Programme of 1961. While Soviet per capita GNP still tends on the whole to grow somewhat faster than that of the USA, the East–West technology gap has remained a real one. A group of case studies of technology level in a number of Soviet industries does not show any clear overall reduction of the gap between the mid-1950s and the early 1970s.[13] One's general impression

12 I have tried to trace the development of Soviet leadership
    attitudes on these matters in 'The import of Western technology'
    in Archie Brown and Michael Kaser (eds.), *The Soviet Union Since
    the Fall of Khrushchev* (London: Macmillan, 1975), pp. 19–23.
13 R. Amann, J. M. Cooper and R. W. Davies (eds.), *The Technological
    Level of Soviet Industry* (New Haven: Yale University Press, 1977).
    In these studies the gaps were assessed primarily in terms of
    lead-times between first commercial production or use of a major
    new product or process in the USSR and in the West; diffusion
    was also reviewed. It is at first sight paradoxical that
    micro-economic comparisons suggest no overall reduction in
    technology gap while aggregate figures indicate a diminution of
    the gap in per capita GNP. (The latter appears to be true per
    head of labour force as well as per head of population.) The most
    likely explanation (if the micro-economic findings are correct and

is that there remains a technology gap between the West and the whole CMEA group, as the data in table 1 on East–West licence trade suggest. (For the sake of comparison we may note that Soviet sources put total world licence and know-how trade at about $2½ billion in 1970. Japan, which purchased far more foreign licences than the CMEA group between 1950 and 1969, was spending about six times as much on licences in the latter year as it was earning abroad.)[14]

An acceleration of negotiable technology transfer by means of machinery, licence and know-how imports from the West might therefore be expected to facilitate technical change in Eastern Europe and improve economic growth performance. Improved East–West political relations during the 1960s (despite Vietnam and Czechoslovakia) favoured such a strategy of import-led growth for the CMEA countries. Their limited hard-currency export earning capacity, however, has been a severe constraint on such a policy.

For this reason the direct contribution to Soviet growth, for example, of Western technology embodied in machinery has in fact increased only very slightly since the late 1950s. Even in 1975–6 not more than 6 per cent of total Soviet equipment investment was composed of imported Western machinery.[15]

> representative) seems to be that the branch composition of Soviet output has changed, relative to that of Western countries, in a manner favourable to the Soviet side of the aggregate comparison and/or that Soviet labour productivity has benefitted relatively more than Western from capital accumulation, as distinct from technical change. An alternative possibility would be that a given lead-time in innovation and diffusion (in years) has been associated, for the Western world generally, with a lead in factor productivity in each field that has tended to decline over time, i.e. that technical innovation generally is exhibiting diminishing returns. This is possible but one would require a great deal of evidence before accepting a hypothesis with such massive implications.

14 E. Ya. Volynets-Russet, *Planirovanie i raschet effektivnosti priobreteniya litsenzii* (Planning the acquisition of licences and measuring their effectiveness), (Moscow: Ekonomika, 1973), p. 48.

15 P. Hanson, 'The international transfer of technology from the West to the USSR' in US Congress Joint Economic Committee, *Soviet Economy*, pp. 796–7.

Comparable figures for the smaller East European countries are higher, of course, but it is almost certainly the case that all the CMEA countries make relatively less use than Western countries of imported machinery that is more advanced and productive than the nearest domestically produced equivalents.[16]

This might be of no consequence for technical change in Eastern Europe if the absorption of new foreign technology by non-negotiable channels and the domestic diffusion of imported new products and processes were highly effective. Are procedures for non-negotiable technology transfer and domestic diffusion so effective as to compensate for any possible disadvantage of the low level of imports from the West? It is possible that they are, but institutional and anecdotal evidence suggests otherwise, at least as far as domestic diffusion is concerned.[17] So does the evidence (for the USSR) of the technology-level studies mentioned above.

Industrial cooperation therefore has a number of attractions for East European governments. It promises to ease hard-

16 For example, US imports of machinery and transport equipment, excluding cars, in 1975 were equivalent to 10.2% of US equipment investment in that year. (Derived from *Survey of Current Business* (March 1977), pp. S-1 and 47.) The equivalent Soviet figure is about 15% for all machinery but most of the Soviet imports come from other CMEA countries. On the inefficiency and doubtful benefits of intra-CMEA machinery trade see Ausch, *Theory and Practice*.

17 Radio Liberty Research, 'The diffusion of imported technology in the USSR', RL 194/75 (1975). On the other hand it should be noted that an assessment of the net total impact (including *via* diffusion) on Soviet agricultural output of the technology embodied in mineral fertilizer plant imported from the West shows an extremely high rate of return: an addition to mid-1970s annual agricultural output of about $4 billion stemming from an import of plant and equipment, 1960–75, totalling about $2 billion (these figures are at early 1970s US prices and subject to a substantial margin of error). Of course, they may not be typical, and the Soviet successes in diffusing technology even in this case were limited. P. Hanson, 'The impact of Western technology: a case-study of the Soviet mineral fertiliser industry' in P. Marer and J. M. Montias (eds.), *CMEA Integration and East–West Trade* (forthcoming, Bloomington; University of Indiana, 1978).

currency problems by providing for repayment to the Western partner in goods. For this reason East European planners favour cooperation agreements that guarantee hard-currency export sales and usually veto schemes that do not. Insofar as the Eastern partner does export to the West under such an agreement, there is the further attraction that he may learn from the experience and enlarge his bridgehead on the Western market.

At the same time the Western partner to a cooperation agreement is expected to have a stronger incentive than an ordinary trade partner to update over a period of time the technology he has supplied, and to help generally in problem-solving for the Eastern partner. In particular, if the Western firm itself uses or re-sells under its own brand name the products it gets from Eastern Europe under licence, subcontracting, co-production or turnkey arrangements, it has a strong incentive to keep its partner's quality level up to the mark.

These benefits to the Eastern partner cannot, of course, be expected to be available *gratis*. Insofar as some of the burden of risk associated with an investment project to Eastern Europe is shifted to a Western partner, e.g. by his entering into a forward commitment to purchase output from the project at an agreed price or according to an agreed price formula, it should be expected that something will be charged (in the terms of the cooperation agreement) for this risk-bearing. The Eastern partner may be thought of, then, as paying for his risk-aversion as well as for Western management and/or marketing expertise. A corollary of this is that not all cooperation agreements should be seen as necessarily providing the Eastern partner with superior technology. He may sometimes have equally effective domestic technology available but enter into cooperation arrangements for reasons to do with export marketing.

One point needs to be added about the European interest in cooperation for the sake of technology transfer: it is not all strictly related to a West–East flow of know-how. The R and D networks in CMEA countries do after all generate their own applied research results. These may often include potentially worthwhile inventions. Indigenous inventions, however, seem frequently to get stuck at that stage in the product cycle. For the USSR, at least, in most areas of civilian technology, there seems to be a systemic weakness at the development and innovation stages.

There should therefore be scope for what might be termed a systemic division of labour in cooperation projects: the Western partner takes unutilized Eastern research results (possibly under licence), does the development, initial production and de-bugging and hands back an improved and commercially viable product or process which domestic efforts would either have been very slow to reach or would not have reached at all.

This line of argument is put forward (not quite so baldly as I have stated it here) by two Soviet authors in a recent article. They estimate that CMEA countries could earn $370 million from some 7300 licence sales relating to unutilized inventions.[18] As usual with Soviet writings, it is not clear how this figure was obtained; it is not even clear if it refers to a stock at some point of time or to an annual flow. As an annual flow it might just balance the early 1970s level of CMEA expenditures on licences from the West that is suggested by the authors' text (see table 1), and that might be the only reason the figure was chosen. The general line of argument, however, is plausible.[19]

The above considerations go a long way towards explaining East European governments' interest in industrial cooperation. How well it is working out in practice is a separate issue, to which the next section is devoted.

4. Cooperation Agreements in Practice

If our knowledge of the number and scope of East–West industrial cooperation agreements is limited, our knowledge of how they are working out in practice is derisory. There have, how-

---

18 Yu. Naido and S. Simanovskii, 'Uchastie stran SEVa v mirovoi torgovle litsenzii' (The participation of CMEA countries in world trade in licences), *Voprosy ekonomiki*, no. 3 (1975), p. 69.

19 There are also, of course, some straightforward cases of the transfer of technology from East to West at the level of fully developed and innovated products and processes. In the Soviet case these are mostly concentrated in the field of metallurgy, especially casting and welding, and there is also a quite widely licensed Soviet surgical process.

TABLE 1 The value of CMEA licence transactions with the developed West – some estimates ($ m)

Country or group of countries	Time period	Revenue from West	Payments to West	Sources and comments
Bulgaria	1966–70	NA	8.5	Yu. Naido and S. Simanovskii, 'Uchastie stran SEVa v mirovoi torgovle litsenzii', *Voprosy ekonomiki*, no. 3 (1975)
Czechoslovakia	1968–72	51	c. 200	G. A. Vlaskin and S. Simanovskii, 'Litsenzionnaya praktika v ChSSR', *Voprosy izobretatel'stva*, no. 2 (1975), pp. 57–61. Revenue figures given in source; payments 'recently' said to be 'about four times' the value of receipts
Hungary	1968–71	1.52	9.38	UN ECE, E/ECE/844, Addendum 1, p. 9
Poland	1970		'About 3 times receipts'	*Ibid.* p. 8
Total CMEA	1960–9		'11.2 times receipts'	J. Wilczynski, *Technology in Comecon* (London, 1974). p. 308, citing DDR source
Total CMEA	1970		'4.0 times receipts'	*Ibid.*
Total CMEA	?Early 1970s (approximate annual averages)	30	(360)	Naido and Simanovskii, 'Uchastie stran SEVa v mirovoi torgovle litsenzii', pp. 67–77. 'Current' (no date) annual revenue figure from p. 67, where it is stated to be about 1 per cent of total world licence trade excluding (p. 68) intra-CMEA trade. Total East–West licence trade put (p. 68) at about 10 per cent world total *including* the national value of intra-CMEA licence exchanges (period not specified), which is put at 24 per cent of world total including intra-CMEA. Hence (apparently) payments to West = about (10−74/100) times 74/100 times receipts, or about 12 times receipts
Total CMEA	mid-1970s		200–300	Moscow Narodny Bank, *Press Bulletin* (23 February 1977), pp. 10–11
USSR and Eastern Europe with UK only (incomplete)	1972	0.2	5.9	International Business Unit, Department of Management Studies, UMIST (private communication). Data are derived from a sample survey of UK firms. They cover 'technological and mineral royalties' *excluding* licence receipts on whole-plant deals which were not separately reported

ever, been several attempts at systematic questionnaire surveys of cooperation partners.[20]

The rest of this section deals mainly with the USSR and Hungary and concludes with some brief remarks about joint ventures. Hungary and the Soviet Union are the two CMEA countries on which most information is available. Fortunately they also represent in some respects the opposite poles of CMEA experience with industrial cooperation.

The Hungarians have the most decentralized economic system in the CMEA; are probably the most active in East–West industrial cooperation; allow joint ventures, and seem to have gone as far as anyone in establishing co-production arrangements in manufacturing.[21] Soviet cooperation agreements are of two main kinds: the rather marginal scientific and technological cooperation agreements referred to above and large turnkey projects, often in extractive industries. In early 1977, according to a Soviet deputy minister of foreign trade, there were about sixty agreements of the latter kind in force.[22]

A. *The USSR*

Current Soviet public statements nearly all display a very favourable attitude towards industrial cooperation with the West. The Soviet approach to industrial cooperation is nonetheless quite different from that of Eastern European countries. All the systematic quantitative studies of the subject (the ECE register, the McMillan survey, an unpublished study of US involvement in East–West industrial cooperation by Paul Marer) show the Soviet projects to be distinguished by their large average size, their concentration in natural-resource projects and in the chemical industry, and their relatively high concentration on

20 See Knirsch, 'Industrial cooperation'. The most comprehensive and thorough report of such a survey that is known to me is given by McMillan, 'Forms and dimensions'.

21 ECE, 1975, tables 2 and 3. McMillan, 'Forms and dimensions', appendix table v, shows a higher percentage of co-production arrangements among Czechoslovakia's than among Hungary's agreements, but the Czechoslovak percentages relate to a much smaller total number of agreements: sixteen as against seventy-four.

22 V. Klochek in *Foreign Trade*, no. 5 (1977), p. 7.

turnkey projects (including licence and know-how purchases) with product payback. There is relatively little Soviet involvement in either the sophisticated forms of cooperation represented by co-production arrangements or, on the other hand, the relatively humble sub-contracting or contract production kind of activity that is a feature of a good deal of East European industrial cooperation deals. The likely explanation of these Soviet–East European differences will be fairly obvious: the greater Soviet political and cultural isolation from the West, the size of the Soviet economy, the strong Soviet natural-resource endowment and the related lack of pressure in the Soviet case to improve the hard-currency trade balance by sub-contracting, marketing and other links with Western firms relating to manufactures.

The beginnings of Soviet involvement in turnkey projects in the post-World War Two period lie in Khrushchev's chemicalization drive, which began in 1958. The first very large deal, however, was a post-Khrushchev development: the \$550 million Fiat motor industry project at Tol'yatti (1966–70). This was not a cooperation deal in the currently accepted sense, since it was once-for-all and did not entail substantial buyback arrangements. However, it involved a long period of close cooperation between Fiat and the Soviet authorities, from initial exploratory negotiations in the early 1960s to full-capacity operation in 1974. Some 2500 Western personnel went to Tol'yatti, and about the same number of Russians went to Italy for training.[23]

The relatively successful experience of the Fiat deal, with its extensive personal contacts between Soviet citizens and Westerners, seems to have opened the way to a large number of projects which involved Western partners in a variety of roles: as general contractors, as contractors for part of the project, as design engineers, equipment suppliers or advisers in the procurement of hardware. Major deals which involve repayment wholly or partially in products from the project (product payback or buyback) are listed in table 2. It should be noted that reported values of such deals are not always reliable, and in any

23 Imogene U. Edwards, 'Automotive trends in the USSR' in US Congress Joint Economic Committee, *Soviet Economy in a New Perspective* (US Government Printing Office, 1973), p. 296.

TABLE 2   USSR: major buyback–turnkey projects signed by early 1976

Western partner-country	Project	Value of deal ($m)	Form of product payment
France	Gas-field equipment	250	Natural gas
Austria	Large-diameter pipe	400	Natural gas
Italy	Large-diameter pipe	190	Natural gas
West Germany	Large-diameter pipe	1500	Natural gas
France/Austria/ West Germany	Large-diameter pipe and equipment	900	Natural gas
Japan	Forestry and forest products	708	Timber, wood chips, pulp
France	Pulp and paper complex	60	Pulp
West Germany	Polyethylene plants	100	Polyethylene
Italy	Chemical plants	600	Ammonia
UK/US	Polyethylene plant	50	Polyethylene
France	Ammonia plants and pipeline	420	Ammonia
Italy	Chemical plants	670	Chemical products
US	Ammonia plants, and pipeline and fertiliser storage and handling	400	Ammonia
Italy	Polypropylene and detergent plants	100+	Chemical intermediates, surface-active detergents
West Germany	Ethylene, oxide/glycol plant	80	Related products
Japan	Oil exploration	150	Oil and gas
Japan	Coal development equipment	450	Coal
West Germany	Steel complex	1200	Pellets, steel products
France	Aluminium complex	1000	Aluminium

Source: Adapted from Maureen R. Smith, 'Industrial cooperation agreements: Soviet experience and practice' in US Congress Joint Economic Committee, *Soviet Economy in a New Perspective*, pp. 767–86.

case are normally different from either (*a*) the total investment cost of the project or (*b*) the total value of agreed product-payback flows.

In the size of product flows planned, these agreements appear to dwarf both other forms of industrial cooperation in which the USSR has so far engaged, and also the industrial cooperation agreements of all kinds entered into by the smaller East European countries. It is all the more important to see them in perspective. It is useful, for example, to consider projects that have *not* been agreed upon.

Several large Soviet cooperation projects have been discussed with Western firms and subsequently shelved, at least for the time being. These include schemes for Japanese participation in pulp production, in the development of the Udokan copper deposits and in Tyumen oil; they also include the much publicized oil and natural gas projects involving US firms.

Any area of business negotiations is bound to include proposals that come to nothing. The reasons for failure in the above cases, however, shed some light on the peculiarities and prospects of industrial cooperation with the USSR. We cannot at present establish the importance of particular obstacles in these negotiations but we can at any rate list (in no special order) the different sorts of difficulty that have arisen.

(i) Military considerations have sometimes hampered or completely stopped negotiations (though the excuse of government pressure may sometimes be a useful pretext for a Western firm to back out without loss of goodwill from a deal which it has decided against on commercial grounds): for example, US government reluctance to licence Ford or Mack Truck (under the strategic embargo) to act as general contractors for the Kama River lorry complex; the Chinese government's representations to Japan about the military implications of an oil pipeline serving the Soviet Far East.[24]

(ii) Broader foreign-policy considerations have also intervened as in the US Congress veto on Eximbank credit to the USSR; this source of credit was probably a pre-requisite for the major US–Soviet natural gas deals.

(iii) A sufficient explanation of the breakdown may in at least some cases be a simple failure to agree on the terms of the deal. (*a*) In the big natural-resource projects there has been plenty of scope for disagreements on costing and on likely

24   It does not appear that any Soviet–Western negotiations over a cooperation project have yet been brought to a halt because of Western government limitation on the extent of dependence on the USSR as a source of supply of a fuel or raw material. This could, however, happen if East–West trade expands substantially. For information on the negotiation of cooperation projects involving Japan I am indebted to Dr K. C. Davis, who has recently completed a PhD thesis on Soviet–Japanese commercial relations at the University of Birmingham.

future product prices. Expectations about the future distribution of costs and benefits between the participants have
therefore been hard to reconcile during negotiations. The
sheer scale of many of the Soviet projects must often create
uncertainties about the outcome which are unacceptable to
the Western potential partner except on terms that the
Soviet negotiators cannot accept. (*b*) One characteristic difficulty about product payback deals for turnkey or similar
projects is one that is inherent in the nature of barter
transactions generally: the Western plant contractor has to
want (or be able to dispose of at a cost he can build into his
price) the product in question. Where there is already expected to be excess capacity in the West for the product over
the period in question there are severe limits to what can
be arranged. This problem is exacerbated by the fact that
the product is usually one supplied by the customers of the
Western plant contractor or machinery supplier; considerations of goodwill in his Western markets therefore make
the Western partner especially reluctant to take responsibility for additions to total Western supply.

When negotiations have been successful, however, the question
is whether subsequent implementation of the contract has been
successful too.

This is a point on which quantitative evidence is lacking and
on which Western businessmen are coy. Experience in Eastern
Europe, especially in Hungary and Poland, is rather better
documented. The best test I can propose – and even this is far
from conclusive – is a strictly behavioural one: do both participants in a cooperation deal go on to conclude further East–West
cooperation deals, either with one another or with other partners? If they do, there must be at least a presumption that they
thought the original deal worthwhile. It was presumably either
profitable by itself or at any rate formed part of an overall
strategy of East–West business arrangements that promised to
be profitable.[25]

25 Of course, both parties to an agreement may be quite satisfied
    with it without subsequently having the occasion to embark on
    another, similar agreement. Conversely, cooperation partners
    entering into second or third cooperation agreements may, like

I have seen no systematic information about the number of Western firms that have concluded successive cooperation agreements with Soviet agencies. There are several well-known examples, though, of firms which have come back for more. Constructors John Brown, in the Polyspinners Consortium with ICI, put up a 50 000-ton-per-annum polyester fibre plant at Mogilev in the late 1960s, supplying machinery, know-how and technical assistance valued at $40 million. They have more recently contracted to design and help build another major chemical plant, with repayment partly in high-density polyethylene from the plant. They have also undertaken to extend capacity at Mogilev. ICI entered in 1977 into another joint arrangement, this time with Davy Powergas (mentioned above) in which they will accept deliveries from the methanol plants to be put up in the USSR by Davy. A whole series of large ammonia plant deals have been entered into in the 1970s by Toyo Engineering of Japan, apparently with some element of product payback to other Japanese companies. Renault have provided designs, know-how and hardware successively for the Moskvich plant at Izhevsk and for the Kama River lorry complex.

It is true, on the other hand, that Fiat declined to act as general contractor for the Kama River project. It is also alleged that one reason why other Western firms turned the offer down was that they were deterred by Fiat's experience at Tol'yatti. The different scope of the later project, however, and its even vaster scale, not to mention US government intervention, may be quite enough to account for the lack of volunteers. It is worth noting that the Russians, at least, wanted to appoint a Western firm as general contractor again.

It appears, in short, that examples can be found of both apparently happy and of apparently unhappy experience of cooperation deals in the USSR on the part of Western firms.

What problems have Western participants in Soviet projects encountered? Again we have only scattered, anecdotal information. The difficulties usually reported are uniform and predictable, however, and one is tempted to regard them as

> people marrying for the second time, only be demonstrating the triumph of hope over experience.

representative. Supplies of materials and equipment for the Soviet share in construction work tend to be poorly coordinated. Soviet targets are often far too ambitious. Soviet construction bonuses can have perverse results. There is often a shortage of important skills in the Soviet labour force available to operate the new capacity created. (This is often a regional problem. It may be resolved – as it apparently has been at least in part at KamAZ – by proper coordination of housing and infrastructure investment so that the new location attracts the skilled labour required.) Soviet middle management seems always to be reported as weak; Soviet senior managers (enterprise directors; senior ministry officials) usually impress their Western partners, but too many decisions are pushed up to them, causing delays.[26] All these problems would be predicted from the nature of the Soviet planning and management system.

Possibly for reasons such as these, there have been some notable delays in some cooperation projects in the USSR. Tol'yatti was at least two years late reaching full capacity operation. Production facilities were not built quickly enough to make use within the specified time limits of an imported licence to manufacture disc brakes.[27] Of the sixteen float-glass licence sales made by Pilkington's up to May 1970, the one sold to the Russians (in 1967) took the longest to be exploited. The shortest time taken between licence purchase and start of production was fifteen months by a Japanese firm. The average was twenty-seven months. The Russians took forty-one months, one month longer than Vidrio Plano de Mexico.[28] On the other hand some projects

26 These remarks are based on interviews with British and American executives with experience of turnkey projects in the USSR.
27 *Pravda* (12 March 1974), p. 1.
28 Derived from G. F. Ray, 'Float glass' in L. Nabseth and G. F. Ray (eds.), *The Diffusion of New Industrial Processes* (London: Cambridge University Press, 1974), table, p. 265. The only other CMEA country included in the table is Czechoslovakia. The Czechs have a traditionally strong glass industry but they also took an above-average time (thirty-four months) to exploit the Pilkington licence. By 1975 Pilkington were complaining to the Department of Trade about dumping of horticultural glass by East European exporters. Whether this was in any way a boomerang effect of their earlier licence sales, I do not know.

have been completed in good time – for instance, the Mogilev polyester fibre plant referred to above.

Whatever the problems of implementation may be, they do not seem so far to have blunted Soviet enthusiasm for industrial cooperation. In a Western press interview in 1973 the deputy chairman of the State Committee for Science and Technology said that a foreign firm which built a plant in the USSR could have 'say, thirty or forty per cent of its production' on a long-term basis.[29]

This reference to 30 or 40 per cent may represent typical Soviet experience but there is no obvious reason why the figure should be set at any particular maximum level for all projects. In principle, Soviet planners will seek a cooperation deal in preference to a domestic project where, for a given total domestically available supply over the period of payback to the foreign partner, cooperation lowers costs at least enough to repay the foreign contribution (with interest). In making such calculations, Soviet planners are expected to convert the resultant foreign currency into domestic rubles at a rate determined by the 'coefficient of effectiveness' of trade with the country or group of countries in question: this is, essentially, the estimated domestic ruble cost of earning a unit of the foreign currency.[30] It is doubtful if these 'criteria' are often useful in practice, since the outcome of the 'effectiveness' formulae will no doubt be heavily dependent on the choice of forward estimates that are subject to very large margins of error. But there is every reason to believe that Soviet planners see the general principle of cooperation deals as a highly attractive one.

This perception appears to have led to continuing modifications of Soviet organizational structures and policies to allow

29 Cited by James Ramsey, 'In East–West trade "Cooperation" is in', *Fortune* (November 1973), p. 180.
30 This is the gist of four pages of algebra in V. Savin, 'The effectiveness of cooperation on a compensatory basis', *Foreign Trade*, no. 5 (1977), pp. 24–9. His formulae are a variant of the usual sort of Soviet 'foreign-trade effectiveness' criterion. They appear to make no allowance, in comparing 'domestic' and 'cooperation' variants of a project, for differences between the two in the time-distribution of output and costs, though there is the usual condition of a minimum 15% rate of return.

more flexibility in cooperation deals. Soviet openness to Western participation in management of Soviet facilities, and Soviet readiness to engage in contract manufacturing arrangements, remain much less than in the case of Hungary, Poland or Romania, but there is evidence of change in the direction of such involvement. A spark-plug factory deal under negotiation with the Bendix Corporation in early 1977 would apparently allow Bendix control over quality and allocation of output for exports under the Bendix name.[31]

B. *Hungary*

Hungarian experience with industrial cooperation is very different from that of the Soviet Union. The Hungarians have substantially more cooperation agreements (if Soviet scientific and technological cooperation agreements are excluded); they are typically much smaller than the Soviet agreements; more often classified as co-production or licence deals rather than turnkey projects, and more heavily concentrated in mechanical engineering and clothing and textiles. Those, at least, are the characteristics displayed by the 1975 ECE data.

The McMillan sample of seventy-four Hungarian cooperation agreements (excluding equity joint ventures and all cooperation agreements with US firms) appears to be consistent with this ECE picture, and in addition indicates some other features of the Hungarian agreements: a larger proportion of the agreements (twenty-eight out of seventy-four) were consumer-oriented than was the case with any other CMEA country; the elements of co-production and of contract production were especially prominent; there were more agreements (in the McMillan sample) in electrical engineering and electronics than for any other country; and Hungarian agreements were mostly relatively small, and had a correspondingly greater involvement of Western partner-firms that were not classified as multinationals.[32]

---

31 *Business Week* (31 January 1977), as cited in Moscow Narodny Bank, *Press Bulletin* (26 January 1977), p. 8.

32 McMillan, 'Forms and dimensions'. In the McMillan sample the share of multinationals in all interfirm non-equity cooperation agreements in the CMEA was 46.5 (by number of agreements).

Another feature of Hungarian cooperation is the relatively prominent role of direct cooperation with Hungarian producing enterprises without the mediation of foreign trade organizations or with only limited participation by them. This reflects the special features of the Hungarian economic system. The Hungarian New Economic Mechanism (NEM), introduced in 1968, transferred production and other current decision-making powers to the enterprise management level and gave a number of enterprises the right to participate directly in foreign trade. The intention was to establish a competitive market-socialist economy substantially more open to foreign trade than before. A complex system of exchange controls, import licensing, foreign exchange 'multipliers' (resembling multiple exchange rates) and tariffs was to replace direct administrative control of imports./

In practice the NEM has not evolved as intended. Many large, multi-plant enterprises have acquired monopoly power in a small domestic economy. The tariff structure influences import decisions but import prices (plus tariff) are insulated from domestic prices by subsidies as well as the foreign exchange multipliers. Competiton from abroad therefore does not make up for the lack of domestic competition.[33] Price control is quite extensive and so is centralized investment decision-making.

The Hungarian government has encouraged industrial cooperation with the West by offering tariff concessions on imports under cooperation agreements and preferential investment credits to Hungarian partners whose cooperation schemes will raise net exports. Equity joint ventures in Hungary have been possible since 1970, and two were in existence in 1975. Cooperation agreements have proliferated but there has been some dissatisfaction with the results. Two recent papers describe and

The corresponding share for Hungary at 39% was the lowest for the group. The share for the USSR in the sample was not a great deal higher (45.5%) but McMillan estimates (p. 42) that out of thirty-six such agreements known to him for the USSR, at least twenty were with multinationals.

33 At the same time, the government has not been able to insulate the domestic economy from Western inflation, which has to some extent been imported.

analyse the main issues and a number of case studies have been reported.[34]

Radice points out that both the allocation of investment funds and the approval of cooperation proposals are still in fact highly centralized, so that on the Hungarian side market forces play only a very constrained role in the establishment of cooperation arrangements. Many large Hungarian enterprises prefer to deal only with the CMEA market. This, Radice suggests, is partly because CMEA (especially Soviet) orders are more often large and long-term, guaranteeing long production runs and corresponding cost reductions; they may also in many cases be less demanding in quality and technology-level requirements.

Hewett agrees with Radice that the competitive pressure on Hungarian enterprises to obtain substantial inflows of new technology *via* cooperation is not very strong. 'Hungarian enterprises are not really interested', he observes 'in being "transformed". Their market situations are far too comfortable for that.'

Both authors go on to suggest that many Hungarian cooperation agreements involve small or medium-sized Hungarian firms and are frequently only 'normal' trade disguised in order to get preferential tariff and investment credit treatment. Many are subcontracting arrangements in which the Hungarian partner specializes in the less research-intensive, skill-intensive

34 E. A. Hewett, 'The economics of East European technology imports from the West', *American Economic Review*, vol. 65, no. 2 (May 1975), pp. 377–82. H. Radice, 'East–West industrial cooperation and transition to socialism', paper prepared for a conference on New Approaches to Trade, Institute of Development Studies, Brighton (1975). A number of general points which are undoubtedly relevant to Hungary also emerge from the case studies of Polish and Romanian cooperation projects in Eric W. Hayden, *Technology Transfer to East Europe: US Corporate Experience* (New York: Praeger, 1976). An interesting account of three agreements is given from a Hungarian point of view by Béla Bojkó, 'Results and problems of cooperation with Western firms in Hungarian light industry' in Saunders (ed.), *East–West Cooperation*, pp. 152–66. Bojkó also states that in late 1975 there was a total of over 400 cooperation agreements involving Hungarian and Western partners.

and/or capital-intensive parts of the production process. Hewett argues, further, that the Western partner usually does the R and D and marketing; such agreements therefore tend to reinforce the monopolistic domestic market situation which keeps the Hungarian enterprise focussed on current production and therefore ill-equipped to innovate and to market its products in the West.

Hewett concludes that industrial cooperation will probably not prove to be an effective means of technology transfer from the West into Hungary. Radice makes no predictions but he does not consider technology transfer under cooperation agreements so far to have been very striking.

The two papers I have quoted are by Western economists. They are based, however, on Hungarian published sources and on interviews in Hungary, and they express a scepticism shared by several Hungarian specialists. Other Hungarian officials and economists stress, however, that disappointment with the technological impact of cooperation agreements is a natural consequence of exaggerated initial expectations; it should not obscure the fact that many of the agreements do contribute to Hungarian technical change.[35]

One example is an agreement between Findus and a Hungarian state farm. Apart from earning hard currency, this is said to have introduced quick-freezing and packaging technology of substantial value to Hungarian agriculture and food-processing. Critics would presumably point out that the research and development input has come entirely from the Western partner and the latter is also responsible for marketing. Nonetheless there will have been some real gain, one must assume, in the ratio of output to inputs.

Similarly with the complex Anker Werke co-production agreement for cash registers, involving West Germany, Austria, Czechoslovakia and Hungary: the fact that Anker Werke retain all marketing rights outside Hungary and Czechoslovakia, and locate the more advanced manufacturing processes (the electronic components) in the West must presumably be set against

35 These remarks stem from my own conversations with Hungarian economists and officials, as well as from the paper by Bojkó.

some hard-currency and productivity gains for the Hungarian partner, IGV.[36]

The scope that may exist for productivity gains is indicated by one of Bojko's case studies, involving a Hungarian textile enterprise. The Hungarian enterprise and its Western partner are described as closely similar in total output, product-mix and degree of vertical integration; the Western firm, however, is said to have a productivity level (presumably labour productivity, though whether per man-hour, week or year is unclear) 2.4 times the Hungarian partner's level. The cooperation agreement began in 1974 and entails the transfer of production and management know-how for all stages of production. The Western partner takes an agreed proportion of the improved output and sells it under its own brand name, and also has various market-sharing arrangements with the Hungarian enterprise. Apparently this agreement contributed substantially to an increase in sales on Western markets in the first full year of its operation, but the point to be noted is the very large potential gain in productivity; even if the gap between the two partners' labour productivity levels were only halved, the gain for the Hungarian enterprise would be very substantial.

The question for Hungarian policy-makers is not whether industrial cooperation can totally transform the economy but whether it can, on balance, do some good without precluding alternative policies that might be more effective. The Hungarian authorities continue, at all events, to encourage industrial cooperation. In May 1977 they went so far as to revise the joint-venture legislation to make it more attractive to Western firms (see below). Nor does interest on the Western side seem to have slackened. As in the case of the USSR one can point to Western firms which have entered into more than one cooperation agreement with a Hungarian partner: Siemens of West Germany, according to Radice, has signed at least fifteen.

C. *Joint Ventures*

Hungary and Romania have both passed legislation (in 1972 and 1971 respectively) allowing joint ventures on their territory. So,

36 Ramsey, 'In East–West trade "cooperation" is in'.

more recently, has Poland (see above). As in Yugoslavia, the maximum foreign equity participation is 49 per cent, though certain exceptions to this limit may in future be allowed in Hungary.[37]

In Hungary joint-venture companies could not until 1977 engage directly in the production of goods, but had to sign production contracts with domestic enterprises. The foreign partner could have a say in production management by means of this contract. New legislation passed in May 1977 is reported to allow the formation of joint ventures directly engaged in production in Hungary. It also seems to be intended to increase the attraction of joint ventures to Western firms by (a) replacing a progressive (two-tier) profits tax of 40 and 60 per cent with a flat-rate tax of 40 per cent and (b) envisaging the possibility of majority Western equity in joint ventures in the financial and services sectors. Until 1977, at least, the Hungarian policy has been to treat joint ventures as a long stop arrangement: to be resorted to only when other forms of cooperation cannot be negotiated which will yield the results wanted on the Hungarian side. Few have in fact been set up, but two that appear to be well-established involve Siemens (West Germany) in electrical machinery and electronics and Volvo (Sweden) in the motor industry.

Romania has been more active in encouraging joint ventures. By the spring of 1975, however, only five had been established. These five were in the fields of computer peripheral equipment, marine engine gears, acrylic fibres, electronic medical apparatus

37 Details of Hungarian, Romanian and Yugoslav joint-venture legislation and experience are given in a number of sources, including C. H. McMillan and D. P. St Charles, *Joint Ventures in Eastern Europe: A Three-Country Comparison* (Montreal: Canadian Economic Policy Committee, 1974) and I. Spigler, *Direct Western Investment in Eastern Europe*, Papers in East European Economics, no. 48 (Oxford: St Antony's College, 1975). The original Hungarian legislation was passed in 1970 but became operative only with a Ministry of Finance decree of 1972. The new (1977) Hungarian legislation on joint ventures is reported in Moscow Narodny Bank, *Press Bulletin* (1 June 1977), p. 9. An informative account of the Control Data corporation's joint-venture experience in Romania in 1973–5 is contained in Hayden, *Technology Transfer to East Europe*, pp. 82–90.

and the manufacture of yeast and protein-based foodstuffs. More recently several more have been set up, including joint ventures in the fields of medical instruments manufacture, the motor industry (with Citroen) and gear-making (with a subsidiary of the West German GHH group).[38]

The foreign partner in a Romanian joint venture can ensure that major decisions require a majority vote of more than 51 per cent. In other words, he can exercise a veto on key decisions despite his minority shareholding. On the other hand he can repatriate his share of profits (after tax) on foreign operations only; he cannot sell his share in the venture without Romanian agreement (though in the gear-making joint venture, at least, arrangements to withdraw the initial investment are said to have been allowed for in special legislation); the joint venture's production plan (annual and five-yearly) must be approved by the Romanian authorities.

The joint venture has the advantage, for each partner, that the other partner has committed resources to a long-term relationship. Yet it appears to be chiefly a device for attracting the Western partner into a cooperation arrangement he might not otherwise enter. Much of the Western equity contribution seems typically to be in the form of the capitalized value of know-how, i.e. the real cost and risk to the Western partner is often small. A Western firm may prefer a joint venture because it provides more control over the Eastern partner's use of the transferred technology than does, for example, a licensing agreement.

On present evidence, however, it is hard to detect a clear cut general advantage of joint-venture arrangements over other forms of cooperation, for either partner. Many major aspects of a joint venture are specially negotiated in each separate case, and the outcome can be hard to distinguish from, say, a non-equity co-production arrangement in which the Western partner had a say in quality control and also as a management consultant. Thus the Romanian computer peripherals joint venture, Romcontrol Data, entailed an initial $1.8 million Control Data investment in Romania to be recouped over five years by deliveries to the US partner of Romanian-made peripherals

38 For details see Moscow Narodny Bank, *Press Bulletin* (3 November 1976), p. 15; (19 January 1977), p. 12; (23 March 1977), p. 8.

at below the normal US price. One attraction to the US firm was the use of relatively cheap Romanian labour for labour-intensive assembly processes; this is reflected in the terms of the venture, but these terms were reached only after negotiation down from an original Romanian request for an 800 per cent 'social cost' mark-up on wages. Another attraction to the Control Data Corporation was – as in many non-equity cooperation deals – the hope of a spin-off, *via* goodwill, in sales in 'normal' trade outside the joint venture: in this case, for computer main frames.[39]

Thus, while experience in individual joint ventures may be regarded as satisfactory for both parties, it looks as though the joint venture as such is so far only a variant of very modest significance within East–West industrial cooperation.

Conclusions

I have argued that East–West industrial cooperation is, from the East European point of view, desired chiefly as a vehicle for technology transfer. It is only part – and, at present, a small part – of a growth in East–West commerce in which technology is a dominant Eastern concern. In some respects it is a substitute for direct Western investment in Eastern Europe. The East European policy-makers would like the technological benefits of direct investment without what they would regard as its political costs.

The Japanese government also pursued a policy of planned and active technological borrowing with very little foreign direct investment between 1950 and 1967. Only from 1967 and only in a limited number of industries was it possible for a foreign firm to acquire or establish a wholly owned subsidiary in Japan. By that time Japanese firms had spent almost $1.5 billion on licence purchases abroad and had probably done more to absorb technology of licensing than the CMEA group has yet done.[40]

Can East–West industrial cooperation, together with licensing

39 This paragraph is based on Hayden, *Technology Transfer to East Europe*.
40 See M. Y. Yoshino, 'Japan as host to the international corporation', in Kindleberger (ed.), *The International Corporation*, pp. 345–70.

and machinery imports, promote East European industrial modernization and export competitiveness *à la Japonaise?* Well, economic miracles do happen, according to the newspapers. Can we envisage a Japanese economic miracle in Eastern Europe?

If the relatively poor technological performance of the CMEA economies so far could be explained largely by their relative isolation from economies with higher levels of technology, cooperation and other commercial links with the West could transform the situation. If, on the other hand, the administrative economic systems of CMEA countries are in themselves a fundamental impediment to technological dynamism, cooperation, licensing and machinery imports will not greatly reduce the East–West technology gap, except insofar as they contribute to the fundamental modification of the domestic economic system.

If the administrative economic system really is poorly adapted to rapid technological innovation and diffusion in an industrialized country, and if it is not fundamentally modified, the likelihood is that East European governments will eventually be disappointed by the results of industrial cooperation and of closer East–West commercial links generally. This is perhaps most likely in the Soviet case, where the size of the economy relative to its foreign trade flows is so large that internal diffusion must as a matter of arithmetic be the major channel of technical change in an aggregate sense.

In a small economy such as Hungary the direct effect of technology transfer from abroad can be much greater relative to the indirect effect. Hungary, moreover, has a significantly less 'administrative' economic system.

The evidence so far available suggests that in the CMEA countries generally cooperation arrangements can produce substantial economic improvements within the framework of existing organization, but that there are limitations to this process which make a Japanese-style transformation of the CMEA countries into technologically dynamic competitors appear a remote prospect.

This is the picture that emerges from our review of Soviet and Hungarian experience in the previous section. It is reinforced by evidence for other CMEA countries, notably in Hayden's eight case studies for Poland and Romania. On the one hand there are inducements for Western firms to transfer technology under cooperation agreements: in particular, the prospect of a relatively cheap manufacturing source for exports to other countries; the prospect of additional revenue from proven technology whose development is a sunk cost; the prospect of product (e.g. component) sales associated with the early stages of an East European project, before the East European partner is able to manufacture all the components; the prospects of product sales unrelated to the cooperation project as a spin-off (goodwill) effect. Hayden's case studies show the US partners exercising considerable care in transferring know-how and proprietary technology in such a way as not to set up a competitor, but they also show substantial and useful transfers occurring, often of the latest proven technology; the Western partner protects himself either by market restrictions or by the lead time in his own development of technology as yet unproven.

At the same time, the usual experience of Western partners seems to be that East European weaknesses in production techniques and quality control are considerable and not easily rectified. One major reason for this seems to be the low morale, skill and initiative, and the general apathy of East European labour: this was reported to Hayden by executives of all five of the US companies who were carrying out their technology transfers at the time he interviewed them.[41] It seems to be a commonplace of Western experience of East–West industrial cooperation, together with the perceived weakness of East European middle (though not senior) management.

These are predictable consequences of an economic system in which initiative is highly concentrated at 'the top' and virtually precluded lower down, and in which the incentive effects of payment by results are often negated by shortages. This systemic weakness seems to be reflected in a finding of a recent survey of US businessmen engaged in trade with the USSR: the greater their experience of the Soviet market, the more willing they were to consider selling advanced technology to the USSR

41 Hayden, *Technology Transfer to East Europe*, p. 108.

and the less anxious they were about thereby creating a dangerous competitor.[42]

On the other hand, it would be wrong to conclude from this that the mutual benefits of East–West industrial cooperation will in the long run be shown to be illusory. The evidence is that they can be significant; at all events, such cooperation is likely to increase.

42 R. W. Clawson and W. F. Kolarik, 'Surveying US businessmen engaged in Soviet–American Trade', *ACES Bulletin*, vol. 18, no. 2 (summer 1976), pp. 71–83, especially p. 77.

6

Western Investment in Eastern Europe

RICHARD PORTES

It is not yet too late for Western countries to develop jointly sensible policies towards investment in Eastern Europe. There are already signs that the initial wave of enthusiasm has moderated, and I am certainly not the only skeptic among those who have studied the problem. But individual Western governments continue to extend their commitments, and although few of the proposals for immense investments in raw material extraction have proceeded beyond the initial visions of economic journalists, the hard-currency indebtedness of East European countries continues to rise very rapidly indeed.[1] It may therefore be useful to put forward a case for much more caution, coordination and control by Western governments and their international organizations in their economic relations with CMEA countries, with particular attention to investment.

We have come a long way from 'Western economic warfare'[2] and the restrictions of COCOM, doubtless excessive even at the height of the Cold War. Now Western governments and banks compete in offering favourable credit terms to East European borrowers, the banks hasten to organize consortia to float Eurodollar loans for these countries, and the multinationals occupy hundreds of new hotel rooms (many built with Western participation) in East European capitals, aggressively seeking business. Given our earlier abstinence, détente did open up real unexploited economic opportunities, but these at first appeared

1 For a detailed study of Eastern Europe's hard-currency debt and its policy implications, see R. Portes, 'East Europe's debt to the West', *Foreign Affairs*, vol. 55, no. 4 (July 1977), pp. 751–82.
2 G. Adler-Karlsson, *Western Economic Warfare 1947–1967* (Stockholm: Almqvist and Wiksell, 1968).

so rich as to prompt indulgence. The prime virtue of the competitive system is its quick and massive response to any rents created by changes in market conditions. In this instance, it worked perhaps too well.[3]

In reaction, the bandwagon has slowed down, even before the current difficulties in US–USSR relations, and despite the contrary efforts of some governments. It would therefore seem an appropriate time to reconcile the interests of drivers and passengers by putting it on a steady and controlled course. Central planning also has considerable virtues, not least of which is the coordination of foreign trade in the light of national economic and political objectives. The advantages of the 'foreign trade monopoly' in dealing with decentralized systems are most important for capital flows, which have such wide-ranging ramifications. There is no reason why Western countries should not exercise some similar powers, judiciously and in concert. I will suggest below specific reasons why they should do so, and indeed why this might in the long run promote more harmonious and mutually beneficial East–West economic and political relations.

First, some definitions. 'Western countries' will be the advanced industrialized non-communist nations, roughly coincidental with the OECD. 'Eastern Europe' will be the CMEA (Comecon) with some reference also to Yugoslavia, and of course a special role for the USSR. 'Investment' is acquiring title to an asset expected to yield some future return. I shall not be concerned with the multitude of licensing and minor industrial cooperation agreements, which can be of some use and little harm, and which are anyway often merely a gloss on straight trade transactions.[4] Some care is needed here, because of the widespread tendency to see all East–West industrial cooperation

3   For example, a comprehensive survey made at the height of American enthusiasm for investment in Eastern Europe set out a remarkably wide range of initiatives (many of which did not subsequently bear fruit): see J. Hardt, *et al.*, *Western Investment in Communist Economies*, prepared for Committee on Foreign Relations, US Senate, 93rd Congress, Second Session (Washington, DC: USGPO, 1974).

4   See above, chapter 5.

as a form of investment. I shall similarly disregard normal short-term commercial credits.

Investment may be undertaken by various types of transactors and may take a wide variety of forms. I shall consider the activities of Western and Eastern producing firms, banks, and governments. Western transactors may acquire equity or debt liabilities of Eastern transactors. A special feature of investment in Eastern Europe is the frequency with which debt may be repayable in kind (output), while equity may be the title to a specified share of output or profits, rather than the physical assets which generate them. 'Title' itself is ambiguous in this context, because here it normally carries only limited powers of control over financial, production, and marketing decisions, and even more limited rights to liquidate or otherwise dispose of the asset.

In all investment transactions, the expected time pattern of returns and the degree of certainty of these expectations are important variables. We must distinguish clearly between types of investment opportunities in these respects when considering policies towards them. Assets may be purchased with cash or commodities (Western exports), or acquired in exchange for the capitalized value of technology. Western firms have so far used the latter form particularly often. The essential characteristic of investment, its risk, may be borne by a firm, bank or government. Western governments have been very active in offering insurance against 'non-commercial' risk and in otherwise encouraging the private sector to undertake the special risks they might perceive in investment in the East.[5]

One might think that Western policies towards private investment in and government lending to Eastern Europe would be guided by past experience in the West itself and in less developed countries (LDCs). Such transnational activities by Western firms have generated continuously increasing interdependence, but we have become correspondingly conscious of

5 For thorough surveys of Western government and export credit agency policies towards credits for Eastern European importers, see S. Porter, *East–West Trade Financing* (Washington, DC: US Department of Commerce, 1976); and a series of articles in *IMF Survey* (1976).

the political and economic frictions this can bring, and many analysts have questioned the purely economic benefits to both 'home' and 'host' countries. Even foreign aid, whether by grant or loan, is no longer regarded as unambiguously beneficial to the recipients, while donor governments have always found it difficult to justify to their electorates. Why have these lessons not dictated greater caution towards investment in Eastern Europe? Perhaps Western policy-makers believe that the multi-national corporations will be able to exploit these countries as they do the LDCs. Planned economies are better able to defend their interests, however. On our side, there are good reasons to believe that Western firms and governments may overesti-mate the benefits and underestimate the costs and risks of investment in the East, and that government encouragement has widened the divergence between the net social benefit and perceived net private benefit of this investment.

When the strategic embargo relaxed, one expected a rapid expansion of trade, taking advantage of the many previously unutilized opportunities for profitable exchange. There were of course strong arguments (which I shall not discuss) for the normalization of East–West trade relations,[6] and it should be noted that medium- and long-term financing of large CMEA import surpluses on ordinary commodity trade is responsible for a substantial proportion of their debt to the West. It was however remarkable that the removal of constraints on current transactions should be accompanied by similarly extensive re-laxation of those on capital transactions, and that only the United States Congress (for rather special reasons) should even-tually have called a halt.[7] For the assessment of the economic

6 And Peter Knirsch is certainly right to conclude, in a
   wide-ranging essay on post-war East–West economic relations, that
   'trade with the East has hitherto certainly resulted in an increase in
   the prosperity of the Western economies'. 'Interdependence in
   East–West economic relations', presented to Marshall Plan
   Commemoration Conference, Paris (June 1977). I am questioning
   only some aspects of capital flows, not the gains from trade.
7 At the end of 1974, legislation renewing Eximbank authority, as
   well as the 1974 Trade Act, imposed limitations on American
   lending to Eastern Europe (the Stevenson and Jackson-Vanik
   Amendments). For details, see P. Marer (ed.), *U.S. Financing of*

and political implications of capital transactions is much more complicated, and the dangers of uncoordinated activity are much greater.

Let us assume that private firms do act as long-run profit maximizers. We may then ignore the effects of other possible objectives like sales or growth maximization, empire-building within large multinational corporations, etc; these have no special relevance to investment in any particular region. We may also disregard the motivations of businessmen who have historical associations with investment in the USSR, and the more recent and wider recognition of the pleasures of being entertained with the best caviar and vodka at banquets in Moscow. Even a profit-maximizing firm, however, may make incorrect decisions, or decisions which while correct for the firm are not in the national interest (we also make the assumption that there *are* some 'national interests', and indeed 'Western interests').

Specifically, a private firm may have inadequate data to make a good decision. The firm's judgement of the information available may be poor. Its interest in making profits may differ from that of its home country. And if one firm's actions are imitated by others, they may all consequently suffer and thereby damage the national interest. The home country itself may be pursuing policies detrimental to its interest, and in particular giving incorrect incentives to firms. Finally, policies beneficial to any one country may be harmful to Western countries as a group, especially if the others are simultaneously but without conscious coordination following similar policies. There is obviously a game-theoretic problem here, of the same kind that appears in the theories of oligopoly, externalities, and public goods.[8] Indeed, the strongest reason for investing in Eastern Europe is to establish an 'insider' position, a market presence, which is weakened precisely to the extent that other firms or countries follow suit.

East–West Trade (Bloomington, Ind.: International Development Research Center, 1975); and M. Kaser, 'American credits for Soviet development', *British Journal of International Studies* (forthcoming).

8 Compare the discussion of 'positional goods' in F. Hirsch, *Social Limits to Growth* (London: Routledge and Kegan Paul, 1977).

There are many other reasons for investing in Eastern Europe, and there are corresponding arguments that perceived private or social net benefits may diverge from actual social net benefits. We now consider these in detail.

First, we take the viewpoint of the private firm. Some of the obvious costs and difficulties of investing in Eastern Europe are straightforward and carry no special danger that private firms might underestimate them. Thus the 'transactions costs' of negotiating with East European bureaucracies will certainly be clear to any firm which follows the process to the point of reaching an agreement. The difficulty of obtaining information about the domestic market and consequent dependence on the East European partner is a straightforward informational asymmetry which the firm should be able to evaluate. Any institutional impediments to the repatriation of profits or capital will be specified in advance (we discuss later the possibility that the host country may subsequently change the rules). The East European preference for projects involving export promotion rather than import substitution, although the latter would often be more attractive to the Western firm, may limit the possibilities for agreement but will not bias estimates of the profitability of any given project.

On the other hand, there are many costs and risks which a Western firm might well not fully appreciate. If it were insufficiently familiar with the systemic problems of centrally planned economies, for example, it might not expect the frequency of delays in construction on a project and difficulties in obtaining skilled labour or material supplies. It might also overestimate the ability of its partner to absorb and utilize new technology; in trying to remedy this deficiency it will have to become more deeply involved and more dependent on its partner than it had intended (this is of course just the incentive which Eastern countries hope will operate in such circumstances).

There might be a form of 'adverse selection' operating in the Eastern country's choice of investment projects for which to seek Western participation: since all major investments are screened by the planners, they may select those which they know to be the riskiest for assistance from Western firms. Similarly, the Western firm might encounter 'moral hazard', insofar as the asymmetries of information may allow its partner to conceal responsibility for poor performance. And whereas the insurance companies from whose operations these terms arose develop enough experience to set premiums accordingly, many firms will be unaccustomed to the capacity of closed societies to conceal or distort relevant data.

Finally, there is 'country risk': the problems of debt-service capacity, the stability of the political leadership and their policies, and the relative strength of any political or economic leverage to induce the country to repay a debt which it might suddenly find onerous. We return to these questions below, but we note here that Western businessmen tend to see more of Eastern technocrats and managers than of politicians. They consequently may be excessively inclined to believe optimistic forecasts of decentralizing 'economic reforms', currency convertibility, and the convergence of socialist and capitalist economic systems.

They may also overestimate the supposed benefits of investing in Eastern Europe. There may be little or no labour unrest because there are no unions, but even British Steel or Leyland might find overmanning, featherbedding, and low productivity beyond their expectations. Thus the cost savings from 'cheap labour' might be illusory. In any case, it is unclear what this often-cited advantage might mean in the context of East European price and exchange rate systems and the consequent terms on which investment agreements are concluded.

Entering into a joint venture or a deferred-payment co-production agreement may give a firm the feeling of greater control over its East European operations than the mere sale of equipment or semifabricates would do, but it is hard to see how this 'control' would be exercised in any disputed matter, or to what end. Such an agreement may also bring liberal tariff treatment for the Western firm's exports, but Eastern countries are themselves becoming more reluctant to let Western firms purchase this advantage with a relatively small investment commitment (e.g. Yugoslavia). The argument that investing in any particular East European country might offer a 'gateway' to the entire CMEA market, and especially the USSR, has little apparent weight now that all these countries are so actively seeking Western trade partners.

East European planners are thought to offer monopoly positions to Western firms which establish their *bona fides* by concluding investment agreements, partly because the planning bureaucracies prefer dealing with firms they already know well. To the extent that this is true, it is likely to be transient (e.g. Czechoslovak planners have given explicit warning that they will not continue this practice). In any case, the situation is one of bilateral monopoly, in which the distribution of the benefits between the partners is purely a function of relative bargaining power, and there is no guarantee that the Western firm will be able to extract much surplus.

When Western firms or banks have been able to obtain fairly complete and reliable information on individual projects, they have often appeared very attractive indeed. Thus the Polish copper industry is an excellent risk on its own, virtually regardless of what happens to the world price of copper, because natural conditions are so favourable that it may well be the lowest cost producer in the world. But although Western investors are accustomed to assessing such projects on their own, this project-oriented approach is simply not applicable to investment in Eastern Europe. Whether a centrally planned economy will be able to offer foreigners an adequate return on any given project will depend on its *overall* rate of return on investment *and* whether it can ensure that increases in output go into exports or import substitutes. As Wiles has stressed,[9] there can only be a single borrower, a single project: the entire state plan. There can be no significant distinction between 'project' and 'programme' lending, nor between borrowing by the State Bank and by any individual state enterprise. Resources are fully transferable internally, at the dictates of the planners. Thus foreign investment in what appears to be a highly profitable project producing eminently exportable output may simply release domestic resources to go into badly selected and implemented projects which will never cover their foreign exchange costs. But

9 P. Wiles, *Communist International Economics* (Oxford: Blackwell, 1968).

the total hard-currency earnings of the country – and its priorities in meeting its foreign obligations – are under the full control of the planners.

So far, there has been no question of the ability of any East European country to meet obligations to Western investors. And although there is some evidence that rates of return on deals with some investment component are not very high, a number of Western firms have entered into more than one such agreement, keeping their stake in each venture fairly small. The 'market presence' consideration is important to them, although the benefit to the home country or the West as a whole of this advantage for any given firm may be nil. Moreover, many have been able to invest by selling R and D, which requires little or no actual outlay. Thus, despite Western government encouragement and a great deal of publicity, especially for the proposed massive mineral extraction projects, there has so far been relatively little actual direct private investment. The main Western commitment so far is in bank and government loans.

I should expect private corporations will continue to be reluctant to invest substantial amounts unless insured and possibly subsidized. But Western banks have been more enterprising, and their vigorous competition for Eastern European business has led them to lend very substantial amounts, often at rates comparable to those available to Western customers. Given recent rates of inflation in the West, in real terms these rates are close to zero or negative. Whereas one might say that should they wish to lend to Western firms at such rates, this is their own (perhaps bad) business, when similarly cheap finance is extended to Eastern Europe broader questions of the public interest arise. These questions are the more pertinent since the banks are acting independently and do not have the hard information on Eastern countries' debt-service burdens which they would normally demand from LDCs, for example.

It is fair to reply, however, that the banks have acted with encouragement from their governments and often jointly with government credit or credit insurance provision. We must therefore turn to the background for Western government assessment of the costs and benefits of Western investment in Eastern Europe.

We begin with the primarily economic issues relevant to the *capacity* of East European countries to pay a worthwhile return on Western investment and the economic *motivation* they will have to meet their obligations to service equity and debt capital.

The best Western estimates of the total hard-currency debts of CMEA countries are subject to wide margins of error.[10] They are based partly on cumulated estimates of balance of payments deficits ('estimates' because usually only trade figures are available), partly on public announcements of credits. The former are unreliable because of the 'mirror statistics' problem, i.e. the often large discrepancies between East European countries' data for their trade with individual Western countries and the latter's data for the corresponding transactions.[11] Small errors may cumulate over ten to fifteen years to large sums. Attempts to obtain direct information on how much they have borrowed are complicated by the large number of transactions and transactors, not just the range of Western banks (some of which may withhold information), but also of Eastern banks, including those operating in the West and the CMEA banks. *A fortiori*, any guesses at maturity structure and current debt service payments are bound to be highly inaccurate.

This being said, until recently it was plausible to believe that East European central bankers were at least as conservative as their Western colleagues and were fairly well in control of the situation. I continue to accept the former proposition, because central bankers' behaviour (like that of peasants) appears to be one of those system-invariant constants of human nature. It now seems clear, however, that some of them – especially in Poland and Yugoslavia – have bowed to their political masters and are in trouble. These countries have been borrowing vast amounts and have surely exceeded any prudent limits. Bulgaria, Romania, the GDR and Hungary also appear to be rather extended. Czechoslovakia has in contrast followed a very

10   For some detailed data and references, see R. Portes, 'West–East capital flows', Seminar Paper no. 72, Institute of International Economic Studies, University of Stockholm (February 1977; revised March 1977).

11   For a recent discussion of this problem (first analysed by Marer), see *International Currency Review*, no. 3 (1976).

cautious policy on foreign borrowing, with regard to both bank loans and other forms of foreign investment, and the USSR has substantial reserves and export capacity to fall back on.

Indeed, provided that the harvests of 1972 and 1975 are not repeated frequently, the USSR is by far the best placed of the group, because of the tremendous improvement in its terms of trade during the past few years. In the medium term, the strength of its underlying trade position should continue, unless and until the prices of gold, oil, gas and timber fall drastically. But if the USSR takes up the large credits it has been offered by Western countries, then unless it uses them to generate proper exportables, it may be in difficulty by the mid-1980s. The development of dollar exports does require the successful assimilation of Western technology (for industrial products) and capital (for raw materials, especially oil and gas), so resorting to this route is a self-reinforcing process. This holds for both the USSR and the smaller countries, but there is still the major difference that the latter require Western investment with quick payoff in dollar exports, while the Soviet Union is more interested in major projects with long gestation and repayment periods.

Our assessments of the East European *desire* to repay and the *leverage* we may have in future to induce repayment are not very encouraging, given the debt and balance of payments positions indicated above. The smaller countries could possibly find themselves by the beginning of the next decade in a position similar to that which many LDCs may also then face: needing to confiscate foreign investment and default on debts, except those to the OPEC countries. If the alternatives were meeting obligations to the West or to OPEC, who would be surprised if they chose the latter? It has been said that default is a 'tactic of the weak', but this might fit. The major bargaining counter we might have with the Soviets, our grain, would probably not be essential to the others, for which a major problem is the EEC's barriers to their agricultural exports.

In any event, the repayment problem with the USSR would arise later, and perhaps independently of capacity to repay. If the hypothesized debt were a consequence of major Western investment in Soviet raw material extraction, with promise of repayment in kind, the capital and technology inflow would be complete well before the output began to appear. No subsequent investment would be likely to approach this scale, so the prospect of future investment would not be an incentive to comply. If the recent shift in the balance of economic power towards primary producers holds for the long run, they would have the upper hand; if raw material prices fall substantially, they might simply be unable to repay.

It is of course true that the USSR has met its oil supply obligations to its CMEA partners (albeit at higher prices), despite the attractions of selling more for hard currency. This was entirely predictable, however, given the economic dependence which stable Soviet raw material supplies to the CMEA has created and the great importance to the USSR of maintaining it. As far as Soviet dependence on our technology is concerned, if in fact they turn out to be rather poor at using and diffusing the techniques we supply (which is surely a consensus forecast), they may simply give up the whole idea as a bad job. On the other hand, if they are good at it, they may then be able to do without any more. And even for the massive task of developing the Siberian oil fields, the USSR should if necessary be able to cope entirely on its own, though doubtless more slowly than it could with Western participation.[12]

It remains to consider what our real foreign policy interests are in regard to investment in Eastern Europe. Western hopes from détente are obvious, but it is hardly obvious that significant Western investment in the East would in fact further these objectives. I myself would argue that no substantial economic or political 'reforms', of a decentralizing or liberalizing kind, are likely in the foreseeable future, regardless of our policies. If anything, our exports of capital and technology to the East are likely to substitute for rather than to promote such reforms.[13] The Hungarian economic system *circa* 1971 is about as far as

12 See J. Russell, *Energy as a Factor in Soviet Foreign Policy* (London: Saxon House for Royal Institute of International Affairs, 1976).

13 See M. Bornstein, 'Economic reforms', in *East European Economies Post-Helsinki*, a compendium of papers prepared for the Joint Economic Committee, 95th Congress, First Session (Washington, DC: USGPO, 1977).

any country except Yugoslavia is likely to go. Any far-reaching decentralization would be a much more fundamental threat to the basic Soviet-type system than an influx of foreign business-men and technicians, who can be isolated rather effectively from the rest of the economy and society, and the myth that a 'managerial revolution' would replace *apparatchiks* by tech-nocrats and bring liberalization has long ago been exploded. Moreover, to the extent that Western investment in Eastern Europe were successful, this would relax some of the economic pressures which might provoke experimentation with reforms.

Within the CMEA, the shift in the terms of trade towards primary products and power towards their major supplier has resulted in centripetal tendencies.[14] Indeed, the USSR has suc-cessfully demanded investment from the smaller countries in its raw material production. Thus, if the West were to invest further substantial amounts in these countries, it might simply be indirectly financing their investment in the USSR.

Underlying economic détente is the assumption that trade and Western investment in the East will promote interdepen-dence and therefore harmony.[15] Unfortunately, this hypothesis is refuted by our experience with LDCs, as suggested by the concept of *dependencia*, now rather more fashionable than inter-dependence. The converse position of dependence on Soviet raw material supplies is unlikely to be conducive to good rela-tions. And the experience of Chrysler in the UK is a recent example of how foreign investment between advanced countries can also lead to serious friction and conflict. Overall, it seems likely that neither East nor West will – or should – allow their

14 See P. Marer, 'Prospects for integration in the Council for Mutual Economic Assistance', *International Organisation*, vol. 30 (1976), pp. 631–48; and A. Smith, 'Soviet economic influence in CMEA', mimeo (1977).

15 Kaser, 'American credits for Soviet development', quotes Alexander Hamilton: 'The spirit of commerce has a tendency to soften the manners of men and to extinguish those inflammable humours which have so often kindled into wars.' But Peter Wiles argues from historical evidence 'that freer trade makes nations love each other is absurd'. *Communist International Economics*, p. 527.

trade and investment relations to create any more than a strictly 'limited dependence' of each on the other.[16]

I conclude with some positive policy implications of my rather negative analysis. First, the Western countries should require as a condition of any further credits or direct investment for Eastern Europe that we receive full information on the recipient's debt and balance of payments position. Second, we should evaluate in detail the costs of government subsidies to and guarantees for credits[17] and reassess whether these serve Western interests as a whole, or are merely needless, costly competition between Western countries for the favours of monopolistic buyers. A first step was taken in this direction in 1976. The recession beginning in 1974 had stimulated a competitive search for export markets (especially for capital goods), and all the major Western exporting countries except the US had announced large loan guarantee packages for various East European countries. In June 1976, these countries, clearly believing that this competition had gone too far, announced a 'gentlemen's agreement' setting basic minimum terms for all countries.[18] But the need for export orders was so great that already by December 1976, the UK announced a deal in which it was to sell Poland £130 million of ships on 'very favourable financial terms' in a framework apparently constructed so as to avoid the 'guidelines'.[19]

Third, Western countries must take significant steps towards centralized coordination and control of their trade and investment policies towards Eastern Europe. This is necessary to counter their 'foreign trade monopoly' and to eliminate the competitive offering of concessionary terms by Western countries and multinational corporations. This would in practice mean coordination within the OECD and EEC. In particular, the announced EEC policy of negotiating as a bloc with individual CMEA countries would be appropriate, if member countries could be persuaded to abide by it. Even within the EEC,

16 See Knirsch, 'Interdependence in East–West economic relations'.
17 See T. Wolf, 'East–West trade credit policy', in Marer (ed.), *U.S. Financing of East–West Trade*.
18 *IMF Survey* (5 July 1976).
19 *The Times* (17 December 1976).

it is of course difficult to harmonize policies on an issue in which individual country interests appear so directly opposed.[20] But it may be easier in this context than in the OECD, because Congress has so strictly limited US Eximbank activities in Eastern Europe that American motives in seeking to restrict credit competition are bound to be suspect. Only Romania has shown willingness to deal with the EEC directly, however, and a second-best would be bloc–bloc negotiations.

Fourth, we should consider whether if we really desire to invest abroad, our interests might be better served by properly administered credits to LDCs than by substantial investment in Eastern Europe.

This is by no means a policy of hostility, but rather of common-sense. It is fully consistent with expanding normal trade relations with Eastern European countries, with good will and the best of intentions. Indeed, in my view it would be in the long run be much more conducive to harmonious and mutually beneficial economic and political relations than our present uncoordinated free-for-all. Any good central planner should agree.

20   See the discussion in J. Pinder and P. Pinder, *The European Community's policy towards Eastern Europe* (London: Chatham House and Political and Economic Planning, 1975).

7

Financial Relations between the EEC and the CMEA

J. WILCZYNSKI

The European Economic Community[1] and the Council for Mutual Economic Assistance[2] are not only the best known economic groupings in the world, but also represent two different approaches to financial management and economic ilntegration in general. In the EEC, which consists of capitalist market economies, financial dealings are essentially carried on under the conditions of private ownership, the freedom of enterprise, market competition, decentralized decision-making, the private profit motive and the system of government based on multi-party politics. On the other hand, financial processes in the CMEA

1   The EEC, originally established in 1957, now embraces nine Western European countries as full members – Belgium, Denmark, France, the Federal Republic of (West) Germany, Ireland, Italy, Luxemburg, the Netherlands and the United Kingdom. Meetings of its principal organs are held in Brussels, Luxemburg and Strasbourg. The EEC represents the following proportions of the world's totals: area – 2 per cent, population – 7 per cent, national income – 18 per cent, industrial output – 19 per cent and foreign trade – 34 per cent.

2   The CMEA was originally founded in 1949 and it now also includes nine full members – Bulgaria, Cuba, Czechoslovakia, the (East) German Democratic Republic, Hungary, Mongolia, Poland, Romania and the USSR (in addition, there are four other countries which have been accorded kinds of associate status: Finland, Iran, Mexico and Yugoslavia). Its secretariat is in Moscow whilst its 'Sessions' (the highest policy level of authority) are held in turn in the (full) member countries' capitals, as a rule once a year. In most respects the CMEA is much larger than the EEC, representing the following proportions of world totals: area – 18 per cent, population – 10 per cent, national income – 21 per cent, industrial output – 30 per cent but foreign trade – only 9 per cent.

region take place within the framework of the social ownership of the means of production (including banking and finance), central economic planning with laid-down targets within each member country, a hierarchical structure of management and a mono-party system of government (based on the Communist Party).

Up to the early 1960s financial relations between the two groupings were conspicuously restrained and of hardly any greater economic consequence. Neither side was in a particular need of the other, and the Cold War was also waged in the financial sphere when the Eastern 'iron curtain' was paralleled by the Western 'financial curtain'. However, since that time, and especially since the early 1970s, the situation has changed dramatically in favour of varied, far-reaching and even spectacular cooperation.

This newly discovered community of business interests has been facilitated by favourable background developments. In 1963 most capitalist and socialist countries signed the Nuclear Test Ban Treaty, which marked the virtual end of the Cold War. This was followed by several other treaties and agreements designed to reduce East–West tension. As a result of the liberal economic reforms since the early 1960s, the CMEA countries have departed from the old centralized, directive system of planning and management in favour of decentralization and a greater freedom of enterprises. Under this 'new system' the role of profit, financial instruments and banks has been substantially enhanced. Paralleling these developments, in the EEC countries there has been a long-run trend towards the extension of state control and ownership in banking and finance and in other fields as well, and profit is no longer as dominant a factor as it used to be.

As a consequence of these 'converging' trends, the EEC and CMEA economies have shed some of their extreme capitalist and socialist features – finding that they now have more in common, at least in the economic sphere, than they had in the past. In fact, contrary to what one would expect, there is more centralization of power in the EEC than in the CMEA. In addition to its well-known authority over the common external commercial policy, the EEC now exercises functions in consumer, fiscal and social harmonization – none of which powers have been entrusted to the CMEA. The EEC has several supra-national authorities (the EEC Commission, the Council of Ministers, the European Parliament, the Court of Justice, the European Coal and Steel Community, Euratom), but the CMEA has none, as in the latter each country has a right of abstaining or withdrawing from particular forms of cooperation. This fact has created certain difficulties in formal talks and negotiations between the two groupings, as in the EEC's view the CMEA has no corresponding supranational organs with sufficient authority to honour major commitments.

1. The Extent of the EEC-based Banks' Involvement

The analysis of East–West financial dealings indicates that three-quarters of the EEC-based banks and major finance companies have had significant business relations with at least one CMEA country. It is noteworthy that the CMEA partners have displayed a rather un-Leninist strong preference for big banks noted for a large concentration of capital and multinational affiliations, rather than smaller, 'exploited' and struggling entities. Although at first the CMEA countries favoured state-owned banks, they soon took to developing business links with private banks, too. In fact, the latter have outstripped the former in the scope and volume of business transacted. The extension of large credits has naturally become the main object of their dealings with the CMEA countries and this question is discussed in detail in section 3.

But the reader may be surprised to know that many EEC banks have gone further and now participate in other operations, too. They often act as correspondents for the CMEA banks not only in the EEC but also in other parts of the capitalist world, and they provide various banking facilities for tourists and business travellers to and from the CMEA region. To some extent, they also alleviate the CMEA countries' payments problem by arranging or otherwise facilitating multiangular operations through compensation, switch deals and clearing transactions. Some of them also provide expert advice on production and marketing cooperation and act as intermediaries

TABLE 1   The largest EEC-based commercial banks significantly

Name*	Head office	Assets in 1975 in $m
* Banque Nationale de Paris	Paris	38 333
Deutsche Bank	Frankfurt/M	34 639
* Crédit Lyonnais	Paris	34 308
* Société Générale	Paris	33 078
Barclays Bank	London	33 044
National Westminster Bank	London	29 676
Dresdner Bank	Frankfurt/M	28 003
* Banca Nazionale del Lavoro	Rome	24 452
* Westdeutsche Landesbank Girozentrale	Düsseldorf	24 300
* Banca Commerciale Italiana	Milan	21 811
Commerzbank	Düsseldorf	21 492
Midland Bank	London	20 981
Lloyds Bank	London	20 026
Bayerische Vereinsbank	Munich	18 559
* Banco di Roma	Rome	18 175
Algemene Bank Nederland	Amsterdam	17 890
* Credito Italiano	Milan	16 051
Amsterdam–Rotterdam Bank	Amsterdam	15 672
* Bayerische Landesbank Girozentrale	Munich	15 332
* Bank für Gemeinwirtschaft	Frankfurt/M	13 358
* Hessische Landesbank Girozentrale	Frankfurt/M	13 196
Cie Financière de Paris et des Pays Bas	Paris	12 655
Société Générale de Banque	Brussels	12 370
* Banco di Napoli	Naples	9 609
Cie Bruxelles Lambert	Brussels	9 445
Crédit Commercial de France	Paris	5 087
Union Bancaire	Lille	4 441
Banque de l'Indochine et de Suez	Paris	4 257
Crédit Industriel et Commercial	Paris	4 063

* Indicates banks wholly or substantially (50% or more) owned by the state or other public bodies (by trade unions in the case of Bank für Gemeinwirtschaft).

† According to the size of the bank's assets, as in *The Banker* (see *sources*) listing the 300 largest banks located outside the Socialist bloc.

‡ The number of foreign countries is followed (in brackets) by the number of foreign affiliates.

involved in financial dealings with the CMEA countries

Size rank order†	Foreign affiliations in capitalist world‡	CMEA partner countries§
5	23 (33)	Bu, GDR, *Po, Ro, USSR*
6	30 (52)	*GDR*, Hu, *Po*, USSR
7	26 (31)	Bu, *Cu, GDR, Po, Ro, USSR*
8	— (—)	Cu, *GDR*, Hu, *Ro, USSR*
9	38 (60)	Bu, Cz, Hu, *Po, Ro, USSR*
11	22 (68)	*Bu, Cu, Cz, GDR, Hu, Po, Ro, USSR*
14	28 (45)	*GDR*, Hu, *Po*, Ro, *USSR*
20	16 (21)	Cu
21	7 (19)	*GDR*, Hu, Po, *USSR*
24	33 (60)	Cu, *GDR*, Hu, *Po*, USSR
26	24 (42)	Bu, GDR, *Po*, USSR
27	20 (66)	Bu, Cu, Cz, Hu, *Po*, Ro, USSR
31	31 (103)	Bu, GDR, *Hu, Po, Ro*, USSR
37	14 (23)	Cz, GDR
40	13 (14)	Bu, Cu, Hu, *USSR*
42	16 (21)	Bu, Hu, Po, *USSR*
47	5 (9)	*USSR*
48	10 (17)	Cz, Po, USSR
52	3 (3)	Cz, Po, *USSR*
57	6 (11)	Bu, GDR, Hu, USSR
58	6 (9)	Po
63	21 (53)	Hu, Po, *Ro, USSR*
67	12 (16)	GDR, Hu, *Po*
80	5 (14)	Bu, USSR
81	5 (14)	GDR, Po, Ro
122	10 (12)	*Bu*, Cu, Hu, *Po*, Ro
137	3 (5)	Hu, Po, Ro, USSR
141	11 (14)	Cu, Hu, Po, Ro, USSR
148	1 (1)	Bu, *Po*, Ro, USSR

§ These entries should be regarded as minimal, as unreported or undetected dealings as well as those of small size are not reflected. For country abbreviations, see footnote 3, p. 182. Italicized entries indicate substantial dealings in terms of value or extent.

Sources: Based on *The Banker* (June 1976), pp. 653–95; *Who Owns Whom 1976: Continental Edition* and *Who Owns Whom 1975/76: U.K. Edition*, both published in London by Roskill; daily and periodical literature published in Western and CMEA countries.

in purchases and sales of licences embodying advanced technology.

Table 1 provides a select list of the largest EEC-based banks (i.e. those whose parent countries are members of the EEC) which are most active in financial and related dealings with the CMEA countries.[3] The banks chosen are those each with assets in excess of $4000 million (in 1975). The combined assets of these twenty-nine banks alone represent a vast concentration of capital, totalling more than $555 000 million, or twenty-five times the international liquidity reserves held by the nine CMEA countries.

The volume of business of these banks has radically increased since 1972, and so one half of them have decided to open representative offices in the capitals of several CMEA countries, of course with the blessing of the communist regimes. Table 2 shows the location of such offices as of 1976.[4] It may be observed here that the banking outposts established in the East do not carry on full-scale banking operations involving the acceptance of deposits and the creation of credit. Under central economic planning no bank, much less foreign and capitalist at that, can be freely allowed to create credit, unless there is a provision for it in the plan consistent with the planned allocation of resources.

3 Country abbreviations used in this study are: Be, Belgium; Bu, Bulgaria; Cu, Cuba; Cz, Czechoslovakia; Fr, France; FRG, Federal Republic of Germany; GDR, German Democratic Republic; Hu, Hungary; It, Italy; Lu, Luxemburg; Ne, Netherlands; Po, Poland; Ro, Romania; UK, United Kingdom; USSR, Soviet Union.

4 Other capitalist banks which have established offices in the CMEA countries and compete for business are: Bangkok Bank (Thailand) in Moscow (in 1975), Bank Melli Iran (Iran) in Moscow (1975), Bank of America (USA) in Moscow (1973), Bank of Tokyo (Japan) in Moscow (1975), Chase Manhattan Bank (USA) in Moscow (1973), Citicorp (USA) in Budapest (1975) and Moscow (1974), Creditanstalt-Bankverein (Austria) in Budapest (1975), Export–Import Bank (Japan) in Moscow (1975), First National Bank of Chicago (USA) in Moscow (1974) and Warsaw (1974), Kansallis Osake-Pankki (Finland) in Moscow (1971), Manufacturers Hanover Trust (USA) in Bucharest (1974), Schweizerische Kreditanstalt (Switzerland) in Moscow (1976), Svenska Handelsbanken (Sweden) in Moscow (1974) and Union Bank of Finland in Moscow (1976).

TABLE 2   Representative offices of the EEC-based banks in the CMEA countries

Location of office (and year of establishment)	Bank (and parent country)*
Budapest (1977)	Banco di Sicilia (It)
East Berlin (1976)	Banca Commerciale Italiana (It)
East Berlin (1975)	Credit Lyonnais (Fr)
East Berlin (1975)	Société Générale (Fr)
East Berlin (1975)	Société Générale Alsacienne (Fr)
Moscow (1975)	Banca Commerciale Italiana (It)
Moscow (1975)	Banco di Napoli (It)
Moscow (1975)	Banco de Roma (It)
Moscow (1974)	Banque de Paris et de Pays Bas (Fr)
Moscow (1974)	Banque Nationale de Paris (Fr)
Moscow (1974)	Barclays Bank (UK)
Moscow (1975)	Commerzbank (FRG)
Moscow (1973)	Crédit Lyonnais (Fr)
Moscow (1975)	Credito Italiano (It)
Moscow (1973)	Deutsche Bank (FRG)
Moscow (1973)	Dresdner Bank (FRG)
Moscow (1975)	Lloyds Bank (UK)
Moscow (1975)	Midland Bank (UK)
Moscow (1975)	National Westminster Bank (UK)
Moscow (1975)	Société Générale (Fr)
Sofia (1974)	Banco di Napoli (It)
Warsaw (1975)	Banca Commerciale Italiana (It)
Warsaw (1974)	Banque Nationale de Paris (Fr)
Warsaw (1975)	Crédit Industriel et Commercial (Fr)
Warsaw (1976)	Société Générale (Fr)

* For country abbreviations, see footnote 3, p. 182.

Foreign banks are allowed to engage only in foreign trade transactions arising out of the agreed contracts and to provide various incidental services and advice.[5]

5   There is a qualified exception to this generalization represented by the 'branch' (not a representative office) of Manufacturers Hanover Trust (USA) in Bucharest. This branch is allowed to accept deposits and create credit provided they are all in convertible currencies.

2. The CMEA Countries' Banking in the EEC

The CMEA countries have always regarded the present EEC region as a convenient area for financial operations associated with their trade, developmental programmes and various forms of monetary and economic cooperation. Even before the formation of the CMEA in 1949, these countries had begun keeping some of their international liquidity reserves, especially US dollars, in the Soviet-owned bank in Paris – Banque Commerciale pour l'Europe du Nord, also known by its telegraphic name as the 'Eurobank'.[6]

They believed that in the days of the Cold War their dollar balances were safer in Western Europe than in the USA. As early as the mid-1950s they began offering their idle dollars through the Eurobank on deposit with Western European banks in order to earn interest. The latter in turn took to re-lending such deposits to various clients to whom they had access (whilst the Eurobank had not), and in the days of the universal dollar shortage the demand was keen and the business was proving of considerable benefit to all concerned. It is widely believed that the name 'Eurodollar market' originated from the Eurobank. Another socialist bank which contributed to the development of this market is the Moscow Narodny Bank in London.[7] In 1976 the estimated size of the CMEA countries' hard-currency reserves held in the banks within the EEC was in the order of $4500 million.

6   It was originally founded by the White Russian emigrés in 1921, but it was bought out by the Soviet government in 1925. It has grown to become the largest foreign bank in Paris (out-ranking the Bank of America, the next largest, by two and a half times). In 1975 it was the 195th largest bank outside the socialist bloc (with its assets exceeding $3000 million), larger than such banks in the EEC as Bank of Scotland, Bank of Ireland, Nederlandse Kretietbank, Kleinwort, Benson Lansdale, and Banque Worms.

7   It is the oldest and second largest socialist bank in the capitalist world. Originally established by Russian Cooperative Societies in 1916, it was taken over by the Soviet Government in 1919. Its net assets in 1975 amounted to $2400 million and it ranked the 232nd largest bank in the capitalist world. It has established wholly owned subsidiaries in Beirut (in 1966) and Singapore (in 1971) and a representative office in Moscow (in 1975), and according to recent reports it is to open offices in Montreal and New York.

TABLE 3   Banks wholly or partly owned by the CMEA
countries located in the EEC

Name	Location	Year of foundation	Ownership*
Anglo-Romanian Bank	London	1973	Ro; UK, USA
Banque Commerciale pour l'Europe du Nord	Paris	1925	USSR; Fr
Banque Franco–Roumaine	Paris	1971	Ro; Fr
Banque Unie Est–Ouest	Luxemburg	1974	USSR
Frankfurt–Bukarest Bank	Frankfurt/M	1977	Ro; FRG
Havana International Bank	London	1973	Cu
Hungarian International Bank	London	1973	Hu
Mitteleuropäische Handelsbank	Frankfurt/M	1973	Po; FRG
Moscow Narodny Bank	London	1919	USSR
Ost–West Handelsbank	Frankfurt/M	1971	USSR

* For country abbreviations, see footnote 3, p. 182, and for details of the banks owned
  jointly by socialist and capitalist shareholders (Anglo-Romanian Bank, Banque Commerciale pour l'Europe du Nord, Banque Franco–Roumaine, Frankfurt–Bukarest Bank
  and Mitteleuropäische Handelsbank) see section 5 below.
Source: Based on daily and periodical literature published in the EEC and CMEA
countries.

Most CMEA countries' banks have developed correspondent
relations with many banks in the EEC. A number of them have
further established or re-opened their branches or representa-
tive offices in the leading financial centres:
   Bulgarian Foreign Trade Bank – in London
   Commercial Bank in Warsaw (Bank Handlowy w Warszawie)
      – in London
   Hungarian National Bank – in Frankfurt am Main, Paris and
      Rome
   Polish Guardian Bank (Bank PKO) – in Paris
   Romanian Foreign Trade Bank – in Rome
   Živnostenska Bank (of Czechoslovakia) – in London
But five CMEA countries (Cuba, Hungary, Poland, Romania
and the USSR) have gone further and established separate
banks in the EEC region. Some of these banks are wholly owned
by the CMEA country concerned, whilst others have been
established jointly with capitalist banks. There are now ten such
banks within the borders of the EEC. For details, see table 3.
The Soviets also operate two insurance companies in the EEC
– the Baltic and Black Sea General Insurance in London, and

Schwarzmeer and Ostsee Versicherungs in Hamburg (in addition to Garant Versicherungs in Vienna).

The CMEA countries' banks in the EEC engage in a wide range of business. They finance East–West European trade, extending credits not only to the local customers in the EEC but also further afield. They are active in the Eurocurrency market and they assist and participate in the socialist bond issues in capitalist countries. They provide financial and economic advice to their own governments as well as to businessmen in the West. The Eurobank reportedly acts as a bank for the French Communist Party and it trains bankers not only for the USSR but also for some other countries (such as Algeria and Egypt). The Moscow Narodny Bank is used as an agent for Soviet gold sales in London and the Ost–West Handelsbank in Frankfurt am Main for diamond sales in the Federal Republic of Germany. The CMEA banks operating in the EEC have developed very good working relationships with capitalist banks and financial companies. They have established a reputation for sound management and fair dealings and have come to be respected as shrewd and trustworthy business partners.

3. Credits and Bond Issues

Finance usually flows from richer, more developed countries to areas which are less affluent and in lower stages of economic development. This generalization certainly applies to the flow of finance between the EEC and the CMEA. The EEC also has the best developed financial network in the world which can not only mobilize local savings but also attract surplus funds (such as petrodollars) from other countries with less developed financial markets.

Although virtually all countries at one time or another suffer from balance-of-payments difficulties, this problem has always been of a greater magnitude and persistence in the CMEA region. Under socialist central economic planning there is an in-built pressure inexorably operating on both import and export sides, creating a tight foreign exchange position. The planned accelerated economic development based on rapid industrialization necessitating Western equipment and technology, the unsatisfied consumer demand, the non-fulfilment of production targets and the relatively low quality of domestic products place extra demands on imports. At the same time, there are forces militating against a sufficient level of exports. Developmental programmes are not normally geared to export production, the prevailing local sellers' markets reduce the enterprises' inclination to export, and moreover the CMEA exports are discriminated against in capitalist markets, especially in the EEC. The over-valuation of the CMEA currencies at the official exchange rates further tends to induce imports and discourage exports.

However, before 1960 the CMEA countries' need of Western credits was not urgent and was not allowed to assume larger proportions. These countries were still preoccupied with basic industrialization, for which equipment as well as credits could be obtained from within the CMEA region itself. At the same time they were reluctant to incur large debts in hard currencies for fear of becoming too dependent on capitalist countries, they detested paying exorbitant interest (by their standards) and were against 'mortgaging the future'.

But their need of Western credits has increased dramatically since the economic reforms of the early 1960s. Their modernization drive and their determination to develop the most advanced branches of industry have necessitated large imports of costly equipment and complete industrial plants, together with licences and know-how. The EEC is, of course, in a very good position not only to meet such deliveries but also to provide finance of any description. The CMEA's need of Western finance has risen sharply since 1972, since when these countries have stepped up their technological innovations, have experienced serious harvest failures, have been confronted with steeply rising prices in world markets and at the same time have encountered serious difficulties in marketing their exports (especially manufactures) in hard-currency areas suffering from the recession. Furthermore, there has been an inexorable tendency for the diversion of imports away from intra-CMEA channels in favour of the capitalist world. Whilst 70 per cent of the CMEA countries' imports came from other member countries in the early 1950s, the proportion declined to 54 per cent in 1975. In the latter year the EEC claimed 15 per cent of the

CMEA's total foreign trade, compared with half this share in the early 1950s (the nine countries in both cases). But the CMEA's share in the EEC's trade has oscillated around only 5 per cent.[8]

The forms of finance made available to the CMEA countries include government credits, supplier credits, bank loans and subscriptions to bond issues. We shall examine them in turn.

Government and Supplier Credits

In many cases the EEC governments have rushed to the fore-front offering generous credits, whether solicited or not. Such credits are either directly extended by government instrumentalities (export credit agencies or state-owned banks) or sponsored and guaranteed by the government. Examples of major credit commitments officially announced during 1974–6 are as follows: France to Cuba, $370 million; France to Poland, $1700 million; France to the USSR, $2900 million; the FRG to Poland, $420 million; Italy to Poland, $450 million; Italy to the USSR, $2000 million; the United Kingdom to Cuba, $600 million, and the United Kingdom to the USSR, $2500 million (£960 million).[9] The agencies which provide or sponsor such credits are either state-owned or state-controlled and the most active entities in the EEC are:

Belgium – Office Nationale du Ducroire

France – Coface (Compagnie Française pour le Commerce Extérieur)

Federal Republic of Germany – Hermes Versicherungs

Italy – Istituto Mobiliare Italiano

Netherlands – Nederlandse Cretietverzekering

United Kingdom – Export Credits Guarantee Department

---

8 Based on United Nations, *Monthly Bulletin of Statistics.*

9 *Bank i kredyt* (Bank and credit) Warsaw, no. 5 (1975), p. 188. *Eastern Europe*, London (10 March 1976), p. 6. *Eastern Europe Report*, Geneva (16 May 1975), p. 135; (27 June 1975), p. 178; (18 August 1975), p. 222; (22 August 1975), p. 242; (12 December 1975), p. 354. Moscow Narodny Bank, *Press Bulletin*, London (3 April 1975), p. 16; (16 April 1975), p. 2; (7 May 1975), p. 11; (28 May 1975), p. 1. *Rynki zagraniczne* (Foreign markets), Warsaw (13 May 1975), p. 2.

These institutions have been providing credits at low interest rates, subsidized in one way or another, and guarantees to private lenders against commercial as well as political risks. Supplier credits are extended by the manufacturing firm delivering the equipment. The two types of credits have one feature in common: they are more or less specific and tied to particular purchases and/or periods. These credits were predominant up to the early 1970s.

Bank Credits

This form of finance essentially consists in bank-to-bank loans giving the CMEA countries a greater freedom in the choice of suppliers and timing.[10] It is on account of such advantages that since the early 1970s CMEA countries have largely switched to this unfettered form of finance, even though government credits usually carry interest rates about one-third lower. In the mid-1970s, about two-thirds of all credits extended to the CMEA was in the form of bank loans and the proportion in the case of Hungary was as high as 90 per cent.[11] In fact in recent years several CMEA countries (especially the USSR) have not cared to utilize the credits offered to them by the EEC governments.

Eurocurrency Loans

Most of the finance obtained in the form of bank loans (and bond issues) is now raised in the Eurocurrency market. It is one of the ironies of history that this most capitalistic market of all partly owes its origin to the CMEA countries and its growth has been further enhanced by them as both lenders and borrowers. The leading role in this process has been unwittingly played by the USSR, the country which regards itself as the ideological leader and pace setter of the socialist camp. Yet this financial empire has always been viewed by orthodox communists with suspicion. A Polish monetary expert, K. Studentowicz, described the Eurocurrency market as 'a cancerous growth on the

10   Anna Lipińska, 'The economic significance of the burden of medium and long-term credits', *Handel zagraniczny* (Foreign trade), Warsaw, no. 8 (1973), pp. 259–64.
11   *Business Eastern Europe*, Geneva (10 September 1976), p. 281.

international monetary system which should be completely liquidated'.[12]

More than one-half of the finance raised by the CMEA in the EEC now comes from the Eurocurrency market. The amounts raised in this way in publicized major bank loans alone since 1970 have been as follows (in brackets, the percentage of total Eurocurrency loans):[13] 1970, $48 million (1.0 per cent); 1971, $66 million (1.7 per cent); 1972, $274 million (7.3 per cent); 1973, $780 million (3.9 per cent); 1974, $1238 million (4.2 per cent); 1975, $2597 million (12.4 per cent); 1976 (January–July), $1789 million (13.6 per cent). The reader will note the strong tendency for the CMEA to resort to this source of finance. All the CMEA countries except Mongolia have now floated Eurocurrency loans, the last one being Czechoslovakia (with a $60 million loan in November 1975).

Finance raising by the CMEA countries is typically done on a large scale because it is undertaken on a centralized basis on behalf of the whole country, and not by individual end-users.[14] Many of the loans raised are so large that they are beyond the capacity of single banks, however large, so that often a number of banks cooperate in the form of consortia or syndicates. Thus in the $150 million, six-year loan floated by the Hungarian National Bank in 1975, twenty-four banks participated, including Banque de Commerce (Be), Kredietbank (Ne) and Midland Bank (UK).

Examples of large Eurocurrency credits (of $30 million or more) to the CMEA countries in recent years in which the EEC

12 K. Studentowicz, 'Unsettled problems of the reform of the world monetary system', *Handel zagraniczny*, no. 2 (1974), p. 93.

13 Morgan Guaranty Trust Co. of New York, *World Financial Markets* (16 July 1974), p. 5; (July 1976), pp. 8 and 14.

14 An exception to this rule occurred in 1976 when the Polish Steamship Co. was given permission to seek a Eurocurrency loan of $20 million for five years to finance the purchase of two cargo vessels from Norway (originally built by Mitsubishi Heavy Industries of Japan). The loan, which was syndicated by First Chicago Ltd (UK), is secured by a prime mortgage on the vessels involved (instead of an otherwise customary guarantee from the Polish bank of foreign trade). *Business Eastern Europe* (6 August 1976), p. 245.

TABLE 4   Large credits extended by the EEC-located banks
to the CMEA countries during 1974–6

Participating EEC lending bank*	Borrowing CMEA country	Amount in $m	Period in years	Interest % p.a.†
Bank für Gemeinwirtschaft (FRG)	Bulgaria	45	7	NA
Banque de l'Union Européenne (Fr)	Poland	150	5	IBLR + 1.5
Banque Nationale de Paris (Fr)	USSR	250	5	IBLR + 1.125
Banque Worms (Fr)	Poland	45	7	NA
Barclays Bank (UK)	Romania	50	5	IBLR + 1.625
Commerzbank (FRG)	Poland	240	7	IBLR + 1.25
Crédit Commercial de France (Fr)	Poland	70	7	IBLR + 0.625
Crédit Lyonnais (Fr)	Cuba	350	10	NA
Crocker National Bank (UK)	Romania	50	5	IBLR + 1.375
Frankfurter Bank (FRG)	Poland	40	5	NA
Interunion Bank (Fr)	Poland	40	6	IBLR + 1.5
Kredietbank (Ne)	Hungary	150	6	IBLR + 1.375 − 1.5
Lazard Freres (Fr)	USSR	250	5.5	IBLR + 1.125
Lloyds Bank (UK)	Poland	100	6	IBLR + 1.5
Midland Bank (UK)	Cuba	60	5	NA
Morgan Grenfel & Co. (UK)	Cuba	85	5	IBLR + 1.75
National Westminster Bank (UK)	GDR	110	5	IBLR + 1.375
Société Générale (Fr)	USSR	400	5	IBLR + 1.25
Westdeutsche Landesbank Girozentrale (FRG)	Hungary	42	6	8.25
Wobaco (UK)	Bulgaria	30	5	IBLR + 1.375

* As the managing, co-managing and/or a subscribing bank. For country abbreviations,
   see footnote 3, p. 182..
† IBLR Inter-Bank Lending Rate (which may differ from one financial centre to
   another and also at different times) plus the 'spread'.
Sources: Based on daily and periodical literature published in the EEC and CMEA
countries.

banks participated are given in table 4. Late in 1976, it was
reported that Crédit Lyonnais was investigating the possibility
of forming a French banking syndicate to raise $2300 million for
the USSR to finance the 'North Star' project, involving the
supply of Siberian natural gas to the east coast of the USA.[15]

15   *Business Eastern Europe* (6 August 1976), p. 245.

Bond Issues

Some CMEA countries' banks have raised finance in the Euro-bond market by floating medium-term and long-term bonds. The Hungarian National Bank became the pioneer in this type of venture in 1971. To the surprise of many financial observers, both in the East and in the West, the $25 million ten-year issue was oversubscribed. So far four bond issues have been floated in each of which at least one bank from the EEC participated. Details are given in table 5.

Finance Raising by the CMEA Twin Banks

The CMEA countries have established two banks to facilitate economic cooperation and integration within the grouping through monetary and financial channels. The International Bank for Economic Cooperation (IBEC), created in 1963 with its head office in Moscow, is concerned with facilitating payment settlements amongst the member countries and providing short-term and medium-term trade credits. The International Investment Bank (IIB), founded in 1971 and also based in Moscow, is responsible for medium-term and long-term loans to the member countries for investment projects of collective importance, and it also provides economic aid to less developed countries. (These banks correspond to the IMF and the IBRD under the United Nations set-up.)

One of the interesting developments in the EEC–CMEA financing is that these two banks have also entered the Euro-currency market. Their increasing interest has been prompted by four factors. First, the jointly pursued investment projects in the CMEA are becoming more and more ambitious, necessitating increasingly costly equipment and technology from the West. Second, the efforts to multilateralize intra-CMEA foreign trade and to prepare conditions for the convertibility of the member countries' currencies require convertible Western currencies.[16] Third, credits are now extended by the CMEA to less developed countries also in convertible currencies. Finally,

16 The CMEA countries are committed to some sort of convertibility of their currencies in the 1980s. In 1973 they agreed that 10% of the trade imbalance would be payable by the deficit to the surplus country in convertible (capitalist) currencies.

TABLE 5 Bond issues floated by the CMEA countries in the eurobond market

Year	Issuing CMEA country bank*	Participating subscribing EEC bank*	Amount in $m	Period in years	Interest % p.a.†
1971	Hungarian National Bank (Hu)	National Westminster Bank (UK)	25	10	8.75
1972	Hungarian National Bank (Hu)	Bank für Gemeinwirtschaft (FRG)	50	15	8.50
1975	Hungarian National Bank (Hu)	Westdeutsche Landesbank Girozentrale (FRG)	40	6	8.25
1976	Commercial Bank in Warsaw (Po)	Banque Nationale de Paris (Fr)	30	5	IBLR + 1.25 (8.25 minimum)

* For country abbreviations, see footnote 3, p. 182.
† IBLR Inter-Bank Lending Rate.
Sources: Based on daily and periodical literature published in the EEC and CMEA countries.

the CMEA countries believe that in many cases they can secure more favourable terms acting collectively through the CMEA banks, rather than negotiating separately.

The CMEA began appearing collectively in the Eurocurrency market in February 1972, when the IBEC (after eight years of its existence) raised its first loan in the West – a $20 million medium-term loan, subscribed to by several Belgian and French banks. The IIB followed suit in the following year, with a $50 million, seven-year loan. The largest single CMEA financial venture into the Eurocurrency market was the $600 million, six-year loan raised in early 1976; sixteen Western banks participated, each having contributed $40 million. The consortium was headed by the Dresdner Bank (FRG) and amongst the subscribers there were also the following EEC-based banks: Algemene Bank Nederland (Ne), Barclays Bank International (UK), Bayerische Hypotheken- und Wechselbank (FRG), Bayerische Landesbank Girozentrale (FRG), Brandts (UK) and Compagnie Louxembourgeoise de Banque (Lu).[17] For further details, see table 6.

Total CMEA Indebtedness

The total level of the CMEA countries' indebtedness to the EEC creditors is not known precisely. Although most large credits extended by governments and by banks as well as subscriptions to bond issues are publicized, a large proportion of the total actual figure is not reported, especially in the case of supplier credits and loans of confidential nature for one reason or another. The CMEA countries do not publish figures of their external debts, treating them as state secrets.

The writer's estimate of the CMEA countries' total gross indebtedness to the EEC creditors as of mid-1977 was $35 billion, or perhaps more. In this total, the share of the USSR was $12 billion, Poland $8 billion, the GDR $4 billion, Czechoslovakia, Hungary and Romania $2 billion each and the balance of the $5 billion was owed by Bulgaria, Cuba and the twin CMEA banks. On the EEC side, the chief creditor country was the FRG (about $10 billion), followed by France, the United Kingdom,

17 *Eastern Europe Report* (9 April 1976), p. 109.

TABLE 6 Publicized loans raised by the CMEA twin banks in the eurocurrency market

Year	Borrowing CMEA bank	Participating EEC lending bank*	Amount in $m	Period in years	Interest % p.a.†
1972	International Bank for Economic Cooperation	Société Générale de Banque (Be)	20	medium-term	NA
1972	International Bank for Economic Cooperation	Crédit Lyonnais (Fr)	60	5	IBLR + 1.125
1972	International Bank for Economic Cooperation	Morgan Grenfell & Co. (UK)	60	medium-term	NA
1973	International Investment Bank	National Westminster Bank (UK)	50	7	IBLR + 0.5
1974	International Bank for Economic Cooperation	Crédit Lyonnais (Fr)	50	7	IBLR + 0.438 − 0.625
1974	International Bank for Economic Cooperation	Crédit Lyonnais (Fr)	50	5.5	IBLR + 1.375
1974	International Bank for Economic Cooperation	Banque de Bruxelles (Be)	60	5	IBLR + 1.125
1975	International Bank for Economic Cooperation	Crédit Lyonnais (Fr)	50	7	IBLR + 0.438 − 0.625
1975	International Investment Bank	Société Générale (Fr)	70	5	IBLR + 1.25
1975	International Investment Bank	Deutsche Bank (FRG)	400	5	IBLR + 1.25
1976	International Investment Bank	Dresdner Bank (FRG)	600	6	IBLR + 1.25 − 1.375
1977	International Investment Bank	Dresdner Bank (FRG)	400	6.5	IBLR + 1.125 − 1.25

* For country abbreviation, see footnote 3, p. 182.
† IBLR Inter-Bank Lending Rate.
Sources: Based on daily and periodical literature published in the EEC and CMEA countries.

Italy, the Netherlands, Belgium, Denmark and Luxemburg (in that order).

At the same time, the CMEA countries' hard-currency holdings within the EEC area were estimated at $5 billion. This gives the net figure of CMEA indebtedness of about $30 billion. The CMEA countries also owed some $17 billion to other Western countries (or about $15 billion net). This means that to the CMEA, the EEC is the main creditor area, accounting for some two-thirds of the CMEA's total external debts.

It may be noted here that estimates of the CMEA's indebtedness have varied. Although to the writer's knowledge no one has specifically published figures of the CMEA's indebtedness to the EEC, estimates have been made by several researchers concerning the total hard-currency indebtedness of the CMEA. The net figure published by the Chase Manhattan Corporation of New York for the end of 1976 was $46.4 billion (a revised figure in lieu of $45.8 billion given before).[18] The total produced by the Institute for Comparative International Economics of Vienna, also for the end of 1976, was $40 billion, and the figure predicted for 1980 is at least $80 billion and it could be as high as $100 billion or more.[19] The figure arrived at by this writer for the end of 1976 (after several revisions) was about $45 billion.

4. Credit Terms and Creditworthiness

It may appear surprising, but the CMEA countries often obtain their finance on more favourable terms than those prevailing in financial markets and accorded to capitalist borrowers. These countries benefit from government-subsidized credits, the interest rates on which are typically one-third to one-half below those charged in private markets.[20] The privileged position of

18 *Eastwest Markets* (7 March 1977), p. 7; (16 May 1977), p. 6.
19 Reported in *Business Eastern Europe* (26 March 1977), p. 92.
20 Neither are the EEC governments the only ones subsidizing export credits, nor are the CMEA countries the only ones receiving subsidized credits. According to the chairman of the Export–Import Bank of the USA, governments outside the USA alone spend about $1000 million annually in budgetary funds for subsidizing export credits. Reported in *Eastern Europe Report* (14 November 1975), p. 319.

the CMEA borrowers became most obvious during 1973–4 when the rates of discount of the central banks in the EEC reached up to 13 per cent.[21] Complaints were made in the Federal Republic of Germany that whilst the interest rates charged to domestic borrowers were up to 14 per cent, credits to the CMEA countries (such as Poland and the USSR), for up to twenty years, carried only 2–7 per cent.[22] Such cheap credits, it was pointed out, in effect meant free gifts to the East amounting to 200–500 million DM ($75–190 million) annually.[23] A striking case of cheap credits is illustrated by the loan of 1000 million DM (about $410 million) at 2.5 per cent for twenty-five years from the FRG to Poland negotiated during 1975–6, as part of the normalization of political relations.[24]

The 'cheapest' form of finance is represented by the so-called 'swing credits', arising out of bilateral clearing agreements. To provide for the irregular flow of trade during the year, up to 10 per cent of the value of export, if in excess of import, is financed interest free. The point is that it is usually the Eastern side that imports well ahead of its exports.[25]

But even the terms secured in the ordinary commercial markets are quite favourable. Thus in mid-1975 the CMEA borrowers could obtain loans at only 1.25 percentage point ('spread') over LIBOR (London Inter-Bank Offer Rate), when other borrowers were normally charged 1.5–2.0 spread over LIBOR.[26] In fact during 1973 and early 1974 spreads of 0.5 on

21 The rates of discount reached the following levels in late 1973–early 1974: Belgium 8.75, Denmark 10.00, France 13.00, the FRG 7.00, Italy 9.00, the Netherlands 8.00 and the UK 13.00. United Nations, *Monthly Bulletin of Statistics* (September 1974), p. 241; (November 1974), p. 241.

22 *Handelsblatt* (Commercial news), Düsseldorf (21 February 1974), p. 13; (25 June 1974), p. 4.

23 Quoted from *Die Wirtschaft* (The economy), East Berlin, no. 10 (1974), p. 31.

24 *Eastern Europe* (10 March 1976), p. 6.

25 The GDR is the chief beneficiary on this score, especially in trade with the FRG. Thus the amount of swing credits allowed by the latter country for 1975 was 770 million DM ($320 million), which saved the Eastern partner about $25 million in interest payments. *Eastern Europe Report* (21 February 1975), p. 55.

26 *Eastern Europe Report* (3 October 1975), p. 276.

loans for five or more years accorded to the CMEA borrowers were common. Since the mid-1960s there has also been a tendency for the credit periods to be extended.[27] As of 1977, about three-quarters of the CMEA debts to the EEC were of medium or long-term duration.

The CMEA countries' efforts to minimize interest payments is conditioned not only by practical considerations but also by ideological premises. In the orthodox marxist view, interest above the cost of administering credits (1–3 per cent per annum) constitutes 'surplus value' or exploitation. Confronted with the high interest rates in Western markets since 1972, the CMEA borrowers in many cases refused to pay more than 7.5 per cent. But when in bad need they are prepared to make concessions. Rates of up to 10 per cent and even more are known to have been accepted, especially since 1974, by several CMEA countries (particularly those with a lower credit standing).[28] Or alternatively, some interesting practico-ideological loopholes have been found, acceptable to the borrowers and lenders alike.[29]

The favourable terms usually accorded by the EEC lenders are not an outcome of some sinister pro-communist conspiracy,

27 Thus in the case of Poland, the share of long-term credits (exceeding five years) represented 11% in 1966, 40% in 1971 and the estimated proportion in 1976 was well above 50%. Based on *Handel zagraniczny*, no. 8 (1973), p. 262.

28 E.g. *Eastern Europe Report* (10 January 1975), p. 7; (24 January 1975), p. 22.

29 Thus the nominal interest rate charged by the FRG to the USSR on a $625 million loan, to finance the export of pipes by Mannesmann Export (FRG) and Thyssen-Stahlunion (FRG) in 1975, was 7.0% p.a. At that time the prevailing market rate was 12%. The loan was extended by a consortium of West German banks (led by Commerzbank and Westdeutsche Landesbank Girozentrale), but it was compensated by the pipe suppliers for the interest differential. The exporting firms simply 'buried' the interest subsidy into the price quoted to the Soviet Negotiating team, which accepted this arrangement as not unreasonable in the circumstances. The interest rate on paper was not only more acceptable to Stalinist diehards at home, but was also not prejudicial to credit terms that might be negotiated by the USSR with other lenders in the West in the future. *Handelsblatt* (4 November 1974), p. 2.

but largely a question of cold economic calculation conditioned by a variety of factors. The financial deals entered into by the CMEA countries are typically large with the consequent economies of scale to the lenders; lending to these countries is generally considered to involve relatively little risk, and there is usually keen competition amongst the EEC lenders further enhanced by the inroads of the Canadian, Japanese and US banks which were most acute during 1972–4. Furthermore, the CMEA negotiating teams have proved to be very well informed, skilful and tough – utilizing their power of centralized and large dealings to the full – and time and manpower appear not to be a cost factor for them.

It must be realized, however, that credit terms secured by the CMEA countries have varied. The interest rates were lowest during 1972–4, when the spread was whittled down to 0.5 percentage point and even less. Since that time the spread has risen to 1.0–1.75 and in some cases more. On the whole, the USSR and Czechoslovakia have received a more favourable treatment than Poland and Romania, because the former have a greater capacity in relation to their indebtedness to repay their loans than the latter have.

The generally favourable terms accorded by the EEC lenders so far have been rationalized by a high 'credit rating' or superior 'creditworthiness' of the CMEA countries. In the past, these countries showed a most commendable degree of financial restraint and responsibility, both in domestic and external policies. They have exercised strict controls over their price levels, have kept their standards of living low (in relation to the reasonably high levels of economic development attained) and they have used Western finance primarily for expanding their production capacity and not for current consumption.

In comparison with many capitalist nations, especially the less developed ones, the CMEA countries' level of indebtedness is not considered excessive, at least as yet. It is estimated that the latters' debt service ratios[30] are in the range from 20 per cent

30 Interest plus current debt repayment as a percentage of
     hard-currency earnings from the export of visible and invisible
     items.

(Czechoslovakia, the German Democratic Republic, the USSR) to 35 per cent (Poland, Romania).

There have been several attempts made amongst Western countries to coordinate their credit policies, with a view to preventing excessive competition in respect of interest rates and periods of maturity, especially in the case of government credits. First of all, the creation of a central information agency has been advocated either by the OECD[31] or by the banking and other financial entities operating in the Eurocurrency market.[32] Some economists, such as M. Palmer, have proposed that 'the EEC should affect a united financial front against the co-ordination of central policies of Comecon members through the IIB'.[33]

After protracted negotiations, France, the Federal Republic of Germany, Italy and the United Kingdom, plus Japan and the USA, concluded a 'gentlemen's agreement' in Washington in October 1974, limiting the minimum interest rate on government export credits of five years or more to 7.5 per cent per annum. It was also agreed not to subsidize such credits if exceeding three years (the FRG and the USA had been pressing for 8.0 per cent at least).[34] In March 1977, the EEC Council of Ministers finally approved the guidelines for government-supported export credits when France agreed to drop her long-standing insistence on national sovereignty on the question. According to the guidelines, exporters must require cash payment of at least 15 per cent of the value of exports at the time of delivery. The minimum interest rate to be charged to medium-developed countries (which include the CMEA countries) on two to five year credits is 7.25 per cent and on long-term credits, 7.75 per cent; the respective interest rates applicable to poor countries is 7.25 and 7.5 per cent, whilst those applicable to rich nations is 7.75 and 8.0 per cent. According to a scale prepared previously by the EEC group of experts, poor, medium and rich nations

31 *Business Eastern Europe* (27 August 1976), p. 267.
32 *International Currency Review*, London, vol. 8, no. 1 (1976), p. 13.
33 Quoted from M. Kaser, 'The EEC and Eastern Europe: prospects for trade and finance', *International Affairs*, London (July 1973), p. 410.
34 *Eastern Europe Report* (7 March 1975), pp. 67–8.

were defined in terms of annual per capita GNP: below $1000, $1000–$3000 and over $3000 respectively.[35]

A question has often been asked in the West in recent years as to whether the CMEA countries might default on their credits and bonds in the future. Although the possibility of this occurring cannot be excluded, in the writer's view its likelihood is remote. First of all, their debt burden is not excessively heavy. Although several CMEA countries have exceeded the internationally accepted 'safety limit' of 25 per cent debt-service ratio, the proportion is higher in the case of at least a dozen capitalist nations, with much poorer prospects for meeting obligations. It must also be realized that in a centrally planned economy, with a more direct and effective control of its external outlays, the safety limit is higher. So far, the CMEA countries have met their obligations and there is no known case of default.[36]

The CMEA countries have too much to lose to default. They have assiduously cultivated an image of absolute integrity and have established a payment record unparalleled in the capitalist world. This commercial reputation, which has paid off handsome dividends to them so far, would be ruined beyond repair in case of a default, not to mention the political and ideological loss of face. These countries would probably forfeit the supplier credits owing to them by the EEC, and perhaps other Western, importers (about $500 million), they would lose their hard-currency holdings in the EEC (about $4500 million) and their

35   *Ibid* and *Business Eastern Europe* (25 March 1977), p. 93.

36   There have been some delays in the payment of outstanding bills in the case of Romania (of up to six months), Bulgaria and Poland (of up to four months), Czechoslovakia and Hungary (of up to two months) and the GDR (of up to one month). *Eastern Europe Report* (11 July 1975), p. 188. Some other socialist countries have blemished their payment record even more. The delays by Yugoslavia have reached twelve months. In 1975 payment delays by the DPR of (North) Korea were also reported, apparently caused by acute balance of payments difficulties and involving a figure of $250 million or perhaps more; Australian and other Western firms were affected and the question was even debated in the Australian Parliament. House of Representatives, Canberra, *Parliamentary Debates* (4 November 1975), pp. 2723–4.

assets in various trading, manufacturing and financial ventures operating in the West (about $500 million). Refusals by the Western interests to extend roll-over or any credits and maybe to enter into any business relations could follow.

Because of the gravity of the consequences for other CMEA countries and owing to the high degree of intra-CMEA cooperation, a member country in difficulties is likely to be helped out by others. There is some indirect evidence of Soviet aid to at least one CMEA country; according to a reliable contact, on one occasion the USSR shipped gold to the West to get a 'fraternal' country out of a predicament.

But owing to the large size of their indebtedness not only to the EEC but also to other Western creditors, the CMEA countries will be experiencing balance of payments difficulties. This, together with their limited capacity for expanding hard-currency earnings, is likely to cause further payment delays and a pressure for extended maturity periods and roll-over credits.

If a default does occur, it will be by the CMEA *en bloc*, rather than by a country individually. It could happen only in some most drastic circumstances and would probably be a prelude to a major confrontation and perhaps an East–West armed clash. However, there is little likelihood of it in the foreseeable future, at least judging by recent developments. On the contrary, there has been a remarkable extension and strengthening of organic links across the disintegrating 'financial' and 'iron' curtains. We shall next examine the closest forms of cooperation along these lines.

5. Joint Financial Operations

The financial relations between the EEC and the CMEA countries have reached the highest form of cooperation in jointly owned banking and other financial entities and in the joint provision of finance to users in the CMEA, the EEC and also in third countries.

There are now five banks located within the EEC borders which are jointly owned, managed and operated, as shown in table 3 above. Thus the Anglo-Romanian Bank in London is owned 30 per cent by the Barclays Bank International (UK), 20 per cent by the Manufacturers Hanover Trust (of the USA) and

50 per cent by the Romanian Foreign Trade Bank. Banque Commerciale pour l'Europe du Nord (Eurobank) in Paris is owned by the State Bank of the USSR (48.3 per cent), the Foreign Trade Bank of the USSR (21.95 per cent) and the balance of the shares is apparently held by the French Communist Party. The shareholding in another Paris-based bank, Banque Franco-Roumaine, is distributed as follows: Banque de Paris et des Pays Bas 8.75 per cent, Banque Nationale de Paris 8.75 per cent, Banque Rothschild 3.0 per cent, Crédit Commercial de France 4.0 per cent, Crédit Industriel et Commercial 4.0 per cent, Crédit Lyonnais 8.75 per cent, Société Générale 8.75 per cent, Union Bancaire 4.0 per cent and the Romanian Foreign Trade Bank 50 per cent. To the foundation capital of Frankfurt–Bukarest Bank, in Frankfurt am Main, Deutsche Genossenschaftsbank contributed 24 per cent, Berliner Handels-Gesellschaft-Frankfurter Bank 16 per cent, the Romanian Foreign Trade Bank 52 per cent and Banque Franco-Roumaine 8 per cent. In another jointly owned bank in Frankfurt am Main, Mitteleuropäische Handelsbank, Hessische Landesbank Girozentrale owns 30 per cent of the share capital and the Commercial Bank in Warsaw (Bank Handlowy w Warszawie) 70 per cent.

In addition, there are two joint leasing companies engaged in financing East–West leasing operations. One of them is East–West Leasing, in London, which was established in 1973 by Morgan Grenfell & Co. and the Moscow Narodny Bank, with the joint capital owned on a fifty–fifty basis. The other is Promolease, in Paris, founded in the same year by Crédit Lyonnais and Eurobank on the same basis.

It will be noted that in each of the seven banking and financial joint ventures, the socialist side owns at least 50 per cent of the share capital, presumably to avoid the possibility of being dominated by the Western side. There are also partnerships of a loose nature, such as 'Gisofra', a banking consortium formed in Paris in 1971, embracing Banque Nationale de Paris, Crédit Lyonnais, Société Générale and the Eurobank. Its function is to finance Franco–Soviet trade and industrial cooperation.

We shall next outline the extent of joint financial operations by giving recent examples of loans in which both the EEC and CMEA banks participated.

Loans to the CMEA Countries

In two loans to the USSR, totalling $20 million, arranged by Morgan Grenfell & Co. and provided by Lloyds Bank (both of the UK) in 1975, the Moscow Narodny Bank of London and the Foreign Trade Bank of the USSR also took part.[37] In the same year Kredietbank (Ne), Midland Bank (UK) and other Western banks cooperated with the Eurobank (of Paris) and Banque Unie Est–Ouest (Lu) in a Eurocurrency loan of $100 million to the Hungarian National Bank.[38] In the preceding year, in a $45 million loan to Bulgaria, in addition to Bank für Gemeinwirtschaft (FRG), Banque Worms (Fr), Crédit Commercial de France (Fr), Crédit Industriel et Commercial (Fr) and Interbanca (It), Bank PKO (of Paris), the Eurobank and the Moscow Narodny also took part.[39] An even larger array of banks joined forces in subscribing to a 150 million DM loan to the National Bank of Cuba, also in 1974; on the Western side the following EEC banks participated: Banca Commerciale Italiana (It), Banque de l'Union Européene (Fr), Banque de Suez et de l'Union des Mines (Fr), Banque Française du Commerce Extérieur (Fr), BfG Luxemburg (Lu), Crédit Commercial de France (Fr), Crédit Lyonnais (Fr), Deutsche Girozentrale International (FRG), Midland Bank (UK), and William & Glyn's Bank (UK); the banks owned by the CMEA countries included Bank PKO (Paris), Banque Franco-Roumaine (Paris), Eurobank (Paris), Havana International Bank (London), Hungarian International Bank (London), International bank for Economic Cooperation (Moscow) and Moscow Narodny Bank (London).[40]

Finance to the EEC Countries

In 1974 the Hungarian National Bank participated with several EEC banks in a $40 million loan to the state-owned Banque Française du Commerce Extérieur (Fr),[41] and the Foreign Trade Bank of the USSR together with the Bulgarian Foreign Trade Bank and in company with several EEC banks provided a $1500

37 *East–West Fortnightly Bulletin* (28 March 1975), p. 11.
38 *Euromoney*, London (January 1976), p. 5.
39 Moscow Narodny Bank, *Press Bulletin* (19 June 1974), p. 12.
40 Moscow Narodny Bank, *Press Bulletin* (26 June 1974), p. 15.
41 Moscow Narodny Bank, *Press Bulletin* (19 June 1974), p. 13.

million loan to the French government.[42] In the same year, the Eurobank in cooperation with several EEC banks participated in a $500 million Eurocurrency loan to the Greater London Council,[43] and in another $500 million loan to Electricité de France;[44] and the same bank together with the Moscow Narodny participated in a $600 million loan to Istituto Mobiliare Italiano (It). Similarly, the Eurobank and the Foreign Trade Bank of the USSR and several EEC banks cooperated in providing a $1200 million loan to Mediobanca (It).[45]

Loans to Other Capitalist Countries

The joint lending activities have also extended to third countries in the capitalist world. During 1974–6 the Eurobank and several EEC banks participated in the following loans to Western countries: $10 million to Impresa Nacional de Autocamiones (Spain), $15 million to Frigg Gas Field Developments (USA), $100 million to the Bank of Finland and together with Banque Unie Est–Ouest (located in Luxemburg) $200 million to the Bank of Greece.[46] But the joint lending has been extended further afield – to less developed countries. During the same period the Eurobank took part in Eurocurrency loans to Algeria ($50 million), Brazil ($120 million), Egypt ($100 million), Gabon (20 million DM), Indonesia ($60 million), Iran ($40 million), Malaysia ($140 million), the Philippines ($200 million), Senegal ($20 million), Venezuela ($50 million) and Zaire ($100 million);[47] and the Moscow Narodny to Brazil ($30 million), Iran ($10 million), Lebanon ($40 million) and other countries.[48] The Foreign

---

42 Moscow Narodny Bank, *Press Bulletin* (8 May 1974), p. 13.

43 *Bank i kredyt*, no. 8 (1974), p. 348.

44 Moscow Narodny Bank, *Press Bulletin* (21 August 1974), p. 11.

45 Moscow Narodny Bank, *Press Bulletin* (25 July 1974), p. 14.

46 *East–West Fortnightly Bulletin* (7 May 1975), p. 9; (28 November 1975), p. 9. Moscow Narodny Bank, *Press Bulletin* (19 June 1974), p. 13.

47 Moscow Narodny Bank, *Press Bulletin* (8 May 1974), p. 13; (15 May 1974), p. 13; (21 August 1974), p. 11; (26 February 1975), p. 14; (2 April 1975), p. 11; (28 January 1976), p. 17; (10 March 1976), p. 16; (14 April 1976), p. 16; (8 September 1976), p. 12.

48 Moscow Narodny Bank, *Press Bulletin* (19 February 1975), p. 12; (2 April 1975), pp. 10–11; (27 August 1975), p. 10.

Trade Bank of the USSR has also cooperated with the EEC banks in credits to Argentina ($60 million) and Turkey ($150 million).[49]

Loans to Other Socialist Countries

Several socialist countries outside the CMEA have also become the object of the joint lending patronage. In 1975 Banque Unie Est–Ouest, Eurobank, Moscow Narodny, Ost–West Handelsbank and Živnostenska Bank participated with several Western banks in a $518 million Eurocurrency loan to Yugoslavia,[50] and in the following year the Eurobank acted as lead manager of a consortium including Bank PKO, Havana International Bank, International Bank for Economic Cooperation and several French and West German banks in a Eurocurrency loan of 100 million DM to the Democratic Republic of (North) Vietnam.[51]

The joint financial ventures outlined above bear evidence of the feasibility of working coexistence between capitalism and socialism at the microeconomic level. This organic symbiosis has come to be known as 'transideological cooperation', where the traditional ideological prejudices and other historical grievances have been forgotten, or at least set aside – as too petty to outweigh the undoubted economic benefits to both sides.

49 *East–West Fortnightly Bulletin* (9 September 1975), p. 10; (13 November 1975), p. 8. It may be mentioned here that Turkey is a member country of NATO.
50 Moscow Narodny Bank, *Press Bulletin* (12 February 1975), p. 16.
51 Moscow Narodny Bank, *Press Bulletin* (4 February 1976), p. 17.

8

Mutual Economic Dependence between the EEC and the CMEA

FRIEDEMANN MÜLLER

1. Trade Structure

A. *The Specifics of East–West Trade*

An attempt to establish the specifics of East–West trade has to proceed from the premise that the volume of this trade does not accord it major importance. Trade volume between the EEC and the CMEA in 1976 amounted to no more than $26.5 billion, that is 4 per cent of the EEC's overall trade volume. It thus did not even reach the same levels as trade between the EEC and Switzerland plus Austria ($31 billion). Another comparison is more conclusive: EEC exports to the CMEA were almost as big (namely $14 billion) as those to the United States ($18 billion). But as far as imports are concerned, the CMEA as a supplier did not even reach half of the US deliveries to the EEC (table 1).

The EEC is a more important partner for the CMEA than

TABLE 1   EEC* trade with different regions (1970–6 in $ billions)

	World			USA			CMEA		
	1970	1976	Growth (%)	1970	1976	Growth (%)	1970	1976	Growth (%)
EEC imports	116.3	343.4	195	12.3	27.4	123	3.82	12.5	227
EEC exports	112.4	325.0	189	9.2	18.1	97	3.78	14.0	274
EEC trade volume	228.7	668.4	192	21.6	45.5	111	7.60	26.5	249

* 1970 EEC including Denmark, Ireland, United Kingdom.
Source: OECD, *Statistics of Foreign Trade*, series A (1971 and 1977).

TABLE 2   Foreign trade–GNP relation of EEC
countries, 1975.

	GNP in $ billions	Exports to EE* in $ billions	Imports from EE* in $ billions	Export:GNP (%)	Import:GNP (%)
United Kingdom	238.5	1.30	1.51	0.5	0.6
Ireland	8.2	0.048	0.084	0.6	1.0
Denmark	33.7	0.30	0.52	0.9	1.5
France	299.6	2.60	1.69	0.9	0.6
Netherland	75.8	0.79	0.79	1.0	1.0
Belgium	58.8	0.85	0.61	1.5	1.0
Luxemburg	2.0				
West Germany	402.2	6.46	3.22	1.6	0.8
Italy	169.6	2.17	1.92	1.3	1.1
EEC	1288.4	14.52	10.34	1.1	0.8

* EE = Eastern Europe (CMEA).
Source: Commission of EC, Com(77)63 (4 March 1977), and OECD, *Statistics of Foreign Trade*, series A (1976).

TABLE 3   Foreign trade–GNP relation of CMEA
countries, 1975

	GNP in $ billions	Exports to IW* in $ billions	Imports from IW* in $ billions	Export:GNP (%)	Import:GNP (%)
USSR	738.1	7.10	10.74	1.0	1.5
Bulgaria	19.0	0.32	1.04	1.7	5.5
Czechoslovakia	45.8	1.49	1.76	3.3	3.8
GDR	57.1	2.29	2.62	3.9	4.6
Hungary	22.1	1.17	1.76	5.3	8.0
Poland	73.6	2.76	5.21	3.8	7.1
Romania	42.5	1.44	1.91	3.4	4.5
CMEA	998.2	16.53	25.04	1.7	2.5

* Industrialized West.
Source: US Department of Commerce (Bureau of East–West Trade), *Selected Trade and Economic Data of the Centrally Planned Economics* (Washington, September 1976).

the CMEA is for the EEC. The EEC share in CMEA foreign
trade is in excess of 25 per cent. However, the share of East–West
trade in the GNP is not substantial on either side. The proportion of EEC exports to CMEA nations in the overall EEC

GNP makes up 1.1 per cent, and the import share is 0.8 per cent (table 2). Conversely, the share of exports to Western industrial countries in the CMEA's GNP is 1.7 per cent with the import share making up 2.5 per cent (table 3).

But the really noteworthy features of East–West trade are first of all the high growth rates since 1970, secondly the complementary character of trade, and thirdly the comparatively close interdependence between East–West economic relations and political issues.

Concerning the growth rates, it is interesting to note that overall foreign trade of EEC nations[1] rose by 192 per cent from 1970 to 1976, while their trade with CMEA countries increased by 249 per cent. By comparison, trade volume with the United States rose only by 111 per cent. Whether these rates of growth of trade volume between the EEC and the CMEA can be maintained is questionable. As main obstacles are cited the high trade balance deficits and hence the debt cumulation of the CMEA. Yet there are indications of a reduction of this obstacle. The CMEA's balance of trade deficit *vis-à-vis* the EEC has declined from \$4.2 billion (1975) to \$1.5 billion (1976), and during the first months of 1977 it was reduced by another 36 per cent as compared to the previous year.[2] This decline of the balance of trade deficit, however, affected the EEC's export growth by a rise of only 6 per cent in the overall trade volume between the EEC and the CMEA.

The complementary nature of East–West trade implies that EEC exports to the CMEA essentially include other commodity groups than imports from CMEA countries to the EEC. If foreign trade is divided into two groups, raw materials (SITC group 0–4) and manufactured goods (group 5–8), it can be seen that 91 per cent of EEC exports consist of manufactured goods, whereas 61 per cent of CMEA exports are raw materials (table 4). If the group of manufactured goods were further broken down according to criteria of technology intensity, the complementary nature would be even more evident. Both factors, technology and raw materials, are scarce in the respective receiver countries, i.e. the economic blocs do not have sufficient

1   Including Denmark, Great Britain and Ireland in 1970.
2   OECD, *Statistics of Foreign Trade*, series A (June 1977).

TABLE 4   Structure of trade between the EEC and the
CMEA (January–September 1976)

SITC groups		EEC exports		EEC exports	
		In million European Units of Account	Share of total exports (%)	In million European Units of Account	Share of total exports (%)
0, 1	Food, beverages, tobacco	447	5.6 ⎫	635	8.7 ⎫
3	Fuel products	79	1.0 ⎬ 9.1	2758	38.0 ⎬ 61.2
2, 9	Raw materials	205	2.5 ⎭	1053	14.5 ⎭
5	Chemicals	1213	15.1 ⎫	386	5.3 ⎫
7	Machinery and transport equipment	3192	39.6 ⎬ 90.9	513	7.1 ⎬ 38.8
6, 8	Other manu- factured goods	2916	36.2 ⎭	1917	26.4 ⎭
	TOTAL	8052	100	7262	100

Source: Eurostat, *EC Trade by Commodity Classes and Main Countries*, supplement to the
Monthly External Trade Bulletin (February 1977).

factor resources to sustain their economic process without
imports. The term complementary thus implies dependence
(leaving aside ways of substitution via third markets). The
magnitude of this dependence will not yet be discussed in this
context.

The interdependence between economic relations and political issues can only be indicated. On the one hand, a correlation
between the high growth rates since 1970 and the political
détente efforts cannot be contested. On the other hand, the
debate whether Western technology exports are actually being
translated on a large scale into military advantages for the
Eastern bloc is by no means concluded.[3] In addition, there are
examples of the use of economic instruments for political
objectives on the part of the West or at least of considerations

3   Organizationally this consideration is manifested in the
Coordination Committee for East–West Trade (COCOM), which
prepares embargo lists for strategic goods. Thus the delivery of
large tubes to the USSR was prohibited in 1963 following COCOM
intervention.

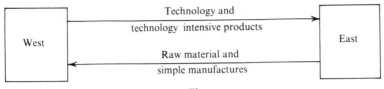

Fig. 1

to that effect.[4] Ever since the raw material crisis in 1973–4, the problem of economic security has gained in importance in the sense that foreign economic instruments could be utilized as either substitutes for or complements to military instruments, which implies that potential areas of military confrontation are at the same time potential areas of economic tension.

Because of these three factors, i.e. growth rates, complementary trade, and linkage between political and economic goals, East–West economic relations are more sensitive to dependence than trade of equal volume between other regions.

B. *Currents of East–West Trade*

As was outlined in the last section, dependence in East–West economic relations may be expected in those areas where there is no substitution for the input. In addition, money circulation plays a role because there is imbalance for two reasons. For one thing Western currencies, as opposed to Eastern currencies, are convertible, which is why East–West trade is handled primarily in Western currencies. Secondly, there has been a disequilibrium in the balance of payments for years which has led to a considerable debt cumulation to the disadvantage of the Eastern side.

A graphic table of simplified trade relations between the two blocs, including this time all industrialized Western countries, would yield the picture given in fig. 1. The monetary relations could be represented as in fig. 2, and if one were to introduce to this very rough scheme an additional factor comprising the remaining countries of the world, the product circulation would be as in fig. 3. This simplified model shows that the West can

4   E.g. US linkage of most-favoured-nation status for the USSR to
    political goals.

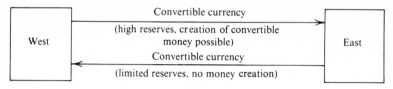

Fig. 2

basically substitute raw material imports by import from the Third World, whereas the East cannot buy technology from the Third World.

A sketch on settlement of payments in this triangle (fig. 4) also points up advantages for the West. Because of the possibility of creating money of convertible currency, which alone guarantees a multilateral trade free of clearance barriers, the West has a much better basis for turning to third markets should problems of an emerging dependence make it necessary.

If not only the qualitative flow of groups of goods and means of payment, but also the quantitative share of these groups in the economic process of the blocs is considered, it can be seen

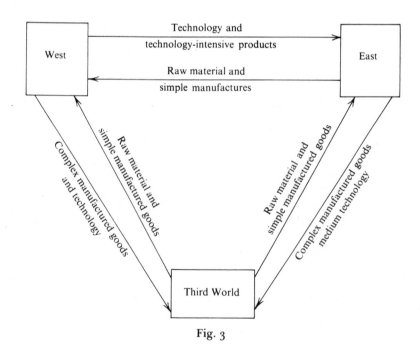

Fig. 3

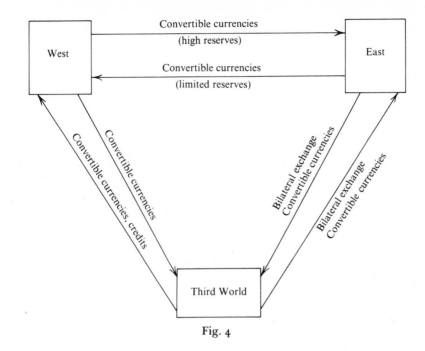

Fig. 4

that these trade currents within the CMEA have a much greater impact on the economic process and hence on dependence.

The GNP of all CMEA states together was $998 billion in 1975 (table 3). The GNP of the EEC countries in the same year reached $1288 billion. If the EEC economic area is extended to include Western allies, among others the US GNP of $1500 billion would have to be added, whereas no significant economic potentials could be added to CMEA figures.

These considerations on the structure of East–West trade serve as the framework for possible relevant dependencies. In order to arrive at more precise statements on the structures of dependence some methodological ideas should be discussed first.

2. Methodological Problems

A. *Definition*

International economic dependence is a rather complex phenomenon. Therefore some explanatory remarks are necessary in order to arrive at a clear definition.

Dependence on the supply of vital goods, above all raw materials, has been at the fore of discussions since 1973. Dependence on the willingness of other markets to absorb export goods was the central issue of the world-wide crisis of 1929–33. Dependence upon financing means and economic control by foreign governments or enterprises as well as the impact upon the socio-economic structure of the countries concerned are an essential element of the North–South conflict. For the area of East–West relations some assumptions will be made to narrow down the study subject.

It is assumed that East–West trade involves two basically equal blocs in the sense that both are sufficiently emancipated to control the degree of mutual trade and thus the influence of trade on their own socio-economic structure. Thus the issue of the asymmetrical dependence evident in the North–South relationship does not apply.

A second assumption further restricts the analysis of dependence. From the Western point of view dependence of non-controlled foreign-economic changes – above all fluctuations of the economy – has different implications than it does within an intra-Western context. During the recession of 1973–5 East–West trade had an anti-cyclical effect with the result of a stabilizing trend of overall international trade. For this reasons unplanned changes in East–West trade from the viewpoint of dependence seem to be of minor importance. In the framework of this study, therefore, only those components of economic relations will be analysed which can be deliberately used as a tool for political objectives by the other side.

Thus dependence exists if a country (or economic bloc), by employing or threatening economic measures (refusal to pay, embargo, termination of economic relations), can jeopardize the other country's (bloc's) security or enforce political objectives against it.

Economic relations between two countries are generally characterized not by unilateral but by mutual dependence. Soviet dependence upon tubes from the EEC implies simultaneous dependence within the EEC on the demand for tubes for the sake of job preservation. Apart from the mutual dependence of an individual business transaction, there is a multitude of additional economic relations with a cumulative or compensating impact with regard to the dependence on tubes. Only the composition of individual dependences to form a dependence structure will permit meaningful statements to be made on economic dependence.

B. *Components of Economic Dependence*

In order to determine the vulnerable areas of foreign economic dependence, the term has to be divided into its components to permit a distinction of the various qualities of dependence. A breakdown into import dependence, export dependence and monetary dependence appears sensible.

Import dependence exists if a country buys from another country (or cartel of countries) a certain import product which it cannot acquire easily from another region or manufacture domestically without suffering a serious dislocation of its economic system (supply, full employment etc.).

Export dependence exists if either foreign demand for a certain product is a necessary precondition for the preservation of the system of values (above all full employment) or if the sale of export goods is the only means to procure currency for the acquisition of necessary imports.

Monetary dependence exists if a foreign partner is in a position to bring about serious shortage of foreign exchange or to hamper monetary circulation in such a way as to upset the domestic system of values via disturbances of the economic process.

Figure 5 demonstrates the impact of the components of dependence upon the production process and thus on the supply situation as well as on the equilibrium of the system.

C. *Parameters of Dependence Components*

Import dependence is determined by the following parameters:[5]

(i) Import share in total domestic consumption

---

5 See F. Müller, 'Wirtschaftliche Abhängigkeit in der Ost–West Zusammenarbeit. Überlegungen zu einem Modell' in G. Zellentin (ed.), *Annäherung, Abgrenzung und friedlicher Wandel in Europa* (Boppard am Rhein, 1976).

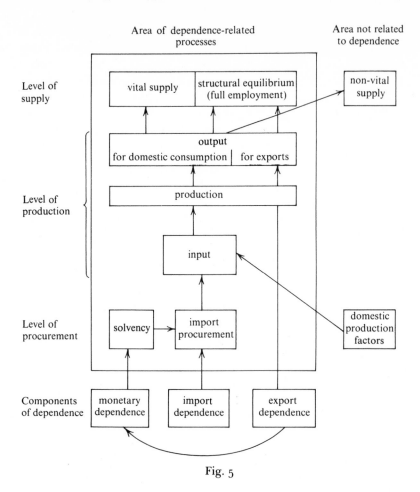

Fig. 5

(ii) Ability to reduce demand (demand elasticity)
(iii) Possibility of acquiring the product from another market (market substitution)
(iv) Possibility of producing the good domestically (import substitution)
(v) Possibility of substituting the product by another available product (product substitution).

These parameters are strictly product-oriented, since in this case supply is dependent upon a specific product. Export dependence, by contrast, involves overall economic parameters where a product-oriented classification is of little interest. For example, it is more interesting to determine the number of jobs dependent on exports to the CMEA than to know which jobs in the field of mechanical engineering or in the automobile industry are in jeopardy. Hence export dependence is determined by the following parameters:

(vi) Ways and means to adjust the economic structure in the event of foreign demand shortfall (guaranteeing full employment)

(vii) Possibility of finding other financing means if revenues are lacking from exports of goods due to an export embargo (see monetary dependence).

Monetary dependence involves all kinds of monetary transactions, i.e. payments for imports, credits, credit repayments. The degree of dependence on such transactions is determined by the following parameter:

(viii) Possibility of compensating refusal to pay by other financing means (from currency reserves, by means of domestic money creation, through indebtedness).

Of course, the components of dependence also have a time dimension. Thus the means of substitution may improve in the course of time, or the necessary import share in consumption may increase by means of stock reduction. Also, the problem of payment may grow with the reduction of currency reserves. Furthermore, it is necessary to distinguish between the types of goods. For preliminary products and consumer goods, dependencies are more immediately effective, but for investment goods the effect is a longer range one.

To limit dependence, the following instruments are available:

(a) regional distribution of imports to several 'politically secure' regions (diversification)

(b) domestic production of goods, if necessary, at increased costs

(c) build-up of stocks and foreign exchange reserves

(d) economic control mechanisms to create jobs

(e) creation of bilateral or multilateral involvement (mutual dependence) with the trading partner in order to render unilateral exploitation of dependence impracticable.

3. Relations of Dependence between the EEC and the CMEA

A. *Present Relations*

Relations of dependence between East and West could only be fully analysed by means of a multitude of detailed case studies, provided that sufficient statistical material is available. For the purpose of this study some global considerations will be made in line with the systematic approach of section 2 above.

TABLE 5   EEC import products (three-digit SITC groups) with more than 10 per cent share of CMEA* deliveries, 1974 (in $m)

	SITC groups	Total imports	Imports from the CMEA	CMEA share (%)
001	Live animal	1456	300	21
013	Meat in containers	749	81	11
091	Margarine	224	24	11
212	Skins	658	89	14
241	Fuel wood, charcoal	64	12	19
242	Wood in the rough	1098	137	12
243	Wood, shaped	3555	612	17
261	Silk	64	46	72
263	Cotton	1288	135	10
274	Sulphur and unroasted iron pyrites	239	62	26
291	Crude animal materials	519	106	20
321	Coal, coke and briquettes	3044	679	22
332	Petroleum products	9466	1224	13
421	Fixed vegetable oils	1358	214	16
515	Radioactive and associated materials	311	31	10
571	Explosives and pyro-technic products	94	10	11
	TOTAL		3762	

* Including other Communist countries.
Source: OECD, *Statistics of Foreign Trade*, series C, 'Trade by Commodities' (1974).

TABLE 6 EEC import products (four- and five-digit SITC groups) with more than 20 per cent share of CMEA deliveries, 1974 (in $m)

	SITC groups	Total imports	Imports from the CMEA	CMEA share (%)
0015	Horses	187	65	35
2421	Pulpwood	164	100	61
2422	Sawlogs	71	15	21
2432	Lumber, sawn	2900	574	20
2741	Sulphur	206	51	25
28391	Ores and concentrates of chromium	59	14	24
3214	Coal/anthracite bituminous	2230	653	29
3323	Distillate fuels	3105	648	21
4215	Olive oil	374	180	48

Source: OECD, *Statistics of Foreign Trade*, series C (1974).

For an analysis of import dependence, therefore, those groups of goods involving a relevant import volume from the other economic bloc in relation to overall consumption or total imports shall be selected. For EEC imports all three-digit SITC groups of goods bought from the CMEA at more than 10 per cent (table 5) and all four- and five-digit SITC goods whose import share from the CMEA is in excess of 20 per cent (table 6) were sorted out. Since no comparative statistical data are available for CMEA imports, Soviet foreign trade statistics were used. The Soviet share in EEC–CMEA trade at 43 per cent is sufficiently great to permit certain generalizations.

EEC imports where the CMEA share exceeds the quoted limits are restricted to raw materials or little processed raw materials. As far as agricultural raw materials are concerned, besides a high import share of silk from the CMEA in 1974, a dependence is above all evident for certain types of wood. However, the distribution of wood imports on the world market is rather favourable. Sixty-one per cent of wood imports (SITC group 24) are acquired from the 'politically secure' OECD area, and 16 per cent from the CMEA area. Since the various types of lumber can be substituted to a limited extent, a high import share, e.g. with regard to pulpwood (SITC group 2421, 61 per cent of the CMEA share) is not too significant. A 20 per cent reduction of the import supply of wood may either be compensated by other suppliers (market substitution) or by a demand adjustment through decreased consumption which would not seriously impair the economic process.

With respect to mineral raw materials and fuels, the demand elasticity is for the most part less, so that a supply shortfall would have major repercussions on the economic process. In the case of sulphur and iron pyrites (SITC group 274) dependence is probably not too serious, since 63 per cent of the EEC imports of these products are supplied by the OECD area. The imports of coal, coke, and briquettes also appear to be without risk, since the EEC exports four times as much as it imports from the CMEA area and because imports play a minor role due to the high degree of self-supply.

By contrast, chrome (SITC group 28391) is a highly sensitive import product. Twenty-four per cent of imports are from the CMEA area. Chrome is a sensitive good because it is a vital product for steel processing which can hardly be substituted. In addition to vanadium and magnesium it is probably the mineral with the most sensitive dependence on imports (low elasticity of demand). This dependence on the CMEA area is further aggravated by the fact that another 25 per cent of EEC imports are supplied by the politically unstable South African region while only 13 per cent are acquired from the OECD countries.

Since a considerably more favorable diversification of the supplier countries is not possible because of the limited distribution of chrome resources, storage would appear to be the best solution. The costs would be relatively low, since the EEC imports only $59 million worth of chrome per year (1974). A two year reserve which would tie up $120 million, could reduce dependence on chrome imports to a minimum.

Since almost the entire issue of dependence on the CMEA centres on raw materials, it would be sensible to examine whether a storage project would be both useful and feasible in financial terms, for raw materials (in contrast to foodstuffs) are

TABLE 7   Soviet import products with more than 10 per cent share of EEC deliveries, 1975 (in million rubles)

	Product groups	Total imports	Imports from EEC	EEC share (%)
101–3	Forge and pressing equipment	113	19	17
10401	Metal-cutting machine lines	84.5	29.4	35
10514	Equipment for automobile producing firms	288	198.4	69
120	Equipment for under-ground and surface mining of raw material	58.1	24.4	42
128	Equipment for geological detection	133	53	40
150	Chemical industry equipment	638	279.2	44
151	Equipment wood cellulous-paper and wood working industry	150	35.4	24
157	Polygraphic industry equipment	55	21	38
19101	Lorries (thousand units)	11	5	46
264	Rolled ferrous metal (million tons)	3.9	1.86	48
26411	Sheet steel (thousand tons)	505	199	39
266	Tubes (million tons)	2.18	1.62	60
304	Plastic material and materials for the production of plastic	217	116	53
	Machines, equipment and transport means	9046	2010	22

Source: *Vneshnyaya Torgovlya SSSR za 1975 god* (Moscow, 1976).

almost without exception well suited for storage. The overall import volume from the CMEA area with regard to the quoted groups of goods, SITC 241 to 332, was $3013 million for the three-digit SITC groups in 1974. If one adds the vulnerable goods of the four- and five-digit groups not contained in the above three-digit groups, the volume amounts to $3027 million. Storage in these orders of magnitude would be absolutely practicable. A critical dependence does not apply to all of these goods, since some of them are of minor importance (high elasticity of demand) or could easily be substituted from other markets. Thus only part of the goods listed in tables 5 and 6 (SITC groups 241 to 332) would have to be stored to decrease dependence.

If we now take a look at Soviet import goods where the EEC share is more than 10 per cent, the classification is as shown in table 7.[6] Soviet dependence, in contrast to EEC dependence, is restricted to the area of investment goods. In 1975 its dependence on EEC imports for some products was more than 50 per cent. Major items in this context are machinery for the automobile industry with a 69 per cent EEC import share and tubes with a 60 per cent EEC share. In both cases dependence on EEC imports has already lasted for a long period of time. A supply reduction would not imply a close-down of individual branches of production in the short run, but would in the medium and long run destroy the chances for planned investment expansions and thus for the growth targets.

Market substitution for products of high technological value outside the OECD area is not possible because of the lack of supplies. An import substitution must be largely ruled out because of the existing technological gap. A product or factor substitution is only possible at the expense of growth losses. A build-up of stocks in the USSR with EEC import products is not possible for two reasons. Firstly, the growth impulses resulting from the new technology diminish with increasing storage time. Secondly, the volume of the then required stocks exceeds the monetary means.

It can be assumed that sensitivities are not as great for export dependence as for import dependence. The share of export production for the other economic bloc in the overall GNP is

6 USSR foreign trade statistics are based on a system different from the SITC system.

1.1 per cent for the EEC and 1.7 per cent for the CMEA. A demand shortfall of such an order of magnitude would still amount to substantially less than the reduction in export demand experienced by both blocs in 1974–5. An embargo of the other bloc's export could thus at best reinforce recessive trends, but could not have a highly disturbing impact during a period of economic boom; it would constitute an effective political instrument only in certain economic situations. Individual branches, such as large-tube industry, would be hard hit by such an embargo, but the multiplier effect of such a decrease in demand would not exceed that of a recessive demand reduction.

In the CMEA area multiplier effects from unexpected demand reductions are hardly noticeable, since the Eastern economic system does not permit such effects to the same degree as a market-type economy. An aggravating factor in the CMEA area, however, would be a loss of foreign exchange revenues, for the EEC would not greatly impair its import capability thanks to its foreign exchange reserves.

Monetary dependence between the CMEA and the EEC is characterized first of all by their basically different situations. Whereas the EEC countries dispose of convertible currencies which enable them to utilize domestic currency to pay for world market products, CMEA currencies cannot be used as means of payment on the Western world market. Moreover, CMEA indebtedness to Western industrialized nations, which amounted to more than $40 billion at the end of 1976,[7] leads to a critical relation between indebtedness (or debt service) and export revenues.[8] This feeling not only is expressed in the Western press,[9] but seems to have led to import reductions in CMEA countries and simultaneous increased export efforts since the beginning of 1976.

Monetary dependence for the CMEA implies that the only

7 Estimated by Chase Manhattan Bank. *International Herald Tribune* (8 November 1976); see also pp. 14 and 194 of this volume.
8 Very high debt service ratios are estimated by Chase Manhattan Bank. *Eastwest Markets* (7 and 21 March 1977).
9 See for example 'Doubts about East–West trade', *The Times* (19 August 1976), p. 13.

means to achieve a monetary margin of action is through exports and that the West, in particular the EEC, can change demand for these exports. For the EEC, monetary dependence means that the CMEA could stop the repayment of credits. This dependence is not that critical, since the dates for repayment cover a long period of time so that a major portion of the debts need not be paid until after 1980.[10] Besides, the annual volume of repayments in relation to the GNP is much smaller than the growth losses during a recession, so that the overall economic repercussions of a refusal to pay would not be serious. But refusal to repay on the part of the CMEA would be rather unwise since the resulting shrinking of East–West trade would have much greater implications for Eastern than for Western growth.

Even though a quantification of mutual dependence is not possible without exact case studies, the data available permit the conclusion that import and monetary dependence of the CMEA upon the EEC is greater than the other way around. For the CMEA has no means of import substitution, whereas such means do exist for most Western imports from the CMEA. In the monetary field Western countries are favoured because of the prevailing asymmetry regarding convertible currency.

Export dependence is, on the one hand, more strongly felt by EEC countries, since their economic system is more vulnerable to demand fluctuations. On the other hand, the linkage between export and the necessity for foreign exchange procurement limits the CMEA's margin of action and makes it vulnerable to EEC restrictive practices.

B. *Prospects for Future EEC–CMEA Trade*

The development of trade between the EEC and the CMEA is characterized by an asymmetrical relationship. On the one side, there is almost unlimited demand for Western technology and Western capital on the part of the CMEA. On the other, the sale of CMEA supplies to the EEC area is limited. This leads to a rapid increase of CMEA debts. In 1976 it exported $21 billion worth of goods to the OECD area and its indebtedness towards these countries amounted to more than $40 billion. That means

10   Figures of the National Bank of Hungary. *Euromoney* (January 1977), p. 17.

that a very high share of export revenues has to be spent for debt service, a higher share than that of almost all developing countries. This high rate is only acceptable because the debts are in large part used for investments designed to create possibilities for future exports. As both sides seem to agree that these rates should not be extended much further, future growth of East–West trade depends on the CMEA's export capability. A number of indicators point to generally smaller growth rates in the future than those prevailing between 1970 and 1975, so that the ratios between export or import and GNP of both blocs are unlikely to exceed 3 per cent in the foreseeable future.[11] Hence, export dependence for the Western side will not create any significant problems.

Monetary dependence of CMEA countries as mentioned above is great at present because of the magnitude of the debt service ratio.[12] Although the indebtedness will rise further[13] the debt service ratio has to decline during the next few years. If the ratio between credits and the Western GNP widens, the EEC's monetary dependence would also increase. At present, however, it remains minor.

The most interesting development will surely take place in the field of import dependence. It appears that Soviet foreign trade policy since 1973 has stopped giving priority to the export of medium-technology products and started to concentrate on the export of raw materials. For the manufacture of medium-technology products, it depends on Western technology. It would like to compensate for this dependence by creating Western dependence on Soviet raw material exports. For this purpose Soviet literature is drawing increasing attention to alleged Western dependence on imports of raw materials[14] with the

11   Of course this is not true for each individual CMEA country (see table 3) but for the CMEA in total.
12   Chase Manhattan Bank estimated debt service ratios from 26% (USSR) to 47% (Poland). *Eastwest Markets* (7 and 21 March 1977).
13   The Wiener Institut für Internationale Wirtschaftsvergleiche expects that CMEA indebtedness will amount to $80–100 billion in 1980.
14   See for example Ju. A. Ersov, *Syr'e, toplivo, politika* (Moscow, 1975), and W. Ongirski, 'The market of chrome compounds', *Foreign Trade USSR*, Moscow, no. 6 (1976).

underlying intention of presenting the USSR as a long-term partner for cooperation, above all in the area of non-ferrous metals.[15]

Whether the EEC should enter into a relationship of increased dependence because of raw material imports is contingent on the one hand on a reverse Soviet dependence upon EEC deliveries. This dependence is certainly relatively great in view of long-term growth targets, but is smaller in the short term. On the other hand, dependence on the USSR has to be incorporated into the global EEC dependence on non-ferrous metal imports. A detailed study could permit the conclusion that overall EEC dependence is reduced if the EEC buys more raw materials from a region with which there exists a relationship of mutual dependence and not, as is the case between the EEC and some of the oil-exporting nations, one of unilateral dependence. The USSR would surely not risk such relations favourable for its growth targets for the sake of minor political objectives. In this sense dependences would compensate each other. Moreover, this type of mutual dependence promotes to a certain extent a policy of détente, since long-term and cost-intensive projects are only worthwhile if the desire for détente is sustained. However, in a crisis situation resulting from other than economic tension, repercussions on Western Europe's supply situation would exceed Soviet growth targets. That could lead to an asymmetry to the disadvantage of the EEC in the event of a strong EEC dependence on the import of vital raw materials from the Soviet Union, unless the West provides for either storage or guaranteed deliveries for example from North America.

15 See I. Russov, 'Possibilities of non-ferrous metal trade with Western Europe', *Foreign Trade USSR*, no. 2 (1976).

9

International Organizations and East–West Economic Relations

MAX BAUMER AND HANNS-DIETER
JACOBSEN

1. Introduction

Discussions about a reorganization of the international economic order have reached an unprecedented intensity during the last few years. The trade and monetary system that emerged following World War Two is becoming more and more obsolete. The collapse of the Bretton Woods system and the decreasing importance of the General Agreement on Tariffs and Trade (GATT) (the two main pillars of world economy in the fifties and sixties), the growing weight of regional integration systems like the European Economic Community (EEC) and the Council for Mutual Economic Assistance (CMEA), as well as the shifting of multilateral negotiations to new institutions such as the United Nations Conference on Trade and Development (UNCTAD) and the Conference on International Economic Cooperation (CIEC), are the result of long-range structural changes in the world economy, where the industrialized Western nations no longer solely dominate. Processes of economic internationalization in trade and production and the emergence of new actors (such as the Organization of Petroleum Exporting Countries (OPEC)) or the increased appearance of traditional actors (such as the CMEA) on the world market can no longer be controlled by the traditional forms of organization.

Since the beginning of 'détente' in the late 1960s, the CMEA member countries have intensified their attempts to put an end to the relative isolation to which they had been subjected for many years. However, their contributions to the formulation of a New International Economic Order have been minor so far. The following analysis will examine how and to what degree the socialist countries of Eastern Europe and the Soviet Union are trying to accomplish their economic and political goals within existing international organizations, how the CMEA contributes to the institutionalization of international integration processes, and finally, how the international organizations (and the Western countries] are affected by these developments.

2. Economic Objectives of the Eastern Countries

The identification of the interests and goals at the basis of the socialist countries' policy towards international organizations such as GATT, the International Monetary Fund (IMF), UNCTAD, the Economic Commission for Europe (ECE) and the EEC, does, however, raise significant problems: not only economic but political issues play an important role – and to a varying degree according to the countries involved.

The smaller East European countries, having relatively poor resource endowments and comparatively large foreign trade sectors, are rather restricted as far as their freedom of choice in economic matters is concerned. Consequently it is one of their main interests to expand this margin by reducing the unilateral dependence upon the Soviet Union, and developing alternative options. By contrast, the Soviet Union's natural resource endowments are much better, and the importance of the foreign trade sector for the national economy is much smaller. Being the CMEA's dominating power, the Soviet Union has more globally oriented goals, and has an interest in controlling and channelling its allies' relations with the West and with Western institutions.

These more general observations require some explaining and narrowing down. With regard to economic development it has to be taken into account that the socialist states of Eastern Europe are deeply committed to the CMEA's process of integration. And indeed by utilizing gains from specialization and importing raw materials from the USSR, the smaller CMEA members have been able to achieve high growth rates. However, the economic reforms in the socialist countries starting in the late fifties and early sixties, which among other things caused a reassessment of the role of foreign trade in the development process of planned economies, led to the insight that the 'technological gap' between Western and Eastern countries could be diminished not only by increased and better use of own resources and a higher degree of division of labour within the CMEA, but also by utilizing Western technology and promoting economic cooperation with the West (acquisition of licenses, cooperation in research and development, co-production, joint ventures). And because of their geographical proximity to the highly industrialized Western European world, an expanded East–West division of labour may grant greater advantages to some East European countries than trade with some enterprises and regions within the USSR (whose location might be less favourable due to higher costs of transportation). Moreover, such endeavors were also seen in terms of helping to cover growing demands on the part of the population of socialist countries caused among other things by the 'demonstration effect' of Western prosperity.

Possibilities of implementing these goals are, however, limited: the structural changes on the world market (in particular the price increase for raw materials and fuels during the last five years) have resulted in more favourable terms of trade for the Soviet Union which, therefore, is striving for increased sales of raw materials to hard-currency (Western) countries: world market prices presently exceed those within the CMEA, whose special price system ensures that this will continue to apply in the next few years.

These facts induced the Soviets in particular to modify their stance *vis-à-vis* their East European partners. They took steps to lower the political and economic barriers between the CMEA and the imperialist world economy, looking for a partial rapprochement with the highly industrialized Western nations and their global and regional organizations. On this premise, the approaches of some of the smaller CMEA countries towards GATT, the IMF, etc., also seem acceptable from a Soviet point of view (much more so now than in the late sixties and early seventies). The attempts of these states to limit political and economic Soviet influence by obtaining more access to the West and Western organizations, now coincides with Soviet endeavors to expand their own trade with the West. But the decisive aspect is the fact that economic constraints narrow down the political margin of action for the smaller East European countries. Thus the above mentioned price rises for raw materials and fuels on the world market (in contrast to much lower increases within CMEA) have placed the smaller socialist countries in the un-favourable position of being unable to reduce their dependence on the Soviet Union by buying a larger share of their raw material needs on the world market.

The Soviet Union seems to have reduced its reservations about East European initiatives to Western countries and their international organizations. This fact becomes plausible when one considers that in the longer run the Soviet Union has a two-fold interest in internationally competitive trading partners in Eastern Europe: to ensure high-quality industrial imports and to reduce its own material exports to Eastern Europe, so that hard-currency earnings can be increased. Considering the high degree of economic and political dependence between the East-ern countries, a possible decline of East European commitment to the CMEA (as a consequence of increased contacts to Western firms and governments) is unlikely to reach substantial pro-portions. Furthermore, the Soviet Union disposes of effective political (through the Parties) and military (through the Warsaw Pact) instruments to control its CMEA partners. On the other hand, the West has accepted the political status quo in Eastern Europe: the signature of the Final Act at the Helsinki Confer-ence in 1975 supports this argument. Finally it is worth men-tioning that Soviet acceptance of a limited sovereignty for the East European countries could enhance the CMEA's attractive-ness *vis-à-vis* third countries.

Thus as far as the incentives for CMEA member states to join multinational economic organizations are concerned, top priority is placed on improved chances for hard-currency earn-ings. For international organizations, this can be achieved through the lowering of tariff and non-tariff barriers to inter-national trade. Secondly, a larger volume of Western credits and better terms of payments might help the Eastern European members of the CMEA (with few natural resources and depen-dent on foreign trade) to reach higher rates of economic growth and to speed up the restructuring of their economies. The participation of CMEA countries in international institu-tions and more cooperation with regional organizations in the

Western sphere could induce processes of adjustment within those countries towards greater economic flexibility and efficiency and may thus have favourable political implications.

But this consequence raises the question of the compatibility of such a development with the principles of the 'socialist' system, i.e. the crucial limit of measures that might jeopardize the scope and stability of socialist economic and political order.

3. Attitudes of the CMEA Countries *vis-à-vis* International Economic Institutions

In this Section we will try to analyse the CMEA countries' position in relation to the EEC, ECE, GATT, IMF and UNCTAD.

A. *Relations Between the CMEA Countries and the EEC*[1]

A most spectacular change has occurred in the CMEA nations' policy towards the European Economic Community which in the past had been denounced as an imperialistic and a peace-hampering organization.[2]

In February 1976, the CMEA presented to the EEC Council of Ministers a proposal for an agreement 'on the foundations of mutual relations'. In November 1976, the Community answered the proposal, but it is premature to envisage negotiations between the two economic blocs in Europe taking place at an early stage.

In the CMEA draft agreement it is stressed – as in the socialist countries' proposal for Basket Two of the Conference on Security and Cooperation in Europe (CSCE) – that Western discrimination affecting trade has to be eliminated in order to arrive at an all-European division of labour.

Some of the subjects for negotiations which the CMEA pro-

---

1 M. Baumer and H. D. Jackson, 'KSZE und die Entwicklung der Beziehungen zwischen EG und RGW' (CSCE and the development of relations between the EC and the CMEA) in J. Delbrück, N. Ropers and G. Zellentin (eds.), *Grünbuch zu den Folgewirkungen der KSZE* (Greenbook on the consequences of the CSCE) (Cologne, 1977), pp. 341–56; see also chapter 2 above.

2 E. Schulz, *Moskau und die Europäische Integration* (Moscow and the European Integration) (Munich–Vienna, 1975).

posed in February 1976[3] should not be too controversial (Article 3 of the draft mentions the following subjects: standardization, environmental protection, statistics, production and consumption forecasts), whereas other demands, like credits at optimum terms (Article 10) and reciprocal most-favoured-nation treatment (Article 11), will create problems. The agricultural sector which was explicitly excluded from the EEC's 'model' agreement of 1974[4] is mentioned in Article 9 of the draft. Furthermore, the CMEA proposals tend to neglect the joint trade policy competence of the Commission by considering bilateral as well as multilateral settlements in questions of foreign trade.

These intentions touch directly upon the state of EEC integration. The legal basis for the EEC's joint trade policy is clearly determined. On 1 January 1973, the competence to conclude trade agreements with state trading countries was transferred from individual EEC members to the Commission. The last bilateral trade agreements expired on 31 December 1974. Since none of the CMEA countries reacted favourably to the 'scheme' which was submitted by the EEC to each state trading country in the autumn of 1974, trade between the EEC and CMEA member countries lacks a contractual basis.[5]

By contrast, the basis for the CMEA's foreign trade policy is not at all clear. The Council for Mutual Economic Assistance, according to its statutes, is not a supranational institution and has no supranational powers. It can only make recommendations. Moreover, national governments are free to announce

3 See the unofficial translation of the draft as published in *Vereinigte Wirtschaftsdienste* (*VWD*), no. 36 (21 February 1976), p. 1/7.

4 The main features of a 'scheme' for trade agreements between the Community and individual state trading countries, as submitted in the autumn of 1974 are the EEC's readiness to conclude long-term, non-preferential trade agreements which ensure equal mutual benefit; the creation of conditions for promoting the dynamic development of mutual trade; MFN treatment in return for reciprocal concessions; the search for possibilities of liberalizing imports; and the exclusion of the Common Agricultural Policy from negotiations. European Parliament, Document 425/74 (9 January 1975), p. 22.

5 In order to bridge the situation, the Community autonomously takes charge of the member countries' import regulations.

that they are not interested in any particular matter under discussion (Article IV of the CMEA statute). The EEC argues that for this reason – the lack of material competence of the CMEA – it can sign foreign trade agreements only with individual CMEA nations, but not with the institution as such.

Moreover, some Western governments are sensitive to the argument that the conclusion of an agreement between the EEC and the CMEA might be interpreted as the EEC's formal acknowledgement and even endorsement of Soviet predominance in the CMEA. To be sure, in the last few years some CMEA countries have tried to compensate at least in part for the USSR's economic dominance in Eastern Europe by intensifying their own relations with the West. However, since the Soviet Union has granted the smaller Eastern nations a greater margin for action towards the West – as has already been pointed out – this argument must be put into perspective. The political levers exercised by the Soviet Union continue to be functional. Agreements between the CMEA and third countries could result in making 'maverick actions' by individual CMEA countries less likely or in lessening the probabilities for direct Soviet intervention because of the existence of a common CMEA framework for extra-bloc relations.

The response of the EEC in November 1976 is rather restrictive insofar as matters of credit granting and trade policy, particularly the demand for most-favoured-nation treatment and non-discrimination, are not mentioned. The argument follows the line that instruments of foreign trade policy decidedly have different functions in centrally planned economies (CPEs) and market economies; hence, realization of the principle of reciprocity would be very difficult. Moreover, in its letter of advice, the EEC refers to its offer of 1974 (to conclude trade agreements with individual CMEA countries) and stresses that its present draft provides for a skeleton agreement which does not exclude agreements between the Commission and individual CMEA members; the substance of such an agreement is limited by the existing asymmetry in material competence, as reflected by the EEC Treaty and the CMEA statute. Finally, the EEC rejects the mention of the CSCE Final Act in the CMEA draft, as this would tend to give binding force to the CSCE recommendations. Furthermore, the listing of CSCE principles in the preamble of the CMEA draft leaves out Basket Three, thereby neglecting one of the essentials of Helsinki, namely equal rank for all three baskets.

The EEC draft concentrates on questions which should be less controversial politically, and where, in the judgement of the Commission, both organizations have equal competence to conclude contracts: economic prognoses, statistics, problems of environmental protection, and standardization. Intensification of information exchange, particularly in these areas, is to provide the basis for improved working relations between the two organizations and their member countries.

B. *The ECE*

The political conflicts of the post-war era as well as the polarization between East and West have hampered the development of cooperative forms of economic relations. For the United Nations Economic Commission for Europe (ECE), created in 1947 as an all-European body for European economic cooperation and development, this meant that it had to be content with playing a minor political and economic role and did not therefore succeed in becoming the institutional forum for increasing economic relations and decreasing politico-economic conflicts in Europe.[6] This was primarily because of the failure of the thirty-four ECE member states[7] to reach fundamental economic decisions 'due to the statutory basis of the organization according to which no member state can be compelled to implement ECE decisions if it withholds its approval. Thus insisting upon majority voting would only lead to tensions within the regional organization.'[8] Moreover, the CMEA countries

6 A copious presentation to the early phases of ECE is given by G. Myrdal, 'Twenty years in the United Nations Commission for Europe', *International Organization*, vol. 23, no. 3 (1968), pp. 617–28; see also ECE, *The Work of the Economic Commission for Europe 1947–1972*, E/ECE/831 (New York, 1972).

7 In this context it has to be noted that not only are most West and East European nations – including the USSR – members of the ECE, but the US and Canada are as well.

8 K. Bolz and B. Kunze, *Wirtschaftsbeziehungen zwischen Ost und West – Handel und Kooperation* (Economic relations between East

considered the ECE as an appropriate forum to try to achieve economic objectives against politically motivated Western resistance. This helps to explain why ECE activities have commonly received little attention from Western governments.

In view of the strains imposed on it by East–West differences, the only way to ensure member states' willingness for collaboration seemed to restrict ECE programs to rather technical matters,[9] e.g. preparation of European agreements on international trade jurisdiction and the standardization of export documents, the creation of ways and means to provide information on trading potentials, the elimination of obstacles to trade (tariffs and non-tariffs) as well as the discussion of preconditions for multilaterization of trade and cooperation. During the last few years ECE activities have concentrated on the promotion of industrial cooperation, technical and scientific exchange, long-term economic projections, and problems of environmental protection.

As a consequence of the results of the Conference on Security and Cooperation in Europe (CSCE), the scope of ECE responsibilities and activities might increase, and the ECE might become the all-European organization providing the framework for quantitative as well as qualitative intensification of East–West politico-economic relations. In the Final Act of the CSCE, the ECE is distinctly called upon to:[10]

examine ways for establishing a multilateral system for diffusing trade laws and regulations;

standardize statistical nomenclatures;

study possibilities for trade promotion, including marketing;

and West – trade and cooperation), edited by CEPES (n.p., n.d.), p. 52 (translation by the authors).

9   I. Bailey-Wiebecke and E. Chossudovsky, 'Folgewirkungen der KSZE im multilateralen Bereich: Die Wirtschaftskommission der Vereinten Nationen für Europa (ECE)' (The consequences of CSCE in the multilateral field: The Economic Commission for Europe) in Delbrück *et al.* (eds.), *Grünbuch zu den Folgewirkungen der KSZE*, pp. 313–40.

10 Deutscher Bundestag, 'Schlussakte der Konferenz für Sicherheit und Zusammenarbeit in Europe' (Final Act of the CSCE) (23 July 1975), Drucksache 7/3867, *passim.*

encourage industrial cooperation by providing information and assistance;

include various aspects of environmental protection in its work;

intensify work of the ECE subcommittee on inland traffic, and standardize traffic rules on inland waterways.

Independent of the question whether or not the ECE will be invited to inform future review meetings of the CSCE on the results of its activities,[11] a precondition for the realization of these rather modest goals is that West and East will give more support by providing necessary information and competence. At the thirty-first session of the Commission, the Soviet delegation submitted a proposal to hold all-European congresses on questions of cooperation in the fields of the protection of the environment, development of transport, and energy. Soviet interest might be greater in the latter two subjects,[12] but it might be the environmental conference in which some Western countries show an interest.[13]

C. *State Trading Countries and GATT*

Among the existing multinational economic organizations GATT seemed to have the greatest attraction for East European countries: all CMEA countries except East Germany and the USSR (Bulgaria has observer status) are now members of GATT. This may in part be explained by the relative success of GATT's Kennedy Round (1964–7) on multilateral tariff reductions. But more important may have been that GATT is increasingly occupied with non-tariff barriers to trade which have

11 J. Stanovnik, ECE Executive Secretary, expects that the Commission will be invited to inform the Belgrade meeting. Cf. UN ECE, *Information*, Press Release ECE/GEN/8 (19 April 1977), p. 13.

12 International negotiations on questions of energy have so far largely taken place without Soviet participation; e.g. the Euro–Arab Dialogue, the Conference on International Economic Cooperation, or within OECD's International Energy Agency.

13 P. Bailey and I. Bailey-Wiebecke, 'All-European co-operation: the CSCE's Basket Two and the ECE', *International Journal*, vol. 32, no. 2 (Spring 1977), pp. 386–407.

been affecting international trade relations to a growing degree. In general, non-discrimination and MFN treatment were the potential gains to be derived from GATT membership.

The principles of the GATT system are based on the classical postulate of free trade between capitalist countries, and it codifies the trade practices of developed market economies (if one ignores chapter 4 on Trade and Development which was added in 1965 and which accords developing countries certain preferences).

On the other hand, through their foreign trade monopolies the CPEs have a different set of instruments at their disposal to regulate and control their foreign trade relations: the 'classical' functions of tariffs, taxes or subsidies may be substituted through the determination of differentials between external and domestic prices; discrimination may be put into effect by determining (e.g. in the import plan) the quantities imported and exported, and by specifying the source of imports or the destination of exports. Hence, when confronted with the application for membership of a state trading country, the contracting parties of GATT were forced to determine what forms 'reciprocal concessions' between CPEs and market-type economies should have.[14]

Since Czechoslovakia was one of the founding members of GATT in 1947, Poland's accession in 1967 served as a precedent.[15] As Poland had no customs tariff system at that time,[16] specific terms for accession had to be worked out. It was agreed that Poland's main concession would be to commit itself to an annual 7 per cent increase of its imports from the other GATT members. Even though this procedure turned out to have some drawbacks,[17] Romania's application for membership (July 1968) was accepted in November 1971. The conditions for

14 For a detailed analysis of these problems see R. Baban, 'State trading and GATT', *Journal of World Trade Law*, vol. 11, no. 4 (July–August 1977), pp. 334–53.
15 'Protocol of Accession of Poland' in GATT, *Basic Instruments and Selected Documents*, fifteenth supplement (Geneva, 1968), p. 46.
16 In January 1976, Poland introduced a comprehensive customs tariff.
17 Baban, *State Trading*, pp. 346–7.

accession[18] provided that other GATT members pledged to reduce their tariffs *vis-à-vis* Romania to the level already applied in their mutual trade, i.e. tariff discrimination in relation to Romania was 'officially' lifted. In return, Romania pledged to increase its imports from other GATT members at least at the same rate as total imports. The formula worked out, for Hungary's accession (1973)[19] contains elements from the Polish and Romanian Protocols, but tariff bindings were accepted as a main concession.[20]

The difficulty of ensuring that state trading countries behave in a non-discriminatory manner is reflected by the fact that the accession protocols of the three East European countries permit the contracting parties to take safeguard actions beyond the relevant GATT provisions. The intense discussion about the problems of extension or denial of MFN to socialist countries cannot detract from the fact that the economic meaning of this clause has diminished due to a generally lower tariff level and due to the growing non-tariff barriers to trade.[21] It is still undetermined what economic gains the CPEs can derive from MFN.[22] A quantitative evaluation of these gains could be the

18 GATT, *Protocol for the Accession of Romania to the GATT* (Geneva, 15 October 1971).

19 GATT, *Protocol of the Accession of Hungary*, Document L/3908 (14 August 1973).

20 An equivocal attitude among the contracting parties towards the Hungarian tariff system becomes apparent through the inclusion for periodic 'reviews' of the operation of the protocol. J. Reuland, 'GATT and the state trading countries', *Journal of World Trade Law*, vol. 9, no. 3 (May–June 1975), p. 318.

21 G. Schiavone, 'The most-favoured-nation clause and East–West trade limitations and prospects', *La Comunitá Internationale* (Padua), no. 4 (1974), p. 651; P. M. Wijkman, 'GATT and the New Economic Order', *Intereconomics*, no. 8 (1975), p. 247.

22 T. Wolf summarizes the results of his work in this field as follows: 'While there is little persuasive evidence that in receiving MFN, the socialist countries would in fact be able to realize a significant short-term expansion in their exports to the U.S., it is clear that the effect would in any case be positive, and many East Europeans have stressed the dynamic effects of the goodwill and certainty which would be created by the granting of MFN.' T. A. Wolf, 'New elements in US–East–West trade policy', *Forschungsberichte*

basis for reaching 'reciprocity' of mutual economic concessions.[23] The discovery of more practicable means for enforcing the principle of reciprocity, however, remains a task for the future.

There are indications that the countries of the Third World might accomplish a softening of the most-favoured-nation clause and of the principle of reciprocity at GATT's Tokyo Round of Multilateral Trade Negotiations. So far, however, GATT has failed to come up with workable solutions to problems of international trade, e.g. liberalization of non-tariff measures and avoidance of increased protectionism. Considering the fundamental monetary and balance of payments problems at the international level, it seems likely that meaningful reforms of trade measures can only be achieved in the context of more general negotiations on a New International Economic Order. It is too early to predict whether these negotiations will lead to a more direct cooperation between GATT and IMF[24] or to the inclusion of GATT in a new International Trade Organization.[25]

D. Implications of CMEA Countries' Membership in the International Monetary Fund

The expansion of East–West contacts and the rapid growth of East–West economic relations seem to have facilitated chances for CMEA countries to become members of the International Monetary Fund (IMF). The IMF provides its 130 member states with credits at favourable terms for compensation of temporary balance of payments deficits. One quarter of a country's subscription to the Fund must be paid in gold upon accession. As

des Wiener Instituts für internationale Wirtschaftsvergleiche, no. 19 (June 1974), p. 28.

23 C. F. Bergsten, 'Future directions for U.S. trade policy' in C. F. Bergsten (ed.), *Towards a New World Trade Policy*, The Maidenhead Papers (Lexington–Toronto–London, 1975), p. 348.

24 C. F. Bergsten, 'Reforming the GATT: the use of trade measures for balance-of-payments purposes', *Journal of International Economics*, vol. 7 (1977), pp. 1–18.

25 The Soviet Union interestingly proposed the creation of an International Trade Organization at UNCTAD I (Geneva, 1964). Cf. section E below.

these convertible means can be indirectly obtained from the Fund itself, applicants are not confronted with any severe financial strain.[26]

Currently Romania is the only CMEA member of the IMF.[27] The main reason for Romania's accession to the IMF and the World Bank at the end of 1972 was probably to increase its credit ceiling.[28] Romania enjoys a special status within the CMEA as far as foreign policy and foreign economic policy are concerned, which has enabled it to act more independently than other members. Romania's application for admission was approved on the basis of Article 14 of the IMF statutes. In accordance with this article, economically weak members have the right to restrict current transactions during a transition period. It makes no distinction with respect to the motives underlying the payment restrictions. CPEs lacking sufficient convertible currencies can therefore also take recourse to this article.

The collapse of the Bretton Woods agreement and the uncertain future of the international monetary system may have diminished incentives for CMEA countries to join the IMF at present. Also there are only very minor indications that in the current process of reconstructing the international monetary system, the specific requirements of centrally planned economies are taken into account. For this purpose some basic modi-

26   Simultaneous membership in the International Bank for Reconstruction and Development (IBRD, World Bank) enables countries to obtain long-term credits in convertible currencies at favourable terms.

27   As was again pointed out recently, the Soviet Union actively campaigned for the International Currency Agreement during World War Two but did not sign the Bretton Woods agreement of 1944. Y. Shiryaev and A. Sokolov, 'East–West business relations: possibilities and realities', *International Affairs* (Moscow), no. 2 (1977), p. 40. Poland and Czechoslovakia, two founding members, left the IMF at the beginning of the 1950s. In 1968 there were indications of a Hungarian application for IMF membership. The main objective of this step did not seem to be a raise of the credit ceiling – as was later the case with Romania – but rather to benefit from political implications of IMF membership.

28   Since 1972, Romania has borrowed over $620 million from the IBRD (RFE special, Washington, 9 June 1977), and has drawn SDR 285 million from the IMF (IMF, *International Financial Statistics*, vol. 30, no. 1 (1977), p. 8).

fications would be necessary in both East and West. Each side claims to be interested in reaching a mutually acceptable international monetary order. But this can only be achieved if, on the one hand, processes of price formation are made compatible among CMEA countries and adjusted to the price structure of the world market combined with the objective of reaching at least partial convertibility, and if, on the other hand, the regulations of a new monetary system take into account the specific characteristics and needs of centrally planned economies. In other words, the scope of the provisions must be wide enough to encourage socialist countries' participation (for example, Article 8 of the IMF statutes may have to be modified to no longer provide for unlimited international capital flows).

The actual developments of the last two years, however, permit only minor hopes for increased involvement of CMEA countries in the international monetary system, although the trend towards a new system of exchange rates and the planned replacement of the main currencies (primarily the US dollar) and of gold as main reserve units through Special Drawing Rights appeared as first steps in the right direction.

The failure to establish internal convertibility within the CMEA – perhaps a problem of the socialist economic system – and the increasing importance of Western currencies in intra-socialist trade seem to indicate that there is a long way to go before more CMEA countries can be integrated into the IMF. Suggestions like those of Adam Zwass, who proposed a 'slightly modified concept of convertibility'[29] or of Peter Wiles, who pointed out that 'purely financial convertibility'[30] could solve the problem, have so far had no influence on actual developments.

E. *United Nations Conference on Trade and Development (UNCTAD)*

The original task of UNCTAD was the development of world trade. Since 1964, however, UNCTAD is mainly concerned with

29 A. Zwass, *Zur Problematik der Währungsbeziehungen zwischen Ost und West* (On the problems of monetary relations between East and West) (Vienna–New York, 1974), p. 192.

30 P. J. D. Wiles, 'On purely financial convertibility' in Y. Laulan (ed.), *Banking, Money and Credit in Eastern Europe*, NATO Colloquium (Brussels, 1973), pp. 119–25.

the problems of less developed countries (LDCs) and is used by the 'Group of 77' (which now consists of about 110 LDCs) as a forum to articulate their economic demands. As long as these demands were mainly directed towards the capitalist countries they were supported by the USSR and her allies. From a Soviet point of view accomplishment of these demands would strengthen the position of the socialist countries. In supporting the LDCs' demands at UNCTAD, the CPEs expected in return to get support from the LDCs as far as socialist conceptions on East–West economic relations were concerned.

This strategy seemed to work. In the Declaration of Lima of November 1971,[31] the 'Group of 77' differentiated between 'market economies' and 'socialist countries of Eastern Europe'. At the Manila meeting in February 1976, market economies and CMEA countries were dealt with separately. At the same time, however, the 'Group of 77' stressed the point that they expect more development assistance from the socialist countries and better support for their demands for a New International Economic Order.[32]

Fundamental problems of the less developed countries, like stabilization of export earnings, have not been dealt with by

31 UN, 'The declaration and principles of the action programs of Lima', adopted on 7 November 1971, Documents MM/77/II/11.

32 Specifically, the 'Manila Declaration' lists fifteen points of complaint as far as CMEA countries are concerned. The most important ones are the following: the share of development aid in GNP is too low (approx. 0.01%); aid is mainly granted on a bilateral level; the more developed CMEA countries are not sufficiently promoting the marketing and consumption of the LDCs' products; preferential tariffs are not granted for imports from LDCs; the CMEA countries are quite passive when it comes to take up concrete measures for realizing the declarations and principles; in trade with CPEs the same problems are encountered as in trade with the industrialized market economies: use of world market prices and other instruments of the capitalist trading system (UNCTAD, 'Manila declaration and program action' Document TD/195 (12 February 1976)).

The 'Joint Statement' which the CMEA nations submitted at UNCTAD IV and which provides for a number of beneficial measures, is a non-binding declaration of intent (UNCTAD, 'Joint statement by Socialist countries at the fourth session of UNCTAD', Document TD/211 (28 May 1976)).

GATT (which the LDCs label as 'rich man's club'[33] with rules designed and operated only for the benefit of the wealthy industrialized countries). The lasting discussions of these problems in UNCTAD, however, may have caused the industrialized countries to consider earnestly the introduction of some sort of raw material programme.

In this sense it seems conceivable that UNCTAD could play a more important role in a new international economic order, e.g. by closer cooperation with the IMF and GATT.[34]

4. Conclusions and Perspectives

A fuller development of the potential for trade and cooperation between Eastern and Western Europe is dependent upon a number of factors. As far as the subject matter of the foregoing analysis is concerned, some of the more important ones can be stated as follows:

(i) Economic gains and losses arising from intensified relations have to be equally distributed between the cooperating partners. The resulting economic interdependence could help to reduce the risk of conflicts and contribute to the improvement of East–West relations.

(ii) Economic cooperation has to be supplemented by cooperation in other fields and by institutionalization. The main problems of finding functional mechanisms which are mutually acceptable to countries with different social and economic systems, and ensuring that reciprocal concessions are balanced and controllable can only be solved with considerable good will on both sides.

(iii) The autonomy and identity of the social and economic

33 E. Wyndham-White (former Secretary-General of GATT), 'Negotiations in prospect' in Bergsten (ed.), *Towards a World Trade Policy*, p. 337.

34 In his speech at UNCTAD IV in Nairobi, the Soviet foreign trade minister Patolichev did not want to exclude the possibility that UNCTAD may become an International Trade Organization which has competence over GATT problems (*Aussenhandel*, no. 7 (1976), p. 8). This argument is reminiscent of the Soviet proposal for the creation of an International Trade Organization which was made to UNCTAD I in 1964 and which explicitly mentioned the Havana Charter of 1948 (UNCTAD, E/Conf. 46/50 and E/Conf. 46/51 (5 February 1964)).

systems in East and West must not be questioned by the other side. For instance, it is not surprising that the socialist countries have political reservations against integration into economic organizations dominated by the West. These institutions might jeopardize the socialist system if their interests are not sufficiently taken into account. Closer institutional cooperation might entail problems of delimitation which could develop particularly within the CMEA. A more open approach to the West may in the long run impair genuine 'socialist' objectives due to the effects of penetration and demonstration inherent in this process and could thus in fact provoke social and ideological conflicts within and among the socialist countries.

As far as relations between the two economic blocs in Europe are concerned, it is hard to envisage how these can be established without regular official discussions on a whole range of subject matter. In this sense it would be necessary for each organization to consider the potential negotiating partner as a basically parallel organization; differences in opinion between the CMEA and the EEC about the competences of each organization to conclude agreements in various economic fields should be solvable at the negotiating table.[35] Generally speaking, increased contacts by socialist countries with organizations of the Western world economy may promote economic and social development in CMEA countries. The Soviet Union seems to be interested in improved access of its CMEA partners to Western markets as it directly and indirectly might derive benefits for itself (social stabilization in Eastern Europe through better consumer satisfaction via intra-bloc imports, acquisition of advanced technologies, and higher growth rates).

A further result of integrating CMEA countries in international economic organizations can be the fact that these institutions which were originally founded by the industrialized countries could cease to fulfill their original purpose (uniform articulation of interests to the outside, obligatory solution of problems within) because of divergent interests and economic

35 J. Pinder, 'The Community and COMECON: what could negotiations achieve?', *The World Today*, vol. 33, no. 5 (1977), pp. 176–85.

systems. Under these conditions, these organizations would form a generally acceptable and thus broad context within which various regional and/or multipolar interest groups could agree upon functionable arrangements. For this reason, from a Western point of view it may seem that the inclusion of countries with lower levels of development and/or other social systems would only be plausible if, at the same time, an institutionally secured and strengthened formulation of own interests can take place, for instance, within separate organizations (such as the OECD), or by building factions within global organizations (such as the Club of Ten within the IMF).

It cannot be expected that the Western countries will fully endorse a far-reaching institutionalization of economic relations with the CMEA countries at a multinational level, as long as their priority is the realization of national objectives which may very well conflict with those of another capitalist country. Assuming that the Western economy will not experience a sharp decline, and that the EEC integration process will continue, it seems possible, however, that in the long run such competitive positions might gradually be replaced by a more unified approach.

It seems plausible to argue that institutional regulations of East–West economic relations may be embedded in a New International Economic Order, and cannot be reached within the traditional organizations. In this context, the historical ideas on the creation of an International Trade Organization may be reconsidered. Such an organization could not only work on the solution of GATT problems, but on problems of capital transfer ('GATT for investment') and raw material supply as well.

Index

DATE DUE	
L R MAR 1 8 1983	AUG 11 1994
L R APR 7 1988	
L R MAY 2 1983	
L R OCT 2 8 1983	
L R FEB 1984	APR 2 9 2003
MAY 1 1 1989	
AUG 1 1989	
JUN 0 8 1990	
AUG 2 7 1990	
NOV 0 9 1991	
AUG 1992	

MP 728